THE EDUCATION OF
EVERETT RICHARDSON

Silver Donald Cameron

THE EDUCATION OF EVERETT RICHARDSON

The Nova Scotia Fishermen's Strike: 1970-71

McClelland and Stewart

ISBN: 0-7710-1845-2

McClelland and Stewart Limited
The Canadian Publishers
25 Hollinger Road
Toronto Ontario
M4B 3G2

Printed and Bound in Canada

Canadian Cataloguing in Publication Data

Cameron, Donald, 1937-
  The education of Everett Richardson

ISBN 0-7710-1845-2

1. Fishermen's Strike, Nova Scotia, 1970-1971.
2. Richardson, Everett.   3. Fishermen – Nova Scotia –
Biography.   I. Title.

HD5329.F653 1970.C35   331.89'28'392   C77-001378-3

CONTENTS

*Along the shores of Guysborough and
Richmond counties in Nova Scotia during
the fishermen's strike, you sized people
up by discovering whether they were
"for the fishermen" or not.*

*In at least three senses, this book is
for the fishermen.*

"When you have no union, you stand alone. And when you're goin' in for fish prices or bait prices, trying to get your bait price cut down a little bit and fish prices raised – goin' in there speakin' alone, they're just laughin' in your face."

> – Edison Lumsden, president,
> Canso Local of the United
> Fishermen and Allied Workers'
> Union, Canso, Nova Scotia.

"The striking fishermen and their union leaders have given an excellent account of themselves, whatever the ultimate result. They have stuck to their guns despite tremendous pressures. . . . When this thing is finally over somebody should write a book about it. It deserves to be remembered as an epic struggle by Nova Scotia workers."

> – The *Cape Breton Highlander,* in
> an editorial, September 9, 1970.

ACKNOWLEDGEMENTS

The Canso Strait fishermen's strike involved thousands of people, and it would be impossible (and, in some cases, imprudent) to list everyone who has helped make this book possible by submitting to interviews, providing documents, pointing out avenues of further inquiry, and so forth.

Some contributions, however, simply must be acknowledged. At the head of the list are the Canada Council and the Ontario Arts Council, which provided small grants to help me finish the book after much of the research had already been done. Kini Savage transcribed tapes expertly and willingly, and served as a critic and encourager into the bargain.

The 4th Estate, the *Cape Breton Highlander*, and the Labour Relations Board of Nova Scotia provided me with many valuable documents, and the Izaak Walton Killam Library of Dalhousie University and the Harriet Irving Library of the University of New Brunswick made their facilities freely available to me. The United Fishermen and Allied Workers' Union, its president, Homer Stevens, and the staff of its newspaper, *The Fisherman*, were unfailingly helpful; so, for that matter, were various officials of the Canadian Food and Allied Workers' Union, although their involvement in the conflict of 1970-71 was relatively brief.

Portions of the book have been published in *Maclean's, Saturday Night*, and *The Mysterious East* and in draft form it was read and criticized by nearly thirty people. Many of these cannot be identified, but I can thank Stephen Kimber, Ruth Misheloff,

11

Ron Parsons, and Doug Gibson, and I am deeply grateful to them and to the eleven fishermen to whom I read the draft aloud in a Canso bait shed. I am particularly indebted to the fishermen generally, and specifically to Everett and Jean Richardson and their family, to Edison and Louise Lumsden, and to such supporters as Ron and Anne Parsons. Nothing I asked of them was ever refused, from a cup of coffee to a bed for the night, to hours of talking into a tape recorder. In a very real way, this is their book, and I hope it is worthy of them.

Finally, I owe a continuing debt to my best friend and lovely lady, Margo Lamont, who has hounded and pestered me to finish the book, who provided a patient ear, a critical eye, entertainment for the guests I neglected, and endless cups of coffee served at my desk. No home should be without such a friend, and happy is the writer who has one.

Silver Donald Cameron
D'Escousse, Nova Scotia
March 1977

WADING THROUGH THE ACRONYMS

The Canso Strait strike involved a vast array of organizations, many of which are known by their initials. The major players:

UFAWU The United Fishermen and Allied Workers' Union, an independent Canadian union headquartered in Vancouver. Its president was Homer Stevens, and it was the chief union involved at Canso Strait.

CFAWU The Canadian Food and Allied Workers' Union, the Canadian arm of the Amalgamated Meat Cutters and Butcher Workmen, of Chicago. The CFAW, which includes the former United Packinghouse Workers, is the major union in the Canadian food industry. Its chief representative at Canso Strait was Jim Bury, a former NDP Member of Parliament from British Columbia. I normally call this union "the Food Workers"; UFAWU fishermen call it "the Meatcutters."

CBRT The Canadian Brotherhood of Railway, Transport and General Workers, an independent Canadian union whose chief interests have been sleeping car porters and other railway employees. Its marine branch has organized tugboat men and small coastal boats. By 1977 it represented most trawlermen in Nova Scotia, including those of Canso Seafoods, successor to Acadia Fisheries. The CBRT is referred to throughout as "the Brotherhood."

LRB The Labour Relations Board of Nova Scotia, a quasi-judicial body with jurisdiction over most labour-management relations in the province. In 1971 its chairman was Horace Read, former Dean of the Dalhousie University Faculty of Law.

CLC The Canadian Labour Congress, the federation of labour unions at the national level, the chief spokesgroup for the mainstream labour movement. In 1971 its president was Donald MacDonald. Its provincial counterpart was

NSFL The Nova Scotia Federation of Labour, of which John Lynk was the president. I usually call it "the Federation." This federation in turn was made up of several more local federations, such as the Cape Breton Labour Council, whose president in 1971 was Winston Ruck, a Sydney steelworker.

NDY New Democratic Youth, a semi-autonomous junior wing of the New Democratic Party which has now been disbanded. At the time of the strike it was a rallying point for many of Nova Scotia's student activists.

CSWU The Canadian Seafood Workers' Union, a small independent Canadian union affiliated with the CLC and headquartered in Canso. Its president was the late Roy Keefe. It had contracts in a number of plants throughout the Maritimes. I normally call it "the Seafood Workers."

PROLOGUE

Everett was down in the engine room, the steel plates vibrating under his feet, the steady clatter of the big diesels beating at his ears. Outside the winter gale was blowing fifty or sixty knots, the decks were icy, and the big stern dragger was rearing half its hundred and twenty-five-foot length out of the water as it plunged and wallowed in the cold North Atlantic.

The deck heaved up and down, but the engine room was warm and noisy. And the cook was coming towards him.

"Here!" the cook bawled in his ear. "Sign this!" He was holding out a little card.

"What's this?" Everett asked, puzzled.

"You're gonna join the union, ain't ya?"

"Yeas," said Everett, "I'm gonna join it. But I mightn't have any money for you right now."

"The money's paid!" shouted the cook. "Your brother Floyd paid it for you. All you got to do is sign the card."

He signed the card. And for Everett Richardson, a good-natured fortyish fisherman from Canso, Nova Scotia, that was where the whole astonishing story began.

Canso has been a fishing port for a very long time. In 1560, when the first Elizabeth had been only two years on the throne of England, when *Gammer Gurton's Needle* was the hottest thing on the London stage, and when William Shakespeare's parents were newlyweds, a young fisherman set out from France, from St.

Jean de Luz, for a summer's fishing. In 1607, when Elizabeth was dead and her successor James I had told his scholars to go ahead with a new English translation of the Bible, when the hottest plays in London were *Macbeth* and *King Lear*, the French traveller and historian Marc Lescarbot met that fisherman, Captain Savalet, on the beach at Canceau, as the French spelled it, and they talked of his forty-two summers of fishing on the Nova Scotia coast. Savalet was by now skipper of an eighty-ton vessel, with sixteen crewmen. Having taken 100,000 fish and cured them on the beaches, he was well satisfied with his season.

Fishermen may have come to Canso before Columbus came to America. By Lescarbot's time, hundreds of little wooden vessels were making the crossing every year from the ports of Brittany and Normandy, of the Basque country and the west of England, of Spain and Portugal, to strain the fat codfish from the cold western sea. When Nova Scotia was French, several proposals were made to move the seat of government from Port Royal, at the mouth of the Bay of Fundy, to Canso, and the rich fishery was one of the chief attractions.

The other attraction was Canso's military importance. The town of Canso perches on the very tip of North America, the most easterly point on the mainland of the continent. It commands the seaward entrance to the Strait of Canso, which separates Cape Breton Island from the mainland and leads into the Gulf of St. Lawrence; from Canso, a couple of days' sailing brings a ship easily within range of almost any important part of Canada's Atlantic coast. In 1688, Louis XIV's Governor, the Sieur de Pasquine, recommended that the town be fortified. By 1720, when mainland Nova Scotia had changed hands, the English Governor had a detachment of troops there "for the security of that fishery, which, by all accounts, is the best in the Universe."

Canso juts into the Atlantic like a rocky wharf, and its history is long, rich, and often bloody. It was harried by the Indians in the early days of English settlement; its men smuggled contraband across the bay to and from the French settlers of Petit de Grat, Arichat, St. Peter's. In 1744 the French recaptured the town, then lost it again. The next year a motley army and navy from New England met in Canso, exercised and planned for several weeks, and went on down the coast to capture the "impregnable" French fortress of Louisbourg. In 1776, a seagoing marauder, a Scottish-American privateer, sacked the town and plundered its merchants, capturing one ship, burning another and sinking a third. Two months later he returned and ravaged the town again. His name was John Paul Jones, and the Americans revere him as the father of their Navy. His memory is less honoured in Canso.

Canso is closer to Europe than it is to Winnipeg, and so, in the 1880s, two great telegraph companies used the town of Canso as the western terminus of their trans-Atlantic cables; their buildings are still there, though the cables are manned no longer. But they were important enough to make Canso a heavily defended point in a world at war.

Above all, Canso is surrounded by fish. The fishery brought Captain Savalet out from St. Jean de Luz four centuries ago, and it sustains the people of Canso to this day. Fishing is not an easy way to make a living, and life in Canso has never been easy. During the past generation, Nova Scotia has turned away from the sea and towards industrial towns, highways, and manufacturing plants; Canso is fifty miles from a main highway, and increasingly it is isolated, its way of life is foreign to the broadloomed offices of the business-suited men who run the lives of Nova Scotians. Sitting at their Danish modern desks twenty storeys in the air over Halifax, they will tell you that Canso is small, and poor, and backward.

So it is, from their point of view. But the men and women of Canso are people of such courage, generosity and humour that it warms one's heart to know them. During the summers of 1970 and 1971 a handful of fishermen in the tiny ports of Canso, Mulgrave, and Petit de Grat – fewer than 300 men in all – fought a battle for the rights of working people which unsettled the opinions and plucked the consciences of Nova Scotians, a battle which very nearly brought the province's economy to an abrupt halt. This book tells their story through the experiences of one fisherman, Everett Richardson, and his wife Jean, a genial mother of six who until the strike never interfered in "the men's business," but who found herself marching on the picket lines and defying the police. This is a story, too, about some of their

17

children – Bertha and Kenny, who worked in the fish plant but would not cross the picket line, and Linda, who went to British Columbia with her husband, Russell Gurney, when the strike ended, to fish where their union was strong.

This is not just the story of the Richardsons; each of the 235 union fishermen has a similar story. But to understand the meaning of the strike one has to move close to the fishermen, and the Richardson's story can stand for the others. In the end this is not a story of the fishermen alone, or even of the labour movement. It is a story about privilege and poverty and injustice in this country, and about the social and political arrangements which cheat and oppress most Canadians, which stunt our humanity and distort our environment. It is a story about learning. In the end, I hope, it is a story about democracy, and the way Canadians might hope to achieve it.

GRADE SCHOOL
Who Needs a Union?

(March, 1970, and its background)

"In the country of Guysborough my first breath I drew;
'Twas the poorest county that I ever knew;
The people were poor, but I think they were proud;
It's no harm to think, if you don't think too loud."

– Nova Scotia folk song

It was a curiously spontaneous strike. It spread like grass fire. It began in Petit de Grat.

"We were at sea," Everett remembers, clenching his fists on the kitchen table, flexing his muscular forearms. "We heard rumours about Petit de Grat walking out. Well, we landed, took our fish out. There was a feller from Prince Edward Island with us that trip, and I called him; Terry, I said, when you come back, I says, bring me over two or three bags of potatoes. You know, you get them cheaper over there. And he said sure."

It's 1972, and we're reliving the experiences of the previous two years: Everett and Jean; young Eddie Dort and Bertha Richardson, who would later become his wife; Linda Richardson Gurney, and occasionally her husband Russell; Edison Lumsden; various others at different times. And a chronicler, with a tape recorder.

"So Terry arrived here at the house two days afterwards, we were scheduled to sail at three o'clock that afternoon. He had the potatoes and he had his sea bag and everything packed, so we jumped in his truck and went.

"Going down to the plant, somebody says, 'I thought you fellas were on strike?' I said, 'I never heard nothin' about it. I knew about Petit de Grat but I didn't know Mulgrave and Canso was going on strike.' Then I put my sea bag aboard and talking there to some of the fellers, and I said to Terry, 'Aw, hell, run me up to the liquor store an' I'll get a quart of rum.' So I went up and got a quart of rum and gone about ten minutes. I came back down and

went out on the wharf and met Jed Roberts, a company feller –
'I'll give you ten minutes,' he said, 'for to get your gear. You're
on strike.' "

"Funny," said Edison, "there was never any talk about us
going on strike." Everett is chunky and easy-going; Edison is
wiry and intense. "We were just holding our meetings, things
were quiet, just going on with normal matters every day, just our
union meetings and even at that there was never any mention of
a strike. That day we was gettin' ready for lobster fishin'. I come
up from the beach, and I was sittin' down having dinner and Con
Mills and Jim Collins walked in."

Conrad Mills, the organizer from Louisbourg. Tough, good-
humoured, burly and almost classically handsome with his
thatch of black, curly hair. The sort of man who wears his body
with the easy confidence an executive brings to his three hundred
dollar suit. And Jim Collins: tall, quiet, balding, many times a
father, and the president of the Mulgrave local.

"They said, 'What're you doing, eating dinner – don't you
know you're on strike?' " Edison smiled, "Well, they were always
joking anyway. And I says, 'Yes, the strike will soon be over
now, I'm getting ready for fishing.' I was referring to the unemployment insurance I'd drawn all winter. 'No,' Con says, 'it's
true. Petit de Grat walked out today.' I couldn't believe him. He
said, 'We're going to call a meeting in Mulgrave now, and call a
meeting here in Canso. See what the men want to do. Put it to a
vote.' So that's the way it started. I think they voted – what was
it, Everett, 98 per cent to strike, wasn't it?"

"Think so," Everett nodded.

"And Mulgrave was the same. Lord Jesus! Then we were into
it. The groundwork wasn't really laid – oh, Homer says it was,
but no way. It would have happened, I daresay, in maybe a year
or so when things were more stable, because we figured in order
for us to gain anything, we were gonna have to go on strike
sometime. This was in the back of our minds but it wasn't talked
about. We knew it ever since Homer was down here in February
that year."

Homer Stevens, the compelling, controversial national president of the United Fishermen and Allied Workers' Union which
had grown in the West Coast salmon fishery and was trying to

unite the unorganized East Coast fishermen. Homer Stevens: inspiration or abomination, prophet or pariah, depending on your viewpoint.

"Homer and Con, Jim Collins and Jim Allen" – an organizer from the proud old German port of Lunenburg – "went up to the plant office to speak to Cadegan, and Cadegan wouldn't listen to him at all. He refused. 'You got the majority of the fishermen in the union,' Cadegan said, 'or you claim you have – well, you know what you can do. Tie up the boats,' he says, 'if you can.' "

Alphonsus L. Cadegan, manager of the Acadia Fisheries plants in Mulgrave and Canso, son of a fish merchant in Glace Bay, a blunt and angry man with no sympathy for loafers, whiners, or leftists. He has his own story. So, no doubt, does Earl Lewis, manager of Booth Canadian Fisheries in Petit de Grat.

"But they did pull the pin on it in Petit de Grat, because when they went in to speak to what's-his-name over there across the bay –"

"Lewis," said Everett.

"Lewis – he said *No spika da English.* So I guess they got pissed off over there quicker than what we did here. That was about the size of it."

Fishermen are the foundation of a whole reach of the East Coast economy. The fishermen support the boat builders and cordage manufacturers, the dealers in engines and other fishing gear, the machinists and the painters and the cutters in the fish plants, the truckers who drive the refrigerated semi-trailers to Boston and Montreal, the executives in Halifax and Chicago who organize and control the industry. In a town like Canso, *everything* depends on the fishery: fishing is what the town is all about. The schoolteachers, the half-dozen clergy, the shop-keepers, the furnace-oil dealers, the bank clerks, the telephone operator, the fellows in the liquor store, the man who shows the occasional films, even the guys who maintain the wharves and buoys, and the man in the lighthouse on Cranberry Island – there would be precious little call for any of their services without the fishermen; and the big modern fishplant which is the town's chief employer would have to close down. Even Canso's own spectacular government-assisted failure, the Cardinal Protein plant, could never have been proposed without a steady supply of fish offal. Fishing has declined over the years, but it is still an enormously important industry, and nowhere more so than in Canso, Petit de Grat, and, to a lesser extent, Mulgrave.

But the importance of fishing is not merely economic. The success of Halifax's own Samuel Cunard in establishing a trans-Atlantic steamship line wiped out the great international trade Nova Scotia boasted in the days of home-built wooden ships; and ever since, the people of the province have gone to sea primarily to catch fish; fishing is nearly all that remains of the province's great seagoing tradition. And yet the sea has made Nova Scotians what they are, to a considerable extent; it has a profound influence on their vision of the world and their sense of human life. Men in little villages building wooden ships and taking them to sea for a living. Men whose competence and courage allow them to survive an environment which in winter seems determined to obliterate everything alive. Half the people of the province today live and work in Halifax, commuting between the downtown towers and the bedroom suburbs as though they were Torontonians, but they are connected with the villages, they have first cousins and in-laws in Lower Economy or South West Pubnico, and their image of themselves is not bounded by the limits of metropolitan Halifax. "We come from Petit de Grat," said an Acadian girl to me once at a party in the city; but she was born in Halifax and so were her parents. No matter: her ancestors probably fled the siege of Louisbourg in 1758 when the French empire was crumbling, and after two centuries they are from Petit de Grat however long they may live in town.

Death by sea looms large in Nova Scotia's vision of life. Gail Fitzpatrick of Mulgrave, who with her fisherman husband Eric was one of the strongest supporters of the strike, lost her father and her only brother at sea. When Everett Richardson and Edison Lumsden fall to gossiping and reminiscing, they identify their friends by the places they were drowned. *You remember old so and so?* No. *He's the one that was drowned off Scatarie Island.* Oh, him! Fishermen's gossip is full of deaths: men swept overboard and left behind by a skipper intent on his fishing; men caught up in nets or winches and crushed or drowned; men trapped in ice-covered ships which became top-heavy and turned turtle. Death by sea is a possibility every working day of a fisherman's life.

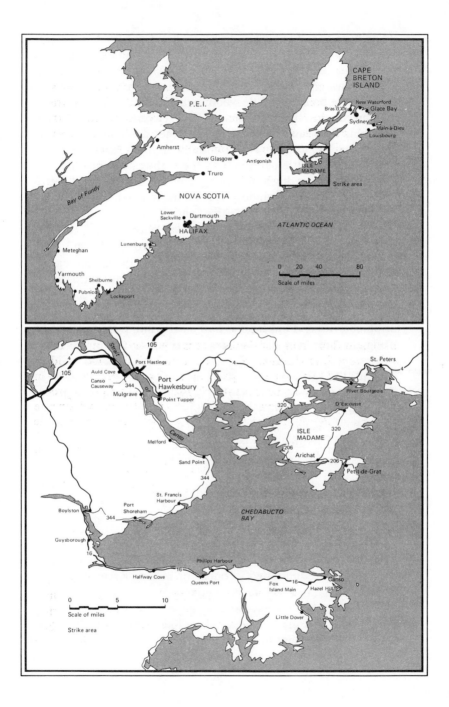

The fishermen I know are therefore very direct, very practical, very good at savouring their pleasures. They don't sniff around for information: they ask. *Where d'you come from? What d'you do for a living? What brings you down this way?* They have to know a little biology, a little woodwork and naval architecture, a little mechanics. They see no point in paying someone to do something they can do themselves, and they don't respect people who waste money. Slowly, gradually, Everett Richardson is remodelling his little old house by the highway on the outskirts of Canso. He tears down the ceiling, puts up the panelling, opens up the wall for a new window. He can mend a net, caulk a boat, tear a big marine diesel engine apart and rebuild it.

He drinks enough – or did – that I was once worried that he might become an alcoholic. I was quite wrong. He will quit drinking and "go on the keg" for months at a time. The reason he drank a lot is that he enjoyed it, just as he enjoys sitting on a wharf in the sunlight swapping stories, just as he enjoys taking his family to the beach in the summer, just as he enjoys going out for blueberries and bakeapples in the early fall, just as he enjoys eating the preserves his wife Jean puts up or the big lobsters which sometimes come his way.

People like this are a kind of touchstone of value in Nova Scotian life. They are realists, they cut through pretentiousness like a sharp knife through the belly of a codfish. They are not puritans; for them, sex is like drinking, at once a joke, a natural function and a large pleasure. "You ever hear the time Frankie was out screwin' around and brought the clap home to his wife? Lord Jesus. . . ."

Or: "When you gonna get married, Shorty?"

"I'm already married."

"Go on, who you married to?"

"To my left hand."

All this has its dark side. The fishing villages have their limitations: if you are interested in books or music or science, in the world of ideas, you will not find your growth in the village – or not, at least, until you have already gone away and gained your tools. And if you are young, a village like Canso will offer precious little excitement to compare with the urban world you see on television. If you don't want to fish or work in the plant, you leave. Every year the children drain away. In 1956, the population of Canso was 1,261; ten years later, it was 1,190. Some of the drinking is desperate rather than joyful, the consequence of a nameless frustration and resentment built up by the relentless experiences of poverty and manipulation.

In 1972, Everett Richardson's family didn't have a flush toilet. Consider what it is like to take a break from "The Mary Tyler Moore Show" by going out to the backhouse for a crap when the temperature is 20 below zero and a gale from Greenland is slashing between the cracks in the walls. You *know* you work hard and live thriftily, and yet somehow you can't be permitted a flush toilet. You watch the pretty girls turning into butterballs, a consequence of a diet with too much potato and bread, too little meat. In Richmond County, which includes both Petit de Grat and my own village, D'Escousse, diabetes is frighteningly common, the rates of maternal and infant mortality are similar to those of Kenya, and dental care is virtually unobtainable: the dentists thirty miles away are booked a year in advance.

If you're a rural Nova Scotian, what can you do? You put in your own garden and you know how to find the free foods of the woods and the shore, but that skill doesn't deliver fresh green vegetables in winter. Your cousin comes home for a holiday from Ontario in a big new car: he's working in a factory up there and he says it's a soft touch. Your old pickup has been parked in the yard for months because you haven't scraped the licence fee together. Your kid needs braces on his teeth, but that's out of the question. You're nailed for illegal possession of liquor, and you have to drive thirty miles to court and defend yourself; you lose and pay a fine because you can't afford a good lawyer. Your husband deserted you years ago and now there's someone else in your life; you can't afford a divorce, and when you live common law your self-righteous neighbour sniffs at you for bringing down the good name of the town and showing a lack of moral fibre. You dream of being able to buy a big house trailer, and just when you've got the down payment together the prices go up.

All that happens not because you're lazy, but because there's something out of joint in your world. It doesn't matter how hard you work; you never get ahead.

So you drink and mutter, and your family life decays. "I hope he don't ever come back," a fisherman's wife told me. Her husband had quit fishing, gone away to work. "He's a right bastard. I ain't let him touch me for two years – I got six kids now, what the hell do I want wit' another? And him after goin' out and gettin' drunk every two weeks and then come home and beat the shit outa me – Lord dyin' Jesus, I don't need *that*."

When the men tied up the boats, their action came out of all that and more. If fishing tells Nova Scotians what they are, part of what it tells them is not pretty. It tells them that they live in an essentially feudal society. It tells them that the law is irrelevant to the way things work: power rules the world, and the powerful rule the law. It tells them they don't count.

All of the varieties of fishing come down to two basic types: inshore and offshore fishing. Inshore fishermen own their own small boats, put out each day to the fishing grounds, and return each night, fishing from April to December, when the harbours freeze. They sell their fish to buyers at the wharves, or perhaps to the local fish plant.

Offshore fishermen, deep-sea fishermen, work in crews of eight to sixteen on "trawlers" or "draggers," ships of 80 to 150 feet in length. Trawlermen are at sea for a week to two weeks; at Acadia Fisheries before the strike a normal trip ran twelve days. Then you have two days at home, and back to sea. If you don't live in the port you fish from, you have the choice of working steadily or seeing your family; you can't have both. Everett fished offshore in the winter, inshore in the summer. In Mulgrave, all the fishermen worked on draggers. Petit de Grat boasted a fleet of draggers operated by Booth, and a fleet of inshore boats centred around the Isle Madame Fishermen's Co-op.

It was the trawlermen who struck, though they were vigorously supported by the inshore fishermen. And no wonder.

"I was fourteen when I started the fishing," Everett says, "I'm forty-six now, so that's thirty-two years. But I was an inshore fisherman and I spent three years in the American merchant marine during the war, and then I come back and started the inshore fishing again, longlining. In 1955 I went on the draggers, and I'm on the draggers practically year-round till the strike."

What's it like on a dragger? What do you take when you go?

"Well, you take your heavy gear: your rubber boots, your oil-cloths, your heavy clothes, heavy shirts, heavy pants, heavy stockings – stuff you generally don't use in the summertime ashore, but out there you use it mostly all the time. And you're taking out a bottle of liquor into your seakit too." He chuckles. "If you get good weather, the trip's not too bad. If you get bad weather, you've got a miserable trip. And you don't stop for nothing when you're out there. They're going day and night. If they want you to work fifty hours without gettin' below, or sixty hours, that's what you gotta do. I worked sixty-two hours at one stretch.

"See, if you're gettin' a lot of fish, it takes a long while to put them down. You break watches and all hands is up there. When you're puttin' that much time in everybody's on deck, it's not only just your watch, but all the watches, and you just get off long enough to get something to eat and back up on deck again. You got to dress the cod – gut 'em and clean 'em, get 'em ready to be washed and put in the fish room. Then you got to put 'em in the fish room and pen them off an' ice them. You spend the best part of your time dressin' fish."

All this time the dragger is steaming, pounding into the seas of the Grand Banks, or ploughing through the Gulf of St. Lawrence. The trawl itself is enormous, a gigantic bag of net perhaps half as long as the ship itself, its mouth held open by three-inch thick wooden doors bound in heavy iron, the whole affair towed by heavy steel warps. The trawl is "shot away," and the ship tows it for a couple of hours. It's hauled in on power winches. "Haulin' back only takes a short time with these modern draggers now because they're pretty fast," says Everett. "Maybe five or ten minutes. By the time you've gone up and got your oil gear on, and gone on deck, the trawl is hauled back. You open your hydraulic ramp door and untie the fish net, and all the fish run down to the tank. Then you shoot away again and go down and dress the fish.

"I've seen fifty and sixty thousand pounds of fish in one tow. That's more than you'll get on a whole trip sometimes. I've been out sixteen days in the summertime and come back with twenty-six thousand pounds. Them big draggers'll carry up to five hundred thousand, and sometimes you'd have fifteen or twenty thousand on deck if the fish room is full. But outside of that, you just want to put your fish room full.

"Normally you work sixteen hours a day, though – you only work them long hours if you're really into the fish. Usually you work eight hours on and four off, that's your regular shifts. Sometimes you're short-handed, but normally you have five or six packing fish in the fish room.

"But like I say, it's the weather. It's not too pleasant when you're working out there in zero weather – or like last winter, where we ended up there in the Gulf with 24 below zero* and a wind chill of 52. You don't dress no fish up on deck then. You can't. Just as soon as you come up on deck you're freezing. But if you got trouble with the gear, if it gets tore up while you're gettin' it in, why then you got to stay on deck, and fellers do get frostbite sometimes. These modern trawlers where you're down below dressin' the fish, they don't seem to be too bad. In the old side trawlers you couldn't dress 'em at all in that cold, you just had to put 'em down round. Before you got 'em dressed they'd be frozen so hard you couldn't do nothin' with them. When the fish come out of the water, the eyeballs would turn right white, you know, all the stuff inside them freezing. It don't take long. They'd be frozen stiff's a stick of firewood.

"And see, in the old days, it was better, because if the weather was too bad then you just didn't go out. But these new steel stern draggers, they go out in all kinds of weather. And when you're out there you're into it, you don't get in any more. You're out there for your twelve-day period. Even if they get a big storm like a hurricane or something like that, now, some of them may come in and some of them might not. But outside of that, you're out in everything, you just take whatever comes. There's lots of people on land say, 'Well, Christ, I wouldn't want to be out there in a gale of wind' – but when you're working for twenty-four hours straight, some of the fellows are right happy to see a wind sometimes, they can get a little rest. But the wind has to blow pretty hard – you know, fifty or sixty mile an hour winds."

---

*Fahrenheit: this was the winter of 1971-72.

It is not easy for shorebound, sedentary people to realize what kind of life this is, what kind of work it entails. Father Thomas Morley, the Catholic priest of Bras d'Or, himself a former steelworker and coalminer, took a trip on a dragger. "On the basis of that never-to-be-forgotten experience I can make the following statement," he wrote. "There is not a unionized miner or steelworker in Cape Breton or anywhere else who would work two successive trips on a dragger; one trip would be sufficient to convince him that here obtains the most foul exploitation of human resources still extant in our land.

"You can work steadily for 20 hours as long as the fish-finder needle keeps pointing out fish. And when the fish are slack and the boat changes course, even then, rest is not assured. There are fish to be cleaned and put in the hatches, ice to be shovelled, bottom-damaged nets to be mended. One of our crew was on his feet for over 30 hours.

"Add to this the wind and the frost, the snow and the sleet of winter trawling, the open decks, the bare hands and the exposed machinery of running winch and speeding steel cables, and you get a faint idea of the hardest life by which men still earn their daily bread.

"This is exploitation," Father Morley concluded acidly. "We used to call it immorality."

A trawlerman working steadily, as Eric Fitzpatrick did the year before the strike, might make twenty-seven trips a year. That works out to 5,000 hours a year, or roughly triple the hours of the average industrial worker. Six out of seven of his days are spent away from his family. For all of this the draggerman was paid between $3,000 and $5,000 a year – a dollar an hour, at best.

It wasn't always like this. As recently as the 'thirties, fish were still caught from wooden schooners, built up and down the shore, and owned by their skippers. Since World War II, however, fishing – like farming and lumbering – has been industrialized, the little local entrepreneurs giving way to the vast corporations, the old manual gear being replaced by massive machinery. First it was side draggers, of which some are still in service, wooden boats of eighty or a hundred feet, shooting away over the side. Now the boats are stern draggers, steel ships with elaborate equipment, shooting away under a huge truss through a specially-designed ramp in the stern. A stern dragger is worth half a million dollars: only a big company can afford one.

So the fishermen, who were once independent businessmen sharing their take with crews made up of their own friends, neighbours, and relatives, began increasingly to resemble blue-collar workers in other capital-intensive industries. An international corporation is different from a friend or relative: it doesn't give a damn about your welfare, it moves only in response to the balance sheet. Like the textile companies of nineteenth century Lancashire, like the mine owners of turn-of-the-century Glace Bay, like the garment makers of New York, the fishing companies paid their men as little as possible, took profits as high as possible. That's only capitalist common sense. And like the workers in the mills and mines and garment factories, the fishermen began to talk about fighting power with power. They began to talk unions.

In British Columbia, the first fishermen's union was formed in 1893. Through a series of strikes, struggles, and mergers it developed into a single dominant union, the United Fishermen and Allied Workers, by 1945. But British Columbia is not Nova Scotia. The boisterous, self-confident frontier community of the West Coast is made up largely of immigrants: prosperous and dynamic, it has generated one of the strongest, most broadly based groups of socialists and labour organizers in Canada. British Columbia's fishermen are Finns and Japanese, Scandinavians and native Indians, Newfoundlanders and Maritimers – an unusually polyglot group, with a wide range of backgrounds and experiences, seeking their fortunes in a new land.

By contrast, Nova Scotia's fishermen have been here a couple of centuries, tracing their descent to the first Canadians to come from Europe. Over the generations, the East Coast provinces have become the most class-structured part of English Canada, and the control of Nova Scotia represented by the elite of the Halifax Club and the Royal Nova Scotia Yacht Squadron is scarcely credible. The old families of the province live quietly, nipping off to Bermuda for a fortnight in mid-winter, or to London for a week of theatre-going. They put their sons into the best private schools and see them through law at Dalhousie before they join a dignified partnership or enter the family business.

Nova Scotian money is discreet, confident, and powerful. Robert Stanfield is of this class, and his style is characteristic. Who ever heard of Roy Jodrey of Hantsport? And yet he was one of the richest and most powerful men in Canada.

Cut from Halifax to Petit de Grat, from the towers of Scotia Square, the downtown development built by men like Jodrey, to the squat little building of the Caisse Populaire de St. Joseph. Carl Boudreau manages the credit union, and explains that it came into being because of the savagery with which the fishermen were exploited. "You fished all summer," he declares, "and you sold your fish to the merchant – there was only one, really. You had to take what he would give you, you had no choice. By the middle of the winter you were out of money, and you had to run up a bill with him just to eat and get the gear to go out again the next season. But then you had to work half that season to pay off your debt, so you were *worse* off the next winter. You couldn't borrow from a bank, the bank wouldn't look at you. These days the banks are *trying* to get you in there to make a loan, but in those days they wouldn't loan to anyone who wasn't pretty well off already. You know even today it's a bit of a status symbol in Petit de Grat to have a loan from the bank, eh? That's true. It shows you're somebody.

"So that's where the credit union came in, something to get the fishermen out of the clutches of the merchants by loaning them money at a *fair* rate, so then they could hold out for better prices." The system came down essentially to a form of feudalism, where the serf relied on the squire to keep him alive, and in return was obliged to enrich the squire. During the strike, Homer Stevens referred to the old families as "the codfish aristocracy of Nova Scotia." It was no mere figure of speech.

Nova Scotia's workers, of course, have fought back from time to time, but they have usually been crushed. As early as 1816, the colonial Assembly was passing anti-labour legislation, directed against workers who "by unlawful meetings and combinations are endeavouring to regulate the rate of wages." Ninety miles from Petit de Grat, in the coal mines and steel mills of Sydney, New Waterford, Glace Bay, and the other towns of industrial Cape Breton, labour unions have struggled for nearly a century through one violent clash after another to win the most rudimentary amenities for their members. These were not gentle clashes around the negotiating table, but armed battles in which the British Empire Steel and Coal Company used thugs with iron bars, and called in special reinforcements from the RCMP and the Army to bolster its own force of 400 armed men. In the 'twenties, people were dying of malnutrition, and BESCO was *cutting* wages; the miners and steelworkers fought back with stones and bare fists.

In all these early years only occasional attempts were made to organize Nova Scotia's fishermen. In 1947, the Canadian Fishermen's Union, an affiliate of the Canadian Seamen's Union, organized trawlermen at Lunenburg Sea Products and won certification as their bargaining agent, only to have the company apply to the Supreme Court to quash the certification. The company argued that the fishermen were not employees at all, but "co-adventurers" who shared both the risks of the voyage and the profits. The court agreed:

> Fishermen operating under such an agreement may toil in stormy seas for days and weeks and may catch only fish enough to pay for the bait, oil, and wages of the cook and engineer. The time of the men and the use of any equipment which they own is a dead loss; equally so is the use of the vessel with its tackle and the provisions supplied by the owner; equally, the captain gets nothing. . . .
>
> But assuming that the owner loses the hire of the vessel and the provisions and the men lose their time and the use of some equipment and that, in this suppositious case, there are no profits to divide, can it be said that the men are employees and the owner an employer?
>
> To my mind the persons in question in the present case were engaged in procuring fish not for the owners or for the captain but for the general account of all. . . . The relationship between the fishermen who share in the proceeds of a fishing voyage under the agreements before us and the owners of the vessels is not that of employer and employee but of partnership in the limited sense which is sometimes described as a "joint adventure."

(21 Maritime Provinces Reports, 323 *et seq.*)

In an earlier day, such a decision might have made sense – but that finding has ruled the fishing industry ever since 1947, and in a day of half-million dollar ships owned by international corporations which also process and market the fish it seems about as relevant as a whalebone corset. In its comments on the "supposititious" fishing trip, the court showed a level of ignorance which even in 1947 must have taken some effort to achieve. Listen to Everett Richardson, reviewing his financial records for 1958-59, ten years later.

"Let's see here," he muses, leafing through the papers. He points out a nine-day trip over New Year's arriving back in Canso January 5, having earned $43.01. "For all these trips, you've got an average of two days in, just about, sometimes not that. Some days you turn around and you're back out again. The biggest part of the trips that year you had under fifty dollars. Here's some good ones – "

January 8 to January 16	$101.33
January 17 to January 24	129.50
January 26 to February 5	115.00
February 7 to February 17	98.49

"Now here's where we get trouble," he says, pointing at the page. "We had to go to Lunenburg, we were up there quite a while with mechanical trouble, and we never sailed again until March the twelfth. We left Lunenburg in a northeast gale that called for sixty to seventy mile an hour winds that night, but we left Lunenburg that afternoon and we went out in it; we were hove-to a couple of days before we started fishing, and we made our first set at 1.00 on March 15. We landed in Canso on March 23. We had a good trip of haddock that time, we had 167,000 pounds of haddock, and I made $234.44. It was the biggest trip of the year."

He leafs through to the end of 1958.

"Here's a good one for a Christmas trip – we sailed December 12 and landed on December 21, with $32.24."

December 25 to January 4, 1959	$70.68
January 6 to January 15	19.31
January 17 to January 26	142.19

"This next one is going to be the smallest trip of the year, 'cause

Credit: Jim Haggarty.

we sailed January 27 and we landed February 4 and we made $2.01 apiece. And the one cent was in the envelope, too, just with the two dollars."

There are some other figures on the side of the page.

"I was in the engine room at this time, chief engineer, and I got $4.00 a day for sailing as chief. The second engineer got $2.00 a day. When we worked in port, the chief got $1.25 an hour. You see here, most of the trips is only two days in. But we had to do all our own maintenance work when we come ashore, *in* this two days and get this boat ready to go to sea. All our engine work, deck work and all, the engineers had to do it, along with a little bit of help you could get from fellas around the plant."

His brows wrinkle, his eyes are intent on explaining.

"Lots of trips we've landed in at eight o'clock in the morning and I never even got home until dinner time, and then I was just the same's a man working in the fish plant. I come home at 12.00 and got me dinner and I'm back at the job again at 1.00. Sometimes we got home for supper, and if we did get home for supper we had to go back and work that night until 9.00 or 10.00. Murray Westhaver and Freeman Boyd and me, we worked together to put a set of rings in the main engine, six-cylinder Crosley. We were in port twenty-four hours, and nineteen hours after we landed we had the rings in the main engine, had her done. In nineteen hours. You work late hours for to get her done."

And sail five hours later?

"Yeah, we got the engine started in the afternoon, I can remember just the same's it was today, Albert Crouse the skipper. We got the engine going and we were running her in at the wharf. I think it was around three o'clock in the afternoon, and I said to the skipper, 'When do we sail?' He said, 'We're sailing six o'clock.' I said, 'I thought we'd get an extra night in.' He said, 'There's no extra night in. We're sailing six o'clock.' I come home and I never even had a chance to change my clothes hardly until I went down to sail."

He laughs.

"Who needs a union?"

Did the Canadian Fishermen's Union come to Canso, back in '47?

"No, there was no time to be unioning then. The conditions we were working under, well sure, a union had to come in, eh? regardless of what union it was. Everybody would have jumped for it. But the way we were then, you do it or else. And at that time we had only three draggers and there was lots of men to go onto them. If you didn't do it they wasn't tied up at the wharf very long before they'd get someone for to go. No, I heard some talk about that fishermen's union, but not enough for to get interested into it. We got a couple of fellas with us here that was actually in that strike at that time in Halifax, though. Yeah, Bill Dollard was one that was into it, and there were others – but at the time you didn't hear enough about it for to worry about it. Until we got into this big strike, and we met different fellows and you talk about stuff like that. Not only in Canso but in Halifax or wherever you went there'd be a little bit more about it, and that's how we came to be familiar with the strike of '47. Before that we hardly knew it existed. Our own strike brought it all in view."

The Canadian Fishermen's Union vanishes after the 1947 strike. Its parent union, the Canadian Seamen's Union, was the victim of one of the most shabby episodes in Canadian labour history, the importation of the Seafarers' International Union. Sponsored by the American Federation of Labor and the Canadian government, the SIU performed an exceptionally messy hatchet job on the CSU, reflecting the changed attitudes of the Cold War and what came to be known as "McCarthyism."

For the CSU was at once radical and national, and such unions are anathema to Canadian capitalism and to "international" – i.e. continental – unionism. The United Fishermen and Allied Workers is similarly national and radical; and it strongly supported the CSU. In 1953, as the varieties of permitted thought shrank rapidly across North America, the UFAWU paper, *The Fisherman*, attacked the national Trades and Labour Congress for suspending another union and then trying to take over its jurisdiction. The action was a raid pure and simple, said *The Fisherman*, and "raiding simply cannot be condoned under any circumstances." The TLC promptly suspended the UFAWU as well, and the Seafarers at once attempted to raid the UFAWU itself. The raid failed, but the union was kept out of the TLC and its successor, the Canadian Labour Congress, for nineteen years, a fact which hurt its cause at Canso Strait.

36

"Actually that was part of the really strong attack on the left in those years," claims Homer Stevens, "an attack which badly weakened the political awareness and the unity of the labour movement."

In most respects, the exclusion left the union virtually unscathed, and by the 1960s it was actually being hurt more by the fact that the Atlantic fishermen were unorganized. Union officers would go to Ottawa to talk about international treaties, hydro projects, unemployment insurance, or any other of the dozens of political issues which affect fishermen. You fellows may know the West Coast, they would be told, but what about the Maritimes? In 1952, in the middle of a bitter trawl strike, the West Coast fishing companies pointed to the Maritime situation with approval and the UFAWU worried that the divided and weakened Maritime fishermen would undercut their own contracts. In the 'sixties, too, the British Columbia herring fishery was closed, due to overfishing, and the BC herring seiners made the long trip through the Panama Canal to begin destroying the Maritime herring, a job they have now virtually completed. With BC boats and companies established on the East Coast, it was time to act.

A union committee visited Nova Scotia and came home recommending that the UFAWU begin organizing in the Maritimes. General organizer Tom Parkin and welfare director Glen McEachern went to Nova Scotia in the spring of 1967, visiting fishing ports throughout the province. Parkin's reports in *The Fisherman* are restrained in their tone, but he was clearly appalled by what he found:

There are no minimum price agreements.

The fishermen have no say in the price of fish or the lay (division of the profits) for the trip. The lay here ranges from 60 to 70 per cent for the boat share and 30 to 40 per cent for the crew.

No delegate of the crew is present when the fish are tallied in the plant.

No proper statement of weights, prices or trip expenses are given in most ports.

No welfare or compensation (even as we know it in BC) or medical plans exist.

Prices for fish may drop even while the boat is unloading. (We saw this happen in North Sydney.)

Demand for a statement or tally can lead to dismissal and blacklisting.

There is no agreement covering sanitary conditions or safety on deep-sea vessels and some vessels are in a deplorable condition.

There is no job security on any vessel. If you are not on the boat or at the dock at sailing time, even if your reasons are valid, you can be canned and blacklisted. We have had cases referred to us where fishermen waited five or six hours, went home for an hour and came back to the boat to find the balance of the crew had arrived in the meanwhile and had sailed without them.

Offshore fishermen here, both draggers and longliners, pay from $75 to $175 per trip for electronic gear, which in the case of older vessels, has been paid for over and over again.

In the absence of a boat delegate, a dragger hauling 300,000 pounds of mixed fish may find that 20,000 or 30,000 pounds has been culled as "white tag" or second grade fish and this comes off the stock. No one has ever been able to find out what happens to the "white tag" fish or where it is sold. You won't find it in store or cafes at a marked down price.

Charges can be made against stock in which no fisherman has a say, or, as frequently happens, any knowledge. We mentioned a case in an earlier report where a crew had "donated" $185 to the annual appeal for charities which they were neither asked about nor given credit for.

Are some boat repairs and gear also taken off the stock in this way? No fisherman has the answer.

Turning to the shore workers, Parkin found Halifax filleters at $1.68 per hour, with maintenance men making $2.23 and female packers $1.16 – and this, he pointed out, was the best contract in the province. (By classifying the same job as a different job when it's performed by women, fish companies routinely fail to pay equally for equal work.) In another port, the same company negotiated with the same union – the Canadian Seafood Workers, a small Maritime union, which Parkin is careful not to blame – a contract in which the top rate was $1.40, and women were paid $1.01. Those were the days of Expo and the kissing Prime Minister; one wonders how many shoreworkers shared in the general euphoria.

And yet these were the *unionized* workers! "We have talked to women in unorganized plants," Parkin wrote grimly, "whose wages are 85 cents an hour. And how about a waitress making 65 cents an hour having to pay for her meals and launder her own uniform?"

Not surprisingly, Parkin and McEachern found the fishermen eager to hear them, and by mid-June they were able to report they had signed up seventy of the eighty fishermen in Mulgrave, and formed organizing committees in Canso, Lockeport, Shelburne, Lunenburg, Pubnico, and Yarmouth. They were also able to boast the first UFAWU local in Nova Scotia, at Louisbourg, twenty miles from the union towns of industrial Cape Breton. Its president was Conrad Mills, who later became their first native Nova Scotian organizer. The union was strongly supported in Louisbourg by a young Englishman, an archaeologist working on the restoration of the old French Fortress of Louisbourg. His name was Jeremy Akerman, and he went on to become the leader of the Nova Scotia New Democratic Party.

Back in British Columbia, the union was embroiled in a bitter trawlermen's strike, with terms like "scab" and "thug" and "goon" being freely handed about. The Prince Rupert Fishing Vessel Owners Association sought and received a back-to-work injunction directing "the Union" to send telegrams ordering some of its workers to handle cargoes which had been declared "hot." The union's officers concluded that "the Union" meant its membership, and asked the members in a referendum whether they were to send the telegrams. Eighty-six per cent of the members said No, and an infuriated Justice Thomas Dohm cited Steve Stavenes, the president, Jack Nichol, the business agent, and Homer Stevens, the secretary, for contempt of court. He sentenced them to a year's imprisonment and fined the union $25,-000.

The UFAW history, *A Ripple, A Wave* says

There is no doubt that the fishing companies' ultimate

objective in the B.C. conflict was to destroy militant union organization in the fishing industry in its traditional stronghold. They also calculated that the UFAWU would be so occupied in fending off the full weight of the forces arraigned (sic) against it – the Social Credit provincial government, the courts, the fishing companies, the Prince Rupert Fishing Vessel Owners, raiders, strike-breakers, and scabs – that it would be unable to concentrate on its organizational campaign in Nova Scotia. And at the same time, the fishing companies used the struggle in B.C. to mount a red-baiting scare campaign against the union in the Maritimes.

The campaign had its effects. In a pattern which would be tragically repeated later, a CLC union stepped in at Lunenburg and harvested the UFAWU work by signing a "voluntary recognition" agreement for the trawlermen at National Sea Products, the towering Nova Scotia-owned giant of the East Coast fishery. "Voluntary recognition" means simply that a company recognizes a union as a bargaining agent without obliging the union to appear before the Labour Relations Board and force the company to bargain with it. Once a voluntary agreement is in force, the union – in this case the Canadian Brotherhood of Railway, Transport and General Workers, which has a marine arm chiefly concerned with tugboat crews – can negotiate a closed shop, and thus secure the membership of a majority of workers *after* it has been recognized. The voluntary recognition route is designed to avoid unnecessary and pointless applications to the Labour Relations Board, but it is obviously open to abuse – to sweetheart agreements and company unions – both devices to thwart the ambitions of the employees.

The UFAWU could not challenge the Brotherhood before the Labour Relations Board because fishermen, being "co-adventurers" and not employees, did not come within the Labour Relations Act. Thus the Brotherhood had deftly eliminated the UFAWU as a possible union for National Sea Products trawlermen – and National Sea, with its plants throughout the Atlantic region, would have been a superb base for the UFAWU. From the viewpoint of the Brotherhood and the company, it was a very tidy solution to a potentially nasty problem.

So the UFAWU concentrated on Acadia Fisheries in Canso and

Mulgrave and on Booth Fisheries in Petit de Grat. Homer Stevens, out of jail and elected president, came east several times, got to know the fishermen and tried to sound out the management of the companies. Because of the co-adventurer fiction, the union could hope only for a voluntary recognition agreement – but in BC, voluntary recognition, extracted from the companies by years of struggle, had formed the basis of the entire union.

By December, 1969, the fishermen were ready to think about the kind of contract they might like to negotiate. Management didn't want to see them. Nothing could be done without consultation with the head offices – Booth's in Chicago, Acadia's in England. By February, when delegations went with Homer Stevens to talk with the managers, the union was strong in all three Canso Strait ports, but the managers weren't dealing.

"I'm not going to talk about it," Booth's Earl Lewis is reported to have said. "I'm not going to admit in any way, shape, or form that you have a union or have a right to talk to me about conditions."

"Why?" someone asked.

"*No spika da English.*"

And in Canso, A.L. Cadegan, "Donnie," as he is known to his friends, said no, Acadia wasn't about to recognize the union. "You know there's another way to do it. You say you have the majority: tie up the boats, if you can."

In March, Petit de Grat "pulled the pin."

"You'll be out there till snow flies!" snorted Cadegan.

Even Cadegan didn't know the half of it.

41

INTERLUDE
Two Teachers

"Up the great hyaline river
Struggled a hundred vessels.
Eagles in the vast air poised to strike;
Fish in the shallows hovered.
Each living form under the frosty heaven
Fought with another for freedom."

– *Mao Tse-tung*, "Midstream,"
translated by Earle Birney.
From *The Collected Poems of Earle Birney*,
reprinted by permission of The Canadian Publishers, McClelland and Stewart Limited, Toronto.

The two symbolic figures, grappling together like some down-
east Hector and Achilles, are Donnie Cadegan and Homer Stevens. In some respects they seem like the same man in different
moods, or children of the same father: both involved in the fishery from early childhood, both bright and energetic, both
stubborn and courageous, both widely admired and hated during
the strike, both moved by a hard and intransigent moral sense.

Cadegan's story is like a capitalist parable: the poor kid who
through sheer force of will makes his way to power and respectability. Born in Glace Bay, Cadegan was one of ten children

whose father, he says, "started the fishing industry in Glace Bay because he couldn't *buy* a job." A friend backed his note for $90.00, and he bought "a 1929 Durant that had been burnt, put in a box where the rumble seat was, and went around from door to door peddling fish he bought from the fishermen." Working for his father as a boy, Cadegan remembers cutting fish all evening after school, and on weekends and holidays working from two in the morning till ten in the evening for fifty cents a week. "You worked to *eat,*" he snaps. "If you didn't work, you *didn't* fucking well eat."

That was 1930. Cadegan dropped in and out of school, finally graduating from St. Francis Xavier University in 1939. He's been in fishing ever since – with Fullam Brothers of Boston, with National Sea Products, with H.B. Nickerson and Sons, and with Les Produits de la Pays in the Gaspé. For two years, the Cadegan family – "The Singing Cadegans" – were in Toronto, appearing as entertainers at the Canadian National Exhibition, at Expo '67 and on TV. "We did sixty-nine shows the second year," Cadegan remembers happily, "we used to earn eleven or twelve hundred dollars a week. Ed Sullivan heard us once. 'You sing well,' he said, 'who teaches you?' He couldn't believe it when we told him, our mother. Oh, we'd do big conventions at the Royal York and places like that. Somebody once said, 'If you whistled a tune, they sang it in parts.'" He laughs, pleased at the memory, almost embarrassed to be showing pleasure. There is a genial fellow buried somewhere under the surface of the choleric businessman.

"This strike was fought for fellows that won't work anyway," he declares. "That's the unhealthy part of it. You take Everett Richardson, that fellow never worked more than six months in a year, he won't work as long as someone else is paying him. Or some of the women that worked in the plant here – they'd work, then go on compensation for some imaginary injury or other, work a bit more, get fired and go on unemployment insurance. There's lots like that. Only 40 per cent of the workforce in Canso are good people. They don't *want* steady work. But Acadia Fisheries was always undercapitalized, and we *had* to have stable labour relations, and a stable supply of fish."

Cadegan's opinions are somewhat intemperate – but then a strike like this makes everyone intemperate. People seek out the most appalling, slanderous, scatological terms to hurl at one another. The strike zone, it sometimes seems, is populated by strange beasts: slimy Red cocksuckers, capitalist pricks, management ass-lickers, fucking traitors, lying cunts, pigs and jackals and vultures and shit-eating sons of bitches. Cadegan's opinions are intemperate, but opinions *about* Cadegan are equally bellicose. The chronicler humbly strives for some semblance of balance.

Cadegan pauses, stalking around the roomy office on the second floor of Acadia's low, square building. Everywhere in Canso you can smell the pungent reek of fish: here it's particularly strong. I mention the fact: Cadegan looks at me in surprise.

"Stink? Hell, this plant smells *good!* You should have smelled some of the old ones."

He wears a pink shirt, dark trousers; his hair is grizzled, his face ruddy and craggy, his dark eyes flash from under his black brown. He's chunky and solid, built like a prizefighter.

"You know what this community needs? About two hundred houses. And some outside people – you're never going to stabilize the industry here unless you stabilize it with people from outside. Look, that's why we would have *welcomed* a union. You have an unstable labour force, and a union would stabilize it, eliminate the drunks and alcoholics. We *tried* to get a union, but the Nova Scotia Labour Federation hadn't done its homework, they weren't in the same class with Homer Stevens. Unions are good things; I'm not anti-union, I'm anti-Homer Stevens. I'm a Canadian from the word go, and Homer Stevens is a Communist. Now what is the Communist credo? If you can't control it, destroy it.

"In August, 1969, after the Brotherhood had signed the contract with National Sea, we suggested to Roy Keefe that his union, you know, the Canadian Sea Food Workers, should organize the Acadia trawlermen. Or we suggested that he should get in touch with the Brotherhood and ask them to come in. Well, much later Keefe said he was too busy – but he had Homer Stevens and the UF organizers staying with him in his hotel here, see? We didn't know that. Then finally we got in touch with Moulton of the Brotherhood ourselves, and he went to Mulgrave. But he didn't have the stuff, and he found the UF was already too strong. He organized three boats and the UF had already organized three boats – we didn't even know the UF was in here at the time."

Roy Keefe; brush-cut, raspy-voiced, unwell during the strike and now dead. Roy Keefe, who during the 1940s had organized his own union of fishplant workers, the Canadian Sea Food Workers' Union, travelling by motorcycle from one plant to another around the Maritime shoreline. He operated the ramshackle Mermaid Inn, Canso's only hotel.

"I told Roy Keefe during the strike," says Cadegan, "that if his people in Mulgrave didn't work they'd be closing down the Mulgrave plant, never to re-open. And you know what that Keefe said? 'To hell with the goddam bastards in Mulgrave! They were never any good and they've been nothing but trouble for the last ten years; I'll be glad to get rid of them.' That's what he said! There were seven witnesses. You go ask him."

I did. Roy Keefe said no, he was never asked to organize the trawlermen prior to the strike, and didn't want to because of their co-adventurer status. Oh yes, he admitted, there had been trouble with the Mulgravers, "same as any other plant; they didn't want to work overtime, things like that. But why would I have taken the executive of the union up to Halifax to see the Minister of Labour and try to get more money for the Mulgrave plant if I'd said that?" Sure, Homer Stevens and the others had stayed with him: "Why should I tell Cadegan the UF fellows were staying here? I didn't bar them out. He must have known they were here two years before the CBRT organized in Lunenburg, they were plain enough to see around town. Why should I tell him? It wasn't none of my business. I'm a trade unionist, I got trade union principles and I stuck to them same's he stuck to his company principles."

And as I left, Keefe called after me: "Tell that Cadegan he's a goddam liar!"

Acadia Fisheries remains a mildly mysterious organization. It had a marketing subsidiary in Massachussetts, and was linked with Port Hawkesbury Shipyards, which did a good deal of its maintenance and repair work. These connections aside, it was the lone North American venture of the Boston Deep Sea Fishing Group, an assemblage of some sixty-one British companies

Credit: Jim Haggarty.

directed from Hull, England, and chiefly engaged in various marine industries – fishing, processing, towing, shipbuilding. Sir Basil Parkes, who appears to have been Boston's leading figure, served as president of Acadia; Boston's A. B. Wilbraham was an Acadia vice-president, but most of the day-to-day liaison seems to have been carried on by A. W. Suddaby, a director of both organizations.

Other Acadia directors tied the company to Nova Scotia's own elite. C. W. Burchell and W. H. Jost were both lawyers, partners in the Halifax firm of Burchell, Smith, Jost, Burchell and Chisholm; Jost was a director of several firms, notably Canada Permanent Mortgage. Around the various Canada Permanent boards cluster a fair selection of the province's movers and shakers – including, in 1970, tycoons like the late Roy Jodrey and the late J. C. MacKeen. MacKeen alone was formerly chairman of Nova Scotia Light and Power, Halifax Developments, Industrial Estates Ltd., Maritime Steel and Foundries, Atlantic Ready-Mix and Maritime Cans. MacKeen's other directorships included the Royal Bank of Canada, three or four pulp companies, and a clutch of insurance firms. And MacKeen is only one: the Canada Permanent circle includes another half-dozen similar Nova Scotia heavies. In the cozy world of Bluenose business and law, Burchell and Jost are well-placed.

Across the bay in Petit de Grat, Earl Lewis resembles Cadegan in his lifelong connection with the fishing industry; his family dominates Louisbourg, twenty-five or thirty miles from Cadegan's native Glace Bay. But his company, Booth Canadian Fisheries Ltd., was part of an American colossus, Consolidated Foods, with head offices in Chicago, 36,000 shareholders, working capital in 1970 of $251 million, and eighty-one subsidiaries in 1969. Among the subsidiaries are such struggling ventures as Electrolux, Sara Lee, Fuller Brush, Chicken Delight, Monarch Foods, WonderBra, and Joe Lowe Corporation. Food accounted for about 70 per cent of its sales, but it had been diversifying for some time, and it also produced cleaning and sanitation products, insecticides, hospital germicides, dishwashing compounds, trimmings and accessories for home decorating and women's swimwear. In 1969 it had sales of over a billion dollars. And Consolidated Foods was itself a subsidiary of Lever Brothers.

According to Cadegan, Boston Deep Sea had no special grudge against Communist-led unions; it dealt with such unions in England, and Suddaby pointed out that Acadia couldn't financially stand a long strike. "He thought the West Coast union would ruin the industry in Nova Scotia, and he expressed this forcefully to others in the industry," says Cadegan. "He had a lot of information on the union's West Coast operation, and he knew they would have demanded ruinous prices. But he thought he could live with the union long enough for Boston to get out what it had to, and after that he didn't care. He thought he could get a good two-year first contract, though it would jeopardize the industry as a whole."

Cadegan chuckles. "He also told me that as a representative of the British Trawlers' Association he realized that if the Canadian fish industry got knocked out it would be a distinct advantage to the British industry. If I can arrange *that,* Suddaby said, I'll be fucking well knighted by the Queen."

And so, in Cadegan's account, Suddaby sent word that he was prepared to negotiate a contract on his next trip to Canada in the spring of 1970. Cadegan says he set it up and gave Homer Stevens the approximate date of arrival. But Stevens didn't respond and didn't show up.

The fishermen flatly deny this story; by their account, they had only one meeting with Cadegan, the time he told them to tie up the boats. "I *knew* Stevens didn't have a majority," snorts Cadegan. "How could he? Men on the boats come and go all the time. We put 445 or 450 fishermen through this outfit in a year." Not so, say the fishermen: the turnover is nowhere near as great as that.

For reasons which still seem unclear, Acadia decided to fight. At some points Cadegan seems to argue that Stevens' failure to meet with Suddaby demonstrated that he couldn't be relied upon; the fishermen have suggested that the other fishing companies prevailed on Acadia not to break their united front by allowing the UFAWU to gain a beach-head in Nova Scotia. On April 9, 1970, Cadegan wrote Suddaby to tell him the boats were being tied up, and that "either we recognize the West Coast union or prepare for the consequences."

"I felt from the beginning that it would be a long strike,"

Cadegan declares. "I remember a meeting here in the board room in the latter part of May. There were twenty-seven of us there, and we took a poll on how long we thought the strike would last. One fellow said mid-August, and five said the beginning of school. The balance agreed with me, not before snow flies, which would be around the middle of November. Our feeling was that the ones who were keeping it going had nothing to lose, and it was at that time that they were really drumming up the support.

"Stevens had a hell of a lot more members ten years ago than he has now. When he came to Nova Scotia, he didn't have any money. Now there's over forty thousand fishermen, forty-four thousand I think, on the East Coast – Stevens wasn't shooting for peanuts. I've been told he said he couldn't afford *not* to strike: he needed the power, he needed recognition as the leader of the fishermen, and the union needed the money he knew a strike would bring in from sympathizers. You can't find any records of how much they got and where it went, but it was a hell of a lot."

Cadegan is not just an individual: behind him stands the Canadian fishing industry, and eventually the whole weight of international capitalism. Homer Stevens would be quick to point out that although much of the strike's controversy swirled around him, he is not just an individual either; behind him stands the tradition of radical politics and the theory of trade unions, and, ultimately, the desire of working people for justice. But symbolic figures both shape history and are shaped by it; if the fishermen had had a different leader, they would unquestionably have fought a rather different fight. Homer Stevens is a strong and dramatic figure. Nobody is neutral about him.

He is a tall, quiet, rather gaunt-looking man. His handshake, like his voice, is extraordinarily soft, as though he were totally devoid of aggression. He is not, of course: his intensities burn out at you from his glittering X-ray eyes. Even in terrible old newspaper photographs those eyes bore into yours, penetrating, unnerving: the eyes of a hypnotist or a shaman. Edison Lumsden says he can't look Homer in the eye: "I just look at him for a sec' and then I've got to look away because his eyes are boring right through you. No, he's a quiet, soft-spoken fellow and things like that, but he's a fellow that I wouldn't want to get wound up."

49

No wonder his enemies yap like foamy-mouthed terriers when they talk of him, for while his voice is all sweet reason, his eyes, perched up there on his Indian's cheekbones, hint at knowledge, at will, at power.

In the fall of 1971, we talked in his roomy bungalow in the Port Guichon district of Ladner, twenty miles south of Vancouver, across the road from a dike which holds back the murky tidal waters of the Fraser delta. His father, who still lived in the family home, was a fisherman and small-time entrepreneur with a fish-collecting and retailing business much like Cadegan's, four thousand miles away. In those days, Port Guichon was largely scow-houses, shacks built on barges and towed up and down the coast to be beached wherever the work happened to be. The community was "polyglot," Stevens remembers: Poles and Yugoslavians, East Indians, Chinese, Japanese, Italians. He himself is a blend of Songhee Indian, Greek, and Yugoslavian.

"We were non-Anglo-Saxons," Homer says. The kids from Port Guichon – "wops and dagoes and hunkies, they called us" – got thumped by the Ladner teachers and fought it out in the schoolyard, then came home and fought among themselves.

"I can remember going out here at the age of sixteen and getting into a fight with the Japanese, a really racist goddam thing. A dozen Japanese and a dozen non-Japanese, and getting into almost a war out here in the middle of the night, fighting for the opportunity to fish." After that scrap, Stevens' father, a union man, a strong co-op member, and chairman of the local CCF, took young Homer aside.

"He said, Look, I've never got to the stage where I've told you I don't want you in the house. But don't ever come back and tell me you've been involved in one of those things again, or I don't want you in the house.

"Well, that made me stop and think, What have I got myself into? And I had to do a real thorough re-examination. But that was strictly an economic thing and when you suddenly wake up, you know, what the hell were you fighting over?"

In Port Guichon in the 'thirties, you soon learned the economic facts of life. One morning Homer's uncle came in from a night of gillnetting with five hundred humpback salmon, which he sold at the going rate of a cent a fish. He had a few extra.

"I got the bright idea, by Jesus, I'll take some and I'll go and sell 'em. So I took them, and drove around on my bicycle and found farmers and other people only too happy to take a salmon at their door for ten cents. I came back, got some more, and kept doing this till I'd sold fifty. So for fifty salmon I had five dollars, and he worked all goddam night out there on the river to produce five hundred, for five bucks. Well, you learn something out of that, you know – the vast difference, the exploitation."

Stevens became a full-time union organizer in 1946, in his twenty-third year. But by then he had already been a fisherman nearly a decade, beginning with summer work on a Fraser River gillnetter. In 1941 he quit Grade 12 to go trawling, and for the next five years he alternated between summer gillnetting and winter trawling. By 1944, at twenty-one, he was skipper of a four-man trawler fishing off the Queen Charlotte Islands and the west coast of Vancouver Island, having been rejected for pilot training by the RCAF due to a weak right eye.

In the 'thirties and 'forties, BC's fishermen were divided up among several small regional associations, and subdivided again according to the kind of gear the various fishermen used. Ultimately most of the small unions merged to become the United Fishermen and Allied Workers, and when the Ladner local was formed in 1943, Stevens, not yet twenty, was elected secretary – "mainly, I think, because the other members figured that here was a punk who could write minutes." Within a few weeks he was a delegate to the Annual Convention, which elected him to the union's governing body, the General Executive Board. He served on it continuously for twenty-four years. From 1945 to 1947 he was vice-president, and from 1948 to 1969 general secretary-treasurer. From 1969 to 1977 he was president.

"Look, the titles don't matter very much," says Ken Campbell, Manager of the Fisheries Association of BC, the companies' organization. "Homer Stevens was the power in that union when he was secretary-treasurer, and when he moved to the presidency the power moved with him." Campbell describes Stevens as "tenacious, intelligent, a very effective bargainer. He's careful, well-prepared, dedicated and sincerely concerned about the welfare of his membership. He's very firm."

True, says a fishing executive who refuses to be named. "When

51

he gives his word he keeps it. He's never reneged on a deal, and a contract with his union, once it's signed, is pretty well honoured – which isn't so with lots of unions. He's done a great deal for the fishermen. You don't have many problems with him – except at negotiating time." Dick Hanham of the BC branch of the Brotherhood calls Stevens "a very effective trade unionist. He's shown the degree of courage that's necessary in a very difficult industry, and he's a man with few enemies on the West Coast."

But he does have enemies, and they describe him as cunning and slippery, a fellow you have to watch, a Communist who wants to disrupt the economic process and so would as soon strike as not. What about his connection with the Communist Party? "It's no secret," Stevens shrugs. "I've been a member of the Communist Party for twenty-five or twenty-six years, give or take a couple or three years that I've been in disagreement on various issues." Precisely what issues? He'd rather not talk about them: every political party has internal disagreements, and its enemies will always use them against the party. "It had to do with the rights and responsibilities of individuals within the party. I try to live by my conscience and when I felt that certain things weren't being handled properly I tendered a resignation. But at the same time I said I was going to discuss those differences further with the Communist Party." Other people say that one of the issues was the Czechoslovakian invasion.

Ken Campbell feels that Stevens pushes too hard, holds on too long to relatively minor demands. "A good labour leader has to know when to quit. It's embarrassing to be repudiated by your membership when you're recommending that a company offer *not* be accepted – but that's what happened to Homer in 1971."

The United Fishermen's practice, says Stevens, is to send out research material to the locals and ask them to suggest negotiating objectives. These suggestions are harmonized at a meeting of all the locals, and company offers are submitted to the membership. During the first vote in 1971, a small turnout voted 86 per cent to strike; the second vote brought out more members, and a drop to 75 per cent. A large turnout the third time voted 54 per cent to accept. Stevens frowned.

"It happened once before, in '57 I think. What we found was that there wasn't nearly as much participation in the earlier stages of the process as there should have been. But okay, we'd say, it's your democratic right to stay away from meetings, it's your democratic right to come in and vote the contract in, even though it's not as good as it should have been, and" – he shakes his head – "it's your democratic right to work under that contract for the next two years."

Is the union sometimes bullheaded about minor issues? "That's a slightly modified form of what the Fisheries Association would say. And of course that *has* to be their pretence: that the strike is not in the interests of the fishermen and that the companies had no part in starting it."

Stevens is very clear about his relation to the companies: they are "exploiting the fishermen," which means profiting from other men's labour, a kind of Marxist Original Sin. As the labour movement has aged, it has largely been incorporated into capitalism. Unionisation, says the United States' Taft-Hartley Act, "promotes the flow of commerce by removing certain recognized sources of industrial strife." In return for economic concessions, the unions deliver a docile labour force.

"Why sure," says Homer Stevens, "trade unions are a product of capitalism. But they're not tied to it, and they provide a vehicle for changing it." A good organizer, he believes, should normally come from the industry and should know it inside out; he should be able to explain things to others, to inspire in them his own conviction that they can win. He should trust them to make their own decisions: it is "absolutely vital" that members should feel the union to be *their* organization, not something managed for them by remote professionals. And the good organizer will deeply identify himself with the workers he serves.

So Homer Stevens spent two to six weeks a year on the union's own boat, out on the fishing grounds. Like secretary-treasurer Jack Nicholls and business agent Glen McEachern, he was paid roughly what a West Coast fisherman makes – $178 a week in 1971. He did not hob-nob with management. With most union leaders, says Ken Campbell, you get together for a drink or a chat after the meeting, but not with Homer Stevens. "I've known him twenty years," Campbell muses, "and I still don't feel I know the guy." Yes, he agrees, Stevens is in a way an old-time unionist who fights companies and doesn't accept the traditional rights of management.

The United Fishermen is not labour's overseer, but its voice – and thus, necessarily, a deeply political union. Stevens believes that the officers may educate and recommend, and at times Stevens' form of persuasion can be forceful indeed. But the officers may not dictate. The defence of that principle warranted a year in jail for defying the 1967 court order directing the officers to tell the members to handle "hot" cargo. "We argued," says Stevens, that the order "was contrary to the whole idea of the right of the membership to decide."

One does not need to share Stevens' particular political view in order to feel that his vision of the labour movement is more relevant to people and more humane than the corporate unionism which has on the whole displaced it. Unions, Stevens believes, have to get back to some real feeling of unity. Not only should unions be reaching out to one another, they should be reaching out to people in the community as well; they are people's organizations, and must draw all kinds of people together, in a common fight for social justice. "An injury to one is an injury to all," he says, "and a victory is a victory for everybody."

Sons of fish merchants in Glace Bay and Port Guichon, peddling fish from door to door. Poor boys, full of intelligence and energy. Boys with a mark to make. Eyeball to eyeball in the Strait of Canso in the spring of 1970.

HIGH SCHOOL
On Strike

(March 1 – June 22, 1970)

"Now boys, you've come to the hardest time:
The Boss'll try to bust your picket line;
He'll call out the police and the National Guard,
He'll tell you it's a crime to have a union card,
He'll raid your meetings, hit you on the head,
Call every one o' you a goddam Red. You're unpatriotic!
Moscow agents! Bombthrowers! Even – kids."

– Woody Guthrie, Pete Seeger, *et al.,*
Talkin' Union Blues

"When we left the dragger that day," said Everett, with a grin, "me and Terry, he left for Prince Edward Island. I still had me quart of rum, and I come in right here in the kitchen and I remember pourin' one drink out. Before I had that down, Paul Gurney come after me. 'You gotta go down at the gate,' he said, 'to see that nobody takes the dragger out.' Well, that was me first hitch down at the plant, for to see that no one took the dragger out. And from then on we kept watchin' on the trawlers.

"I remember the first meetin', too. I had never attended a meetin' before, until after we was on strike. Jean said to me, 'You goin' to the meetin'?' and I said 'Yeas, I'm goin' to the meetin'.' But, I said, 'If there's one thing I want to tell you before I go, I'm not gettin' involved in nothin'.'

"So then when I come back, I *was* involved, and I started tellin' her, and she said, 'Glad you said you wasn't goin' to get involved, anyway! Never go out to a meetin' with the intentions that you're gonna get involved, because Jesus Christ, *then* what'll happen!' "

"I remember sayin' that, too," said Jean, amid the general laughter.

"See, this is what I was tellin' you about the trawlermen," said Edison. "This was only one feller – now there could have been maybe fifteen or twenty men like him, never been to a meetin'. Just the time you have a meetin', the boat sails. This is what makes it so tough amongst fishermen, tryin' to organize."

"At that meetin'," Everett declared, "I was quiet and just set still, but they kept pickin' people – you're on this committee, you're on that, all this kind of stuff. Of course it seemed like an adventure to me, not ever havin' been on strike or knowin' too much about it. So I didn't decline, I accepted wherever they wanted to put me."

"If you were gonna do it, you were gonna do it *right*," said Edison, nodding.

"Yeah. As far as I know, I done what *I* could."

The early days of the strike were pretty quiet – so far as Nova Scotians at large could tell. They were not quiet days for Everett and Edison.

"The day pretty well always started with a bang," Everett chuckled, "because if I *did* plan on sleeping in until seven o'clock, I'd always get a phone call about six-thirty, something wrong with the picket line or some damn thing. I'd have to get up and run down there and maybe get home for dinner and maybe not then. You couldn't figure in advance what the day was gonna be like. I don't know how they ever picked me, but when anything ever happened on the picket line and they couldn't get ahold of Edison, they'd up and call me. Sometimes I don't even think they *tried* to get ahold of Edison, they called me anyway."

"I don't know how many hours I put in on that picket line, those first two months," said Edison, shaking his head. "Lots of times they *did* get ahold of me, I'll tell you."

"The rackets on that picket line," said Everett. "Lord Jesus, some fella'd get down there and have a few drinks and shoot off his face and the gang would leave the picket line. They'd call me, and they'd say, 'There's only two or three down there.' And then you'd have to go around and get fellers off of the other watch and put on, get it straightened up, and then go around all the next day and try to talk them fellers into goin' back on the picket line. Probably the trouble was started by some feller who wasn't even on the picket line in the first place and shouldn't even have been there."

He lit an Export, poured a cup of dark, strong tea.

"You know," he said, "it's the pressure onto 'em. It didn't take very much for to get 'em in the ear anyway. But it seemed that the more things like this here happened, the stronger they got and the more determined they got. Well jeez, they'd say, we're not gonna do *that* any more – and they'd just knuckle right down to it, be right good and savage then."

"You know what made it tough over here, Everett?" Edison demanded. "We didn't have no picket shack. We had to bring the cars, and lots of times there was only one or two cars, and sometimes no cars at all. All the same there was a lot of miles put on that pavement down there."

It's one thing to declare that a strike exists; it's another thing to make it effective. Bookkeeping and morale-building, negotiating and writing leaflets – the strike called for a range of skills men like Everett had to learn from scratch. As one fisherman remarked, striking was almost as hard as fishing. Talking to reporters, allocating strike pay – and picketing, picketing, picketing.

"I put twenty-six hours down there right straight one time," Everett remembered. "It was late that night when I got home, and I was just gettin' a good sleep – and by Jesus, that's the night Russell was down there and got the line all snarled up. I had to turn around and go down there and stay again until daylight."

Russell Gurney, Everett's son-in-law, a hefty, rosy-faced good-natured young man. Linda Richardson Gurney laughed.

"I remember that night."

"Russell went down there, and set to snarling with his brother," Everett explained. "They were drinkin'. Just talk more'n anything, you know, one word bringin' on another the way it is with two brothers. You can get along with somebody else a lot better than you can with your brother sometimes, 'cause you won't say to the other feller what you'll say to your brother. I know I was plenty contrary; I went back down there and me and Russell got into it. 'Lord Jesus,' I said to him, 'it's bad enough for to be down here twenty-six hours let alone you going down and friggin' up the picket line again, making it that much harder for a feller. You're not supposed to be here,' I said, 'stay the Christ clear of the picket line.' All that sort of stuff."

"And then I had to go and straighten *him* out," said Edison, with a laugh.

57

"That's right, you had to go straighten him. But the fellers that just stood their picket duty for the four hours and went home, they'd say you had nothin' to do. You'd be lookin' after the picket line and the strike pay and keeping all the names down. And then you had your committee meetings in Mulgrave, besides your membership meetings here – and they think you had nothin' to do! But them was the fellers that never realized what was goin' on anyway. As long as they stood in the picket line they figured that's all there is to it. The rest is gonna go all by itself."

"I've seen days," Bertha burst in, "where you wouldn't even see Dad. He'd come home, he'd be in bed, we'd be gettin' up. Or we'd be in bed and he'd be gettin' up. We never even seen him. Pass him on the steps maybe if you were lucky. Oh, walk down the picket lines, you might see him there."

The men walked off the boats on March 30 and April 2; on April 5, a hand lettered note from James Allen of Lunenburg, the United Fishermen's general organizer in Nova Scotia, informed Booth's management "that members of the above named union, that are crewmen on 'Booth Fisheries Fleet,' have voted to withdraw service from aforementioned fleet, untill the company (Booth Fisheries Ltd.) recognizes 'The United Fishermen and Allied Workers' Union' as sole bargaining agent for said crewmen." Acadia received a similar note.

Meanwhile in Halifax, the Legislature's Industries Committee was considering the affairs of "a British-based fish processing company" which was "not identified by name, although both Liberal and Progressive Conservative members of the committee know the company." The company, said J.C. Arthur, secretary of the province's Industrial Loan Board, had received a cool $12,-570,320 in government assistance to establish its Nova Scotia operation – $9 million from the province, chiefly in loans, and $3.5 million from the federal government, mostly outright grants for sewer and water, wharves and dredging, and construction of fishing vessels. The mysterious company was $186,000 behind on its provincial loan payments. Opposition Leader Gerald Regan said it was "unfortunate" that ownership of the company was entirely in the hands of non-Nova Scotians, a theme he was finding particularly congenial in those days.

The nameless company was, of course, Acadia Fisheries, whose immediate concern was that the fishermen had asked the shoreworkers not to handle fish landed after midnight April 8. Some Acadia ships were still at sea, said the management; surely it's fair to let us process their catches, even if they do come in after the 8th? The fishermen agreed. The strike went on silently; the picketers, Cadegan testified later, "continued to be in evidence at both plants but did not seriously interfere with our normal operations – apart from the fact that we could not sail our trawlers – until the morning of April 14, 1970."

That morning the strikers refused to allow a truck loaded with offal to enter the Mulgrave plant. In succeeding days, the strikers turned away shoreworkers from the plant, prevented several other trucks from entering or leaving the premises, and began to voice colourful opinions about the ancestry and personal habits of the management.

By April 17, the strike was drawing brief notices in the Halifax papers. Linden MacIntyre, usually one of Nova Scotia's best journalists, outlined the events to date – three plants closed, 230 trawlermen and 800 shoreworkers idle, concern about the ability of the companies to withstand a long strike. He also struck the chord the major papers would sound throughout the strike.

In the thick of the dispute is the controversial United Fishermen and Allied Workers' Union which was involved in labor turmoil on the west coast for years.

The union has been on the decline in western Canada since the turbulent strike in Prince Rupert, B.C. several years ago that lasted six months and ended only after the wives of striking fishermen picketed their husbands.

Homer Stevens, the president of the union was subsequently sued for $494,000 by vessel owners whose ships had been ruined by rotting fish . . . Charles Gordon, regional manager for Booth Fisheries, was in Petit de Grat yesterday to meet with trawler captains and union officials. Mr. Gordon was not available for comment, but it is understood that he told the meeting Booth will not do business with the United Fishermen under any circumstances.

The situation is tense in the three communities and there have already been reports of threatened violence. A trawler captain refused to unload a cargo of herring in Canso yesterday for fear that his ship would be damaged by picketers. Local observers here say that the strike could be 'a calamity' for the whole Isle Madame economy.

On May 11, Acadia Fisheries took the confrontation another step. When the fishermen blocked a company truck loaded with fish trying to leave the Canso plant for the Kennedy Lobster Company in Auld's Cove, the company called the police. A couple of dozen Mounties cleared the way, and the truck roared out. The strikers phoned their local at Mulgrave. Two carloads of union men went to intercept the truck, which had to pass through Guysborough.

At Guysborough, they found the truck stopped at a gas station. They surrounded it; Gordon Baker snatched out its keys and threw them away. Again the RCMP appeared, and told the fishermen to move. They did, though with some reluctance. Move your car, a Mountie told Ray Cooper; he did, leaving the keys in it. A Mountie locked it up and took the keys. "Hey," said Cooper, "Gimme the keys!" He was charged with mischief, others with various similar offences. Five men were held overnight in Guysborough jail, tried, and convicted the next day, then released without being sentenced. Five months later, they still had not been sentenced.

The next day the company took out another truck. As it left the grounds, the angry fishermen pelted it with stones, breaking the windshield and two side windows. Russell Gurney jumped on the bumper and tried to open the hood. As a company witness later testified, with unconscious humour, "the truck was forced to stop as soon as it had gotten well clear of the main body of strickers, (sic) in order to remove Mr. Russell Gurney from his unsafe and illegal driving position." Later the same day the truck which had gone to Halifax returned, and was similarly treated to a barrage of rocks. Acadia Fisheries lost another windshield and pair of side windows, and the watchman was driven back inside the building by another fusillade. Since he couldn't open the gate, the truck driver rammed his way through it.

Suddenly the strike began to be noticed. The union's joint committee, representing fishermen in all three ports, fired off a protest to both the provincial and federal Attorneys-General; the Mounties, it said, were engaging in "provocation and intimidation coupled with strike breaking." The Mounties denied it. New Democratic MP Frank Howard spoke in the House of Commons, demanding that the RCMP "keep their noses out of such matters" and charging them with making inflammatory and provocative statements to the effect that they didn't want the UFAWU in Nova Scotia. The Mounties denied that, too. The picket line increased from the usual five or ten members to nearly eighty; a similar number of townspeople stood by in support.

On May 13, a reporter from the pro-union *Cape Breton Highlander* arrived in Canso to find the town remarkably quiet. A couple of picketers chatted with the Mounties, who drove off as the reporter began taking pictures. Pretty good relations with the police, fellows?

"You should've been here last night," chuckled a fisherman. "Relations weren't so good then. But these fellows here are regulars around here and we get along fine with them. They're friendly enough and they say live and let live. But when they send carloads of 'em to break our lines and take up for the company, we got to take a stand. If we don't there's no point in being here." Another carload of police passed, and the men scowled at it. Not regulars, apparently.

Were they still solid, despite the arrests, despite reported efforts by the priest and the local Member of the Legislative Assembly to get them into the Seafood Workers?

"One hundred per cent solid, sir, and there ain't no one goin' to break this strike. We can stay out six months if we have to and don't you believe any of that talk about another union comin' in here. This is the union that came lookin' for us four years ago, we didn't have to go lookin' for them. Besides it's the only real union for the fishermen themselves, not for some other industry."

It looked to the reporter like tough times ahead. Everett Richardson snorted. "What the hell kind of times the fishermen *ever* had?" he demanded. "It's all tough and it'll probably get tougher, but that's nothin' new for us. We've got food, thanks to the Farmers' Union we've got potatoes. We can always get some fish for ourselves. We're not going to starve. That's one thing the company better realize, buddy: you can't starve a fisherman."

What about the company claims that the union was Communist, that it would drive them out of business with strikes?

"They got themselves a dandy strike by *refusing* to recognize us, so that's a pretty stupid reason. And there's not a union in the country that would have kept so cool as we did with the annoyance that we're getting. It's our union and we're sticking with it to the end."

Since April 27, the union had been able to offer at least minimal strike pay: ten dollars for a single man, fifteen dollars for a couple plus a dollar a child up to a maximum of twenty dollars. By now support was coming in: potatoes from the National Farmers' Union, cash from the United Mine Workers in Cape Breton and Springhill, the Carpenters in Halifax, the Steelworkers in Sydney. Trade unionists sent $5,000 from British Columbia, where UFAWU members were carrying the story of the Nova Scotia strike to other workers. The union hoped to increase the strike pay as its support built up, and did manage to do so for two weeks later in the summer.

The shoreworkers were having an almost equally tough time, wrangling over unemployment insurance benefits. Bryce Mackasey, then Minister of Labour, explained to the House on April 20 that

> where it can be proven that a worker is without work as the result of a strike in which he is not participating, and from which he will derive no direct benefit, that person is entitled to unemployment insurance. It is only in a case where a person is out of work who may not be a member of the union but will benefit from the collective agreement that is eventually signed, that we ask him to share the responsibility of the union members on strike and not draw unemployment insurance benefits.

The company tactic was obvious enough: call the shoreworkers back to their jobs. If they didn't come, they lost their benefits; if they did come, they broke the fishermen's picket lines. Thirty-five workers in Petit de Grat lost their benefits when the company claimed it had work for them, and they refused to cross the picket lines. The Unemployment Insurance Commission handbook says a voluntary withdrawal of labour during a strike is "participation" in the strike; a withdrawal because of fears of violence from the picketers is not "participation." A union fisherman studied the ruling, and concluded the best thing the strikers could do for the shoreworkers was to threaten them with violence. But then, he thought, no doubt the strikers themselves would be in trouble with the law. "Same old Jesus thing," he said. "The regulations got you whichever way you turn."

Shuttling from coast to coast, Homer Stevens had a further complication that May: a meeting of the Canadian Labour Congress in Winnipeg at which the UFAWU, strongly supported by the 160,000-member BC Federation of Labour, was petitioning to rejoin the Congress. But the CLC had taken up a position in favour of merging small unions into a few large powerful ones. The Congress leadership used this as a pretext to keep the fishermen out unless they were prepared to merge with the Canadian Food and Allied Workers, though they made no similar conditions for the affiliation of other unions. "No one told the Mine Workers they had to come in through Steel," Paddy Neale of the Vancouver Labour Council told the convention. "No one told the Seafarers they had to go into the CBRT. And if the Teamsters come back into affiliation, will they be asked to merge first with the CBRT or some other union? I'll bet not."

The real problem, as usual, was the division between the highly political, socially-oriented unionism of the fishermen and the symbiotic unionism which has become characteristic of the American-dominated international unions; that division, in turn, emerged in a widely-publicized outburst of red-baiting by CLC President Donald MacDonald, after a proposal to admit the UFAWU without a merger was defeated by a two to one majority.

"May I say to some of the sinister forces that are operating in this Convention," MacDonald declared, "particularly the Communist Party of Canada, that the delegates who have the honour to represent the workers of Canada today have demonstrated to you what they think of your sinister efforts to pervert the movement."

"MacDonald, I'm no more sinister than you just because I disagree with you!" shouted a CBRT delegate from Montreal.

"If the mukluk fits, wear it!" roared MacDonald.

A Vancouver delegate protested that the sizeable minority

which had supported the UFAWU re-entry bid were being smeared.

"Certain delegates," snapped MacDonald, "are stupid enough to be led around by the Communists." He moved the meeting on to its next item of business.

In Nova Scotia, the *Chronicle-Herald,* which is not noted for its avid interest in labour's affairs, displayed the story prominently. The companies redoubled their efforts to convince Nova Scotians that the union was not a proper union at all, that it would only disrupt the East Coast fishery and work against the interests of the fishermen, that they were "not anti-union," in Cadegan's phrase, "but anti-Communist and anti-Homer Stevens." From this point on, another theme became apparent: if the men would give up the UFAWU and choose a CLC union, the companies would recognize it at once.

Several clergy and minor officials took up the same tack. Con Mills chuckled at that idea. Nobody ever cared about the fishermen, he told a reporter, until the UFAWU signed them up. Now, suddenly, everyone wants the poor fishermen to have a union. They just don't want them to have the union they themselves have picked; they want them to have a union chosen by someone else. But the Brotherhood and the Seafood Workers had made it plain that while the UFAWU was on strike, it was "hands off"; the Brotherhood actually contributed to the strike funds.

Things were moving. On May 20, the *Chronicle-Herald* phoned Chicago to speak with Frank Spencer, vice-president of Booth Fisheries. Spencer said that his firm considered the Petit de Grat situation "grim," and was considering pulling out of Nova Scotia. The workers, he said, had "the choice of going back or staying out, possibly for good" unless the company received "immediate encouragement." He remarked that the company considered it had treated the people of Petit de Grat fairly in the past and he was surprised that the community had not reacted to the possibility of losing its livelihood.

In fact, Earl Lewis had said the same thing in an address a month earlier, calling on the residents of Isle Madame to choose between the UFAWU and Booth Fisheries. "You can't have both," he claimed. Booth would never deal with such an "irresponsible" union. If the strike were not settled by June 27, Booth later announced, it would abandon the plant.

The next day, the governments acted. By now the strike was nearly two months old, and both the union and the companies had repeatedly called on the provincial government, particularly, to act. Fisheries Minister John Buchanan had held "general discussions" with Homer Stevens and the three local presidents; Premier G. I. Smith had remarked in the legislature that the fishermen were not under provincial but federal jurisdiction; and the federal government muttered that Allan MacEachen would have visited the area – part of his own riding, after all – had he not been detained in Ottawa on House business, and that someday a determination of the legal status of fishermen would no doubt have to be made.

But on May 21, Nova Scotia Labour Minister, Dr. Tom McKeough and his federal counterpart, Bryce Mackasey, announced the joint appointment of Judge Nathan Green of Halifax as a one-man commission of inquiry to examine "the cessation of fishing" at the three ports and "any matters incidental or related" to it.

LENGTHY FISHERIES STRIKE MAY END SOON

trumpeted the *Chronicle-Herald*, reporting the appointment. Even the fishermen were jubilant. "A completely new thing is happening, and you're all a part of it," cried Homer Stevens at a meeting of 450 fishermen and sympathizers in Guysborough High School a couple of days later. "This time the fishermen are going to win!"

The Guysborough meeting, like an earlier one in Petit de Grat, had been intended to allow the fishermen to confront the various federal and provincial officials concerned with the fishery – but before the meetings, Judge Green's appointment was announced, and on his recommendation, the officials decided to skip the meeting.

Stevens reminded the audience that the Green commission's findings wouldn't be binding on anyone, and that it was still possible that the union would have to "drag the companies screaming into the twentieth century. I hope not."

"The meeting was an eye-opener for observers who came to

65

watch a firebrand union raising the brand of hell that's been attributed to the UFAWU," reported the *Highlander*.

Preceded by a quiet afternoon gathering at Petit de Grat, the Guysboro meeting was chaired by Canso mayor James Hanlon who wished the fishermen a just settlement. And as MLA W. N. MacLean observed, 'I've never seen a more attentive audience or a more polite one.'

And Homer Stevens' quiet, self-assured platform style wasn't what the average strike-watcher had been prepared for, especially since CLC President Donald MacDonald had linked the UFAW a few days earlier with 'sinister forces' attempting to pervert the labour congress. Stevens didn't belabour that point, but he did emphasize that while the CBC report had emphasized MacDonald's Communist comments, 'the records of that convention will show that in all discussion about readmittance nothing was ever mentioned about the union leadership being left, right, or centre.' He thought MacDonald's statement 'was one of the worst ever made by a CLC president and I think he regretted it as soon as it was out.'

The meeting heard greetings from the Anglican clergy of the area, who said they were "continuing to pray for a speedy and just settlement." It seemed a reasonable prayer: Jim Collins, the Mulgrave local president, felt that a temporary return to work could come as soon as the companies agreed to a memorandum expressing willingness to negotiate with the union. As for the CLC rebuff, Collins remarked that "If Homer Stevens wants to be a Communist, that's his business. He doesn't try to convert me to Communism and he knows that I don't want to. He's been working awful hard for us and we're going to win. You can see why the people are so solid behind him."

A week later, Judge Green met with company officers, with Stevens, and with the presidents of the three Canso Strait locals. The union outlined the conditions under which the fishermen would agree to return to work for eighteen days. Stevens warned Green not to recommend a return to work on company terms, since that would almost certainly destroy his credibility with the fishermen. On May 29, Judge Green destroyed it.

He cabled the two labour ministers in an interim report:

I see no prospect for early settlement of the issues between the union and the plant operators. As the economic welfare of a large segment of the three communities of Canso, Mulgrave and Petit de Grat are (sic) directly or indirectly affected, I recommend that operations resume as soon as possible, that the companies re-open their plants and their trawlers be made ready for fishing and the fishermen return to work on the same terms and conditions as existed prior to March 30, 1970, without discrimination by the operators against any of the union men.

"I don't know," said Everett Richardson. "He never done too much digging into it as far as I could see. He sat down at his desk and set out that this should be done and that should be done. The fishermen should go back the same way they were before they come ashore, and all this bunch of bull. And he thought the fishermen was going to be stupid enough to fall for that."

Homer Stevens thought there was "practically no chance the striking fishermen will return to work on the terms recommended by Judge Green," and the union scheduled meetings of the three Canso Strait locals. The members voted almost unanimously not to return to work and not to offer further voluntary co-operation with the Green inquiry: if they were subpoenaed, they would appear, but they wouldn't volunteer. Green was thought to be about to review the legislation regarding bargaining rights for fishermen: the union strongly opposed that idea, on the grounds that to do such a review would involve hearings right across the country and would delay action on the strike itself. Meanwhile Green was arranging a set of hearings, the first being expected about June 10.

But before that time events had raced far beyond the inquiry.

On June 4, the Supreme Court of Nova Scotia ordered the union, its president, and thirty-seven named fishermen to stop picketing by June 15 or face contempt of court charges. As Linden MacIntyre put it, the injunction, issued by the late Mr. Justice D. J. Gillis, in effect ordered the men to end their strike.

For people who have had little to do with the courts – and particularly with court actions in labour disputes – it is difficult to believe such injunctions are possible. The June 4 order was an *ex parte* injunction; the term means that the judge only hears one side of the dispute. In theory, such injunctions are emergency procedures, used when an immediate problem requires an immediate remedy; they are usually interim injunctions, as this one was, designed to stop some action or other long enough to allow a full judicial hearing. If you believe a developer is about to knock down an irreplaceable historic building, you probably need an *ex parte* injunction to make sure he doesn't knock it down before you get a chance to show it should be saved.

But what is an emergency? Companies traditionally argue that picketing is an emergency which will inflict irreparable damage on their businesses, and the courts have normally been warmly sympathetic to such claims, issuing such anti-picketing injunctions on an almost casual basis. One New Brunswick judge, indeed, has been known to issue such an injunction in his bathroom, while shaving. The *point* of a picket line, of course, is to bring a company to a halt; it is labour's most powerful weapon. Break the picket line, and the company can always find scabs to operate the plant. The strike can go on forever: without a picket line it is pointless.

Homer Stevens heard about the injunction hearing late on the afternoon of June 4. He wired Judge Gillis asking for a postponement so that the union could marshal its arguments against the injunction. At a one-hour hearing that evening, Peter Green, the Halifax lawyer who represented the union, made the same request. Judge Gillis refused, on the grounds that the strike had already gone on too long, and went ahead with the injunction.

A strike two months old, an injunction giving the men ten days to stop picketing: a curious emergency, this.

The fishermen kept marching. The sheriffs of Guysborough and Richmond Counties served their injunctions. The Mounted Police asked their names and took photographs.

The phone rang at the little house on the edge of Canso, and Jean Richardson answered it. "One of the women called and said, 'We should go down too; *we* should go down.' I had doubts about whether I would want to and whether Everett would really want me to, so I said, 'Well, I won't say anything now. We'll let you know what we decide.' Everett wasn't home; Linda was here, and both Everett and Russell were to a meeting. So we talked it over, the two of us, and we thought maybe we should do something. Then, when the men came home we asked them if it was all right, and they said, 'Well, if there was other women, yeah, it was okay.' We were actually down there when they read the first injunctions.

"But once we got started we weren't turning back. They were taking pictures – but I don't like getting my picture taken, so therefore they didn't get any of me. That's once it paid to be camera-shy.

"After that we carried on in the picket line every day; we'd go down and pretty well stay all day. We could see that the men were being drawn off of the picket line. With those injunctions a lot of them wouldn't go and if they got put in jail somebody had to take over."

Linda Gurney is Jean's daughter, but the relationship between them is more like the relationship between sisters. Linda grew up with her grandparents nearby. "When we were married and Linda was born, we lived with Everett's parents," Jean explains. "They had four boys in their family and of course when Linda came along that was something else! Everett's father at that time wasn't too well, and when they moved into this new house, the house that Linda was living in during the strike, he insisted that Linda should come and stay with them. There was just nothing like Linda." The Richardsons are a Canso clan: Everett's brothers, uncles, aunts, and "any amount of cousins," says Jean, "were all involved in the strike."

Two of Jean's own children worked in the fish plant, and "they couldn't have too much to say or do, on account of their jobs there. But Bertha now, she did behind the scenes, because if she hadn't been home I couldn't have went, you know? There's an awful lot of the fishermen that do have sons or daughters and in some cases both, working at the plant. Well, they're not going to go against their own."

On June 8, Jeremy Akerman called on the provincial government to convene a special one-day sitting of the legislature to scrap the Fishermen's Federation Act and change the Trade Union Act to provide for certification of fishermen's unions. "The injunction," he declared, "is an abuse of the judicial system and an ugly, blunt instrument to which the fish companies resorted because they were losing the strike. . . . The neutrality of the courts and the industrial inquiry commission seems to many people to be something of a hoax."

On June 10, the companies once again attacked the alliance between the fishermen and the shoreworkers by calling the latter back to work, threatening their unemployment insurance benefits. The next morning a number of plant workers showed up, under the impression that the picketing was over. It wasn't, so they went home.

The pickets, in fact, now included not only the fishermen and their families, but various other sympathizers – notably members of the New Democratic Youth, the almost autonomous junior affiliate of the New Democratic Party.

"Those students were down all during the strike," says Everett. "They gave us good support, too."

"They were a lot of help," says Jean.

"Some of them stayed all summer, and then there'd be different groups come and maybe stay for a week and go – but when they were going there was another group coming. But quite a few of them stayed here the whole strike, right through from the start to the finish. But the biggest majority of them was in Mulgrave."

"You didn't have the place here to put them up," Jean explains. "You know, this was the problem. In Mulgrave they had a union hall."

"They'd come and bring their sleeping bags," says Everett. "They stayed right at the union hall over there, slept right on the stage. Summertime, and they really enjoyed theirselves, you know. They got around, too: if we were over at the committee meeting in Mulgrave and we had room and a couple of them wanted to come over, well, we'd bring them with us and some would stay at Edison's and Walter Hanlon's and different places around town, wherever we could put them up."

Eric Fitzpatrick, one of the strongest members of the Mulgrave local, also remembers the students with warmth. "There's no way I could describe what those people did for us," he marvels. "It was really wonderful. They walked the picket line, they went to meetings with us, they went to negotiations with us, when we had to go to Halifax they kept us under their roofs. When I first heard about them I figured that they were, you know, like the papers

70

described them, and television – they were just a bad bunch of people. Then I got to know them, and I think they're a *great* bunch of people."

For Everett, those days melt into a constant whirl. The three locals held their joint meetings in Mulgrave, roughly equidistant from Canso and Petit de Grat. Strike pay was co-ordinated with picket duty, so you had to have lists of who had stood picket duty and who hadn't. There were press releases to get out, meetings of the local, demonstrations to organize, fish sales to be organized in Sydney and Halifax.

"The fish sales were for the strike pay," Everett says, rolling a cigarette around in the ashtray. "We'd catch the fish here and take it to Petit de Grat and they'd fillet the fish over there and then a bunch would go down to Sydney and go around and sell it down there, advertise it on the news." They had to prepare the fish in Petit de Grat because the only ice available in Canso was at Acadia Fisheries; across the bay in Petit de Grat the Isle Madame Fishermen's Co-op would let them use their facilities.

"And there wasn't a time that we had a fish sale and got out our gear that there wasn't a screeching gale of wind the next day," says Edison Lumsden, shaking his head. "Men fished in weather like that they'd never even think about fishing in, under normal conditions."

"But you *could* fish in that kind of weather," Everett explains, "because when you put on a fish sale you had a whole boatload of fellers – maybe six or seven or more, instead of two or three. So when you went to haul your gear it was no trouble to haul it. Course when you go and set your gear you like to haul your *own* gear, you don't like to haul somebody else's neither. We went out and some of the boys got snarled up and cut our gear off and hauled it and give us theirs. They had more gear, so we ended up with twice as much gear to haul as what they had." He laughs. "Course it was all for the same place, the fish sale."

"Then we had to get it over to Petit de Grat," said Edison. "Ev, you remember that day Bill wouldn't go with me?"

"Martin Langille was with you," said Everett. "And Billy Ryan."

"No, Kenny Ryan."

"Kenny, right. And Russell."

71

"We had 6500 pounds that day," said Edison. "Gale of wind to the south'ard. Boy, that – well they still didn't know in Petit de Grat how we ever got in there. The seas were breakin' right across the harbour mouth. Oh, she took a shoot goin' in there! I don't know how fast she was goin'."

"Martin Langille," laughs Everett. Martin was an NDY supporter from Halifax. "Martin was standin' up and I could see the colour goin' right out of his knuckles and his face – if you had of cut his arm off I don't think you'd have got a drop of blood out of it. You know, it seemed like even the weather was against us, because every time we had a fish sale we had a gale. See, once you get the fish, you want to put them on the market fresh, so you had to get 'em over and ice 'em down right away. You can't keep 'em in your hold all day with no ice and take 'em over the next day."

"We had some good times," sighs Edison wistfully. "Some good laughs."

Picket lines, fish sales, and meetings. Endless meetings. Trying for men accustomed to active work. Edison and Everett don't find patience easy. "Many's the time I felt like quittin'," chuckles Everett.

"It's so rugged, especially when you take a bunch of greenhorns and get into something like this," Edison remarks, "something they've never been into before and never experienced anything even *close* to it! What can you expect?"

"You know," Everett recalls, "you'd get into them meetings and you want something done. So you ask Homer and say, 'Well, Homer, what about this?' And he'll say, 'All right, you fellers tell me what you want done. I'm not telling you what to do.' That made it all that much harder for us, all of us green at it and everything. He'd give us advice, but actually what had to be done, we had to make our own decisions for to do it. A lot of people figured we were only doing what Homer told us to do. But a lot of stuff that we told Homer, he'd just say, "I'm not making up your minds for you. You fellers tell me what you want to do.' "

"I've seen him sit there I'll bet you for two hours and not say one word," marvels Edison, "just listen to us fellers go into it. Someone would say, 'Well, aren't you going to say something?' 'No, I'm not saying nothing. You fellers are the union. You fellers are gonna make the decision. When you make up your own minds what you want me to do, then I'll see if I can do it.' "

"He has more patience than anyone ever I know," says Everett.

"I don't know why he didn't go crazy from it," says Edison. "I remember once we got through a meeting in Halifax at 2.00 in the morning. Everybody had left but Con and I."

"I was there," chuckles Everett.

"That's right, you were there too. And Homer mentioned a certain part of the Trade Union Act. 'You know about it?' he asked me. I said No. 'Well, now's a good time for you to learn.' " Everyone laughs. "Get the books out."

On June 13, the summonses started arriving. Hearings were to be held in Halifax before Nova Scotia Chief Justice Gordon Cowan. The picket lines were still up. Contempt of court.

Homer Stevens, Everett Richardson, and ten other fishermen went to Ottawa, to picket on Parliament Hill and hold a brief, unsatisfying meeting with Labour Minister Mackasey. Mackasey made it clear he would not ask for emergency legislation to settle the dispute; the matter, he said, would be dealt with when Parliament resumed after its summer recess.

On Friday, June 19, thirteen fishermen from Mulgrave appeared in Halifax before Judge Cowan. While the NDY marched outside, leafleting passersby, Cowan satisfied himself that the injunction was legal and that the men knew of its existence. No evidence had been given on behalf of the fishermen, he noted, and no apology or explanation had been offered. He asked Charles O'Connell, the men's lawyer, whether they were prepared to obey the injunction in the future.

"I felt pretty nervous lookin' at the old judge there," Eric Fitzpatrick later recalled. When he wanted us to apologize – well, really, to apologize to the companies – and we said we wouldn't apologize, he broke off for a fifteen-minute session to give us time to talk about it. The judge figured he was kind of scarin' everybody – and he *was,* the way he was comin' around about it. He figured that we didn't know what was goin' on, you know, he figured somebody got to explain it to us. The problem was a very serious problem to *him,* I guess.

"Homer simply told us what we were up against, and the lawyer briefed us, and Homer said, 'Well, you're facing something now that I faced, and you could possibly wind up getting a year in jail. It's in this judge's hands now, and God knows how he'll judge you. But I don't want you to go in there feeling that you don't know all about it. I want you to understand it.' I don't know whether I was the first guy, or whether Jim Lundrigan was the first to say, 'Well, we'll take our chances.'

"When we went back in, I was kind of nerved up, but I was still going to go through with it. If it meant a year, well, I was going to take a year, and I think all the fishermen felt the same way. We never went into it ignorant or anything, we knew what was going to happen."

O'Connell told the judge the men were not ready to apologize. Well, said Cowan, would they obey the unjunction? O'Connell said he could ask them to, but he could not guarantee they would comply.

Cowan turned to Homer Stevens, asking O'Connell to put the question to him. Stevens said he would have to consider the question in the light of the fact that he could not issue orders to restrain picketing.

Cowan had had enough. He told the men they were "pawns who were used, I suggest, by other people who told you to picket." In setting sentence he would have to bear in mind that they had not apologized and had not undertaken to obey the injunction. A fine would be inappropriate, he thought; they should serve some prison time "in order to bring home to you the seriousness of your offence." He sentenced them to twenty and thirty days – in Eric's case, to thirty days.

The next day, the Ottawa delegation headed for home and for Halifax, where they were due to appear in court Monday. A Canadian Press reporter interviewed Everett Richardson.

"At least the people of the country have a better idea of what's going on," said Everett, according to the published report. "Now our situation is known nation-wide." And would the men obey the injunction? Everett, said the reporter, indicated that "the men will continue to picket until their demands are met."

The bus taking the Canso men to their trials was due to leave at 6.00 Sunday; Everett arrived back about ten to six. Russell

Gurney also had to go, and since Monday would be his and Linda's wedding anniversary, Linda decided to go with him. Bertha had hurt her back and was having difficulty getting Workmen's Compensation. The three decided to wait overnight and drive Everett up in the morning. Jean stayed home with the two younger boys.

"Everett said to me that night, 'If the others had got clear, you know, I'd have a little bit of hopes. But I know that I'll get at least twenty days, probably thirty.' And I said, 'Well, with your involvement, you'll probably be one of the ones that get the thirty days."

In the courtroom, Cowan questioned Everett first. Had he said that the men would continue to picket until their demands were met, as the CP report had indicated? Was the report accurate? Well, said Everett, he hadn't seen the report. He couldn't remember just exactly what he might or might not have said to the reporter. Cowan persisted. Everett resisted. He couldn't say. And he couldn't say whether he'd continue to picket, either.

The court recessed, and Everett went into the hall for a cigarette. Bertha came out. "Well, Dad," she said, "from what I heard them sayin' up there, you're goin' for two months anyway. Don't worry; we'll hold the fort till you get back."

They went back inside. You are guilty, the Chief Justice of Nova Scotia told Everett, "of deliberately flouting the order of the court." He would impose a sentence that would deter Everett and others from further picketing in contravention of the injunction. "It will not be tolerated. This has to stop. Continued picketing will be dealt with severely." He remanded the others in custody for a week; their sentences would depend on what happened on the picket lines. Again he asked the men to apologize; again they refused. O'Connell asked that one fisherman, a war veteran named Bill Mosher, be allowed to return home to get in his lobster pots. Cowan said that since he was an older and wiser man, perhaps he could be allowed home if he would apologize to the court.

"Oh, no, your honour, I didn't mean that!" said Mosher. "I'll go with the boys."

"Then you'll go with the boys," said Cowan, and remanded him too.

But it was Everett Richardson's sentence over which Nova Scotia exploded. "I saw smiles and laughs over the twenty and thirty days' sentences on Friday," Cowan snapped. "This is not going to continue."

He sentenced Everett to nine months' imprisonment in the Halifax County Correctional Institution.

"A gasp burst from the packed galleries at announcement of the sentence," reported the *Chronicle-Herald*. "A sister of Richardson was led sobbing from the courtroom by a clergyman."

The "sister" was Bertha. The clergyman was Ron Parsons, Anglican rector of Canso. In the months ahead Nova Scotians would learn his name.

INTERLUDE
The Pulpits and
the Papers

"I preached for the Lord a mighty long time.
Preached about the rich and the poor.
Us workin' folks is all get together
'Cause we ain't got a chance any more,
We ain't got a chance any more."

– Tom Joad
Words & Music by Woody Guthrie

"Ron Parsons only come here in May," chuckles Everett, "and it seemed like when he come here, when he turned at the post office corner, instead of turning right he stumbled and – "

"He ended up in the picket line!" laughs Jean.

"He ended up on the picket line and it was just unfortunate for Ron, I think, that he made that stumble, but he's a good man for us. He was the only one that backed us up right from the start."

When the strike began, Ron Parsons was in charge of a parish in the Halifax suburb of Sackville. He was far from happy. Parsons comes from a large, poor family in a Newfoundland outport. He is married to a fisherman's daughter from Pictou. He knows poverty and powerlessness at first hand. He reckons that

Christianity is not just a matter of the hereafter, but has moral implications right here and now.

"It's my belief," says Ron Parsons, "that the present capitalist system will not stand up under the scrutiny of the Gospels, and in due course it'll be rejected. It remains to be seen whether the church will give leadership in this rejection.

"You know Christ's parable of the vineyard, the man who went out early in the morning to hire workers, and hired more again later that morning and at noon and in the afternoon. And at the end of the day he paid them all the same – 'whatsoever is right,' he said, 'that shall ye receive.' You see? The mere fact that a man hasn't been employed as long doesn't mean that his need is any the less.

"But Karl Marx put the same idea forward when he said, 'From each according to his ability, to each according to his needs.'

"Now!" says this most surprising of parish priests, "if Marx and Christ agree on this point, let's not *knock* it: let's thank God!" And he roars with laughter and delight.

Sitting in ticky-tacky Sackville, Parsons fretted. Down in Canso, his kind of person was fighting back. Ron Parsons wanted to move to Canso. Bishop William Davis agreed. In May, Anne and Ron and the five children moved into the old Anglican rectory on the waterfront, a couple of hundred yards from the picket lines around the Acadia Fisheries plant.

He wasn't in town two hours before he visited the picketers. When the Mounties arrested the Mulgrave men for interfering with the truck at Guysborough, Ron Parsons and Homer Stevens worked together to spring them. The fishermen began to feel comfortable in the rectory. Parsons went out fishing with them, catching cod to sell for the strike fund.

"I remember Parsons was out with us one morning," Everett chuckles, "and it blew a good breeze after we'd got the gear out. We were steamin' back and Parsons was out on the stern and I said, 'Yeh, let me see her' – and I took the wheel and I swung her off just as wide as she'd go over. Well, he wasn't long standin' out there, was he?"

"He just got in before it come in after him," laughs Edison. "It was a nice little puff, eh?"

With the fishermen, with their wives and children, the priest walked the picket line. Parsons makes a small, throaty chuckle. He remembers once a townswoman who supported the company coming up to the picket line, taunting the strikers.

"They're still not breakin' through that picket line, eh?"

"No, they ain't."

"If I was twenty years younger," shouted the woman, "I'd smash right through it: I would!"

"If you was twenty years younger," snapped a union wife, "you'd *fuck* your way through it like you did with the crew of that fourteen-dory Yankee longliner that was in here them days."

And, as Parsons listened with amusement, a woman behind him in the picket line turned to her companion.

"Isn't that terrible?" she whispered. "You'd think with the priest here she'd at least have had the decency to say 'screw'."

Telling the story, Parsons rocks with laughter. There is nothing mean or prim about him; he places no great value on respectability. He loves the fishermen, their raucous vitality, their common sense, their courage, their humour. He loves life, he rejoices in the candour of these beer-drinking, story-telling trappers of the sea. He hankers for the sea himself; he would like to have a boat.

One summer day he gets one. A freighter has been driven on the rocks several miles up the bay; a group of union fishermen take a boat and steam up to the ruined ship. They liberate a lifeboat. They give it to the priest.

When the fishermen went to court, Ron Parsons went with them. When Bertha broke down, Ron Parsons took her out of the courtroom and consoled her. When Jean was still numbed by the notion that Everett would be gone for nine months, Ron Parsons came home from Halifax and came to see her, told her he had been to see Everett, explained the the Correctional Institution wasn't all that bad a place.

In the summer of 1970, a good many fishermen began to attend services in the Anglican Church.

Does this mean the churches supported the fishermen?

Certainly not.

A. L. Cadegan points out the many clergymen both in the Strait area and around the province who *did* lend their efforts to the fishermen's struggle: Anglicans like Canon Mel French of Halifax, Cal MacMillan of Arichat, Gordon Neish of Port Dufferin; Catholics like Father Bob Lauder of Ketch Harbour, Father Georges Arsenault in Petit de Grat and Father Tom Morley in Bras d'Or. When Everett Richardson was sentenced, Morley, himself a one-time union man, published a trenchant commentary in the *Cape Breton Highlander*

"We ourselves should be on the picket lines with the fishermen," Morley wrote, "supporting them, and their wives and children whose simple housing and skimpy table are the true subsidizers of capitalists from Chicago and London who can call long distance and threaten, with impunity, to run away with the people's livelihood."

Donnie Cadegan snorts. "I've been told by a clergyman," he declares, "that that Morley comes into a community and tears it apart and leaves it for someone else to clean up. He went out on an old wooden side trawler out of Alder Point – that's no comparison at all with the conditions on *our* ships. They have comfortable quarters, decent food – I admit they're on duty long hours, but it's not all work time. When the fishing's good they work like hell, but that's not a normal trip. Mind you, I think fishing is a hard, tough way to make a living. I think changes have to be made or we just won't have any fishermen. But that Morley – !"

But for every Morley there was an A.P. Poirer of Arichat, an immovable opponent of the union. For every Ron Parsons there was a Rev. Henry Whiteway, who ran a curious little evangelical mission in Canso and who detested the union and its works, or Father Hector Macdonald, the local Catholic, who won grudging respect from the fishermen for standing aloof.

"Macdonald told us right up and down right there," says Everett, "he told us he wasn't having nothing to do with *no* union. He said he got snarled up once in Cape Breton and he said he wasn't for them and he wasn't against them, he just stayed on neutral ground, and I think what time he was here he was truthful about that. He didn't interfere one way or another."

Rev. Harold Beaumont was the local Baptist minister.

"He was with us on the first of it," remembers Everett. "He come down and talked to us on the picket line. 'Boys,' he said, 'if you want to take your kettles and use my basement up there for to get coffee and stuff, you're welcome to it.' That was only for a couple of weeks and then he just kind of sheered clear of us. So I was over to Edison's one time, Ron Parsons was there, too, and they brought up Beaumont. So Edison says, 'By Jesus, I'm gonna call him up, tell him to come down. We'll have a talk to him, find out what side of the fence he's on.' So he come right down. Edison did most of the talking. I didn't belong to his church, but Edison did, and I figured it was up to Edison. Edison asked him right blank up and down. He said, 'Are you with us or not?' When he left, he said he was with us.

"Two days afterward Edison received this letter. Ron and I got copies. Here."

The letter is in a cheap frame, like a picture. In it Beaumont explains that he has been polling the other local clergy, and has learned some alarming things. Specifically, he mentions

the use of alcoholic beverages in public on the picket line on Tuesday and also of returning a provoking move by the company trucks with force and intimidation. This has been most unfortunate as much backing could be lost in this way. Since the granting of the first liquor license to the public published hearing a year and a half ago, Reverend Whiteway and myself were the only two to oppose this and he appeared alone at a later hearing when I was away and the license was granted. We must still stand unashamedly opposed to its use. I also find that I cannot share your personal viewpoints and as thus I would not be willing to have a Communist organization come in locally. I had a classmate in college killed overseas fighting, and also some Christian missionaries have been killed by Communists. As a minister said at the Mermaid Hotel meeting [of Canso clergymen], 'This is the central issue of our meeting today.' I feel that it is still the central issue and I feel that must come to make the stand of myself as being unable to back communism in any form. As was also brought out at the Mermaid meeting, we would still support the demands of the fishermen for just settlement.

Everett takes the letter back and chuckles.

"When I received that in the mail I said, if it's the last thing I do, when I get to Antigonish, I'm gonna get a frame to put it in. When I went to Antigonish I had seventy-five cents in me pocket and I bought the frame. I think it cost me thirty-seven cents.

"Before the strike we and Beaumont were the best of friends, and he even come to the house here and visited me. But since I got the letter I never saw him again. He's gone to Annapolis Royal now."

In the same letter, Beaumont mentions a parishioner named Windeler. "This Windeler," says Jean Richardson, "rules the Baptist Church. If you don't do it his way, there's likely to be less money in the collection plate." That kind of pressure was brought to bear on Parsons, too, and more heavily as the months went on. That it should be possible for a church to be bullied by money seems to Parsons outrageous. He's fond of pointing out that the Jesus Christ he discovers in the Gospels was not an official, but a worker, a man who chose publicans and customs collectors to carry on his work, and whose first four disciples were fishermen.

"Our standard image of Jesus," he once remarked, "shows him with delicate hands, but those hands were the calloused hands of a carpenter." But the church has drifted away from such people. "The medieval priest wasn't alienated from the people. He was one of them; he was a farmer. When they went hungry, he went hungry. It would be better if I were a fisherman and serving one village, instead of trying to serve six the way I am now."

And when he talks about the roots of his beliefs, Parsons goes back to his own experience.

"When I was seven our teacher showed us a picture of burning wheat on the Canadian Prairies. It was 1934 and wheat was being burned to keep prices up while people were starving. 'You know what that is?' he said. 'It's the people of Canada offering a sacrifice to their god – the Canadian dollar.'

"In those days people I knew were dying of malnutrition. I didn't find out until much later that that was why they had died. It was quite common for people to die of malnutrition in Newfoundland then; the government had put a duty on food. They couldn't put a duty on clothing because nobody in Newfoundland bought clothing.

"If my convictions began somewhere, then that was it. They're convictions that can stay at the back of your mind for a long time – until a situation like this one brings them right out again."

The contempt of court sentences were the high point of the church concern for the fishermen. Bishop Davis, in consultation with Parsons, MacMillan and Rev. Ted Burton of Mulgrave, issued a statement which made headlines: "We deeply regret that so many of our Nova Scotia fishermen should be imprisoned . . . this is the first occasion in a labour dispute in Canada since World War II where all picketing has been outlawed, and convictions have been made under such an injunction." The statement went on to point out the responsibilities of both senior governments, of the Nova Scotia Federation of Labour, and of the companies. "Although technically guilty of a breach of the law, our fishermen need our understanding and concern in their complicated and difficult situation."

The pro-fishermen press was considerably less restrained. Frank Fillmore, who had written for *The 4th Estate* in Halifax an extended report on the strike a month earlier, blasted the court in a full-page commentary headed:

CONTEMPT FOR THE LAW:
WHAT ELSE COULD AN HONEST MAN HAVE?

Fillmore was "dismayed, shocked and revolted" at the contempt sentences, and predicted that they would fail to stop the picketing.

I believe that in pushing on with these unjust injunction proceedings and criminal contempt charges against impoverished and ill-educated workingmen, the companies and the Attorney-General's department have set wheels in motion that will bring about the most severe confrontation between government and labour, the courts and labour that Nova Scotia has ever seen. . . .

And the *Highlander* in Sydney was equally appalled:

To abuse the rights of the people by insisting on enforcement of an unjust law is wrong, and all the judges and courts and lawyers in the world cannot make it right. They can send free men to jail for refusing to allow the law-machine to rob them of their natural and constitutional rights, but they cannot make justice out of injustice.

Anyone who does nothing in the face of this issue condones evil.

But the *Highlander* and *The 4th Estate* were only small weeklies; the paper which covers Nova Scotia like an industrial effluent is the Halifax *Chronicle-Herald* and its evening incarnation, the *Mail-Star*. The provincial Attorney-General of the day was one R. A. Donahoe, a particularly conservative authoritarian whose opinions disturbed even some of his own colleagues in the decaying Tory government. Earlier in 1970, Chief Justice Cowan himself – hardly a bleeding-heart – described Nova Scotia's Dickensian county jails as "horrible and disgraceful institutions." Donahoe's reaction? "Going to jail is *supposed* to be an unpleasant experience."

Against this background, consider the Halifax daily's editorial for June 15, on the eve of the fishermen's trial.

Addressing the graduating class of the Victoria General School of Nursing, Public Health Minister R. A. Donahoe, who also is the province's attorney-general, urged the cultivation of a respect for law and of that sense of responsibility upon which our society is based.

The theme is one which needs to be often sounded in this age when the system of law and order is so often abused and when people, insisting on their own rights, ignore those of others. . . . It is disturbing . . . when, as occurred recently in the Canso area, strikers refuse to heed a court injunction.

More damaging than such ponderous attempts at original thought was the *Herald's* covert editorializing in its news stories and even its headlines. The UFAWU was always "the West Coast union" or "the B.C. union." Fears were always being expressed about the effects of the strike on the community – and somehow the reader was left with the impression that the union was solely responsible for the conflict. Like the companies, the *Herald* insisted on regarding Homer Stevens' politics as a vital factor in the strike, ignoring the central issue: what gives anyone but the men themselves the right to decide which union will represent them?

"We never got no treatment *at all* from the press," Everett argues, thumping a big fist on the kitchen table. "Sure, we got good support from the little left-wing papers, but how far do they travel? They're only here in the community. What we wanted, we wanted coverage to go across the nation. But you ask any of the fishermen what we got from the *Chronicle-Herald.* We never got *nothing* from the *Chronicle-Herald.* We read a lot that was put in for the company, and the fishermen give them statements but they never ever printed it. As far as I'm concerned, they just come down and got statements from us and I think they passed it out to the company and forgot about it. We wanted to get the story across Canada, so that everybody can see what's goin' on –"

"Even across Nova Scotia," said Jean. "And the Halifax *Herald* is really the only daily paper."

"Some of the fellows around Mulgrave said we done a little better with the Cape Breton *Post,*" said Everett.

"We didn't do so bad on radio," Linda Gurney volunteered. "Any time they'd call me I'd talk to 'em just the same's I'd talk to Jean right now. And live on radio, well, we got perfect coverage. There's no reason why the fishermen should feel that they didn't get good coverage – "

In terms of sheer weight of clippings, the press was no doubt overwhelmingly pro-fishermen. The small papers in Nova Scotia and their counterparts across the country backed the fishermen's demands, appealed for funds, reported events: *The Mysterious East* in Fredericton, *New Canada* in Toronto, *Canadian Dimension* in Winnipeg, above all the nationally-distributed *Last Post,* which ran two excellent reports by Robert Chodos. Some, at least, of CBC radio's coverage was sympathetic and thoughtful – notably that of *As It Happens,* then a weekly show hosted by Bill Ronald. The news coverage was less impressive. "The CBC figured that they give the fishermen good coverage?" demands Everett. "They want to come down here and talk to some of the fishermen."

But the point about all these outlets is the one Everett proposes: how far do they travel? What is their weight in forming public opinion? CBC captures well under 10 per cent of the radio audience; *The 4th Estate* and the *Highlander* have circulations of between 10,000 and 15,000; nobody would rank *Last Post* or *New Canada* among the giants of the Canadian media.

But the *Chronicle-Herald is* a regional giant. The Cape Breton *Post* of Sydney, with 28,000 circulation in 1970, was a force of some importance in Cape Breton Island. But the Siamese twins of Halifax (or, as *The 4th Estate* preferred to call them, The Old Persons of Argyle Street) with a combined circulation of 135,000 towered over all the other publications in the province. The importance of their doughy presence in the life of the province can hardly be overestimated.

Like the church, the press was bitterly divided over the strike. Like the church, the press ranged its most powerful forces against the fishermen.

It's worth asking why. Was there a conscious conspiracy of the wealthy and the powerful to thwart the union's drive for recognition in Canso Strait?

To some extent there certainly was. The other East Coast fishing companies covered the market commitments of Acadia Fisheries, and provided the company with a monthly subsidy of $25,000 to help them fight the strike. (Booth, with other plants and affiliated companies close to hand, was able to take care of itself.) All the fish companies also submitted a joint brief to the Green inquiry, maintaining stoutly that the fishermen were, even now, not employees but co-adventurers – even companies which had signed contracts with the CBRT.

"The fishing industry in Nova Scotia has made a decision," Homer Stevens explained, "and that decision amounts to this: to do everything possible to prevent the growth and strength of militant, capable unionism in the industry. Essentially all the strategy and tactics have been worked out in a combination of all the companies."

Stevens' assessment of the situation seems to be accurate. Donnie Cadegan won't comment on the subsidy and the marketing assistance, but he doesn't deny them either. And one can easily understand the companies taking such a joint position: as one fish plant manager told me, "certainly we were all very sympathetic to Acadia. Donnie Cadegan was fighting the common enemy."

It is less easy to understand the sympathy with which the companies were treated by the churchmen, the dominant political parties, the major newspapers, the courts, and even the police. Less easy, that is, until one considers just *how many* fishermen Nova Scotia contains. Inshore and offshore, part-time and full-time, fishing all the different species with various kinds of gear – how many? I've heard estimates ranging from 10,000 to 44,000. And the UFAWU would cheerfully have signed up every one.

Suppose the union had signed up only a few thousand: it clearly would have become the pace-setting union in the resource industries, driving ever-harder bargains, offering its members political education through the union newspaper and other vehicles, prodding the labour movement, challenging the entire economic and political power structure of Nova Scotia just as it challenges the same structure in British Columbia. In a province of only a million people, its political significance would have been enormous.

And it is the political nature of the whole conflict which made it so central, for a season, to Nova Scotia's public life. The political implications of the strike brought the fishermen the support of the NDP, brought the young radicals down to the picket lines, brought the opposition journalists to Canso Strait from Montreal and Halifax, Toronto and Fredericton. It is the political significance of the strike which made Nova Scotia's establishment so determined to break it as to risk a head-on challenge to the whole labour movement and its supporters.

The establishment, I feel sure, entered into no overt conspiracy aside from the coalition within the fishing industry. When Gordon Cowan sentenced Everett Richardson to nine months in prison, he was doing what he conceived to be his unavoidable duty; he was not acting as a puppet of the Cadegans, the Lewises, the Nickersons, the Morrows, or any other member of the codfish aristocracy.

But the law is not impartial when a poor man meets a rich one. The law reflects not justice, but power. Laws are made by those who have the power to enforce them. And them fellers ain't fishermen. Not a single one of 'em.

JUNIOR COLLEGE
Now the Women
are a Great Help

(June 23 – August 9, 1970)

"You girls who want to be free,
Just take a tip from me!
Get you a man who's a Union man
And join the Ladies Auxiliary.
Married life ain't hard
When you've got a Union card,
A Union man has a happy life
When he's got a Union wife."

Union Maid
Words & Music by Woody Guthrie
TRO – © Copyright 1961 & 1963, Ludlow Music, Inc.,
New York, N.Y. Used by permission.

Seven thousand workers walked off their jobs the day after Everett Richardson was sentenced.

Directly across the narrow Strait of Canso from Mulgrave, the multi-national corporations were building mills and refineries which were to make Port Hawkesbury "bigger than Halifax by the end of the century," according to its enthusiastic boosters. On June 23, 1970, those developments came to an abrupt halt as 2,500 construction workers put down their tools and drove by the score across the Canso Causeway to Mulgrave to walk the picket lines with the wives and children of the fishermen. If Chief Justice Cowan was going to break *this* picket line, he would have to build more prisons, and build them fast.

In the old industrial area near Sydney, 3,000 miners wildcatted. Near Pictou, the men who were putting up the new pulp mill for Scott Maritimes stopped work. Construction workers shut down projects in Halifax and Sydney.

The Nova Scotia Federation of Labour was galvanized into

accusing Attorney-General Donahoe of "an open bias against all working Nova Scotians, in favour of foreign corporations who are exploiting our natural resources and who have clearly indicated their total irresponsibility to the people of this province." The Federation called on all working people to "act now to free the fishermen and force the companies to the bargaining table."

Jeremy Akerman damned "a jurisprudence reminiscent of nineteenth century oppression." The NDY cried that "what started as a fight for recognition of the UFAWU has now become a fight for the entire working class of Nova Scotia."

Everett Richardson "didn't feel too good about it" himself.

"But I didn't feel *bad*. I didn't cry or anything. I figured when they sentenced me that the judge had went a little too far. I knew he'd backtrack after a while because he was trying to make an example out of me, he said so right there in the court. But I figured what I done I done right, and I was going to do the nine months fer it."

Bertha Richardson was still crying.

"He was just so wore out!" she exclaims. "When the judge said 'Nine months' you could see it was a shock to him. He just looked awful, looked like he'd been hit or something."

"Even after Bertha came home, you just couldn't do anything with her," Jean recalls. She'd go upstairs in her bedroom and she'd just come down to watch the news and then she'd say, 'If you could have seen Dad! If you could have seen him!' And then she'd go back upstairs ..."

Jean heard the news at about 4.00 that afternoon. Linda called home from Halifax. "Did you hear any news?" she asked. "No," said Jean. "You didn't have the radio on?" "No," said Jean, "I didn't." "Well," said Linda, "Everett was sentenced to nine months."

"I said, *WHAT?*" Jean remembers. "And after that all I could say was *Nine months!* because I couldn't think of anything else."

There were only the two young boys, Everett and John, at home at the time. Jean told them what had happened. Young Everett went to the calendar and worked it out. "Mom," he said, "Daddy won't even be home at Christmastime!"

Jean was worrying about Everett's mother.

"I knew that she'd get so worked up, and that I should tell her before she probably did hear it on the radio. I called her several times, but the line was busy. So I thought, okay, we'll go down – she lived just down the road at that time. I took the two boys and I went down there, and there was a woman there in the yard talking to her and she said, 'Did you hear anything from Everett?' I told her, 'Yes,' and I told her what had happened. It really didn't sink in, but this other woman just sat right down on the ground. 'You're kidding!' she said, 'Nine months!' I said, 'No, I'm not; nine months is what Linda told me.'

"Well, Everett's mother went out to her other son's, and then in to the Lloyd Richardsons and when she came home it really sank in, I guess. She called me then, and she was determined – it was kind of funny, she said, 'Well, I'm damned if I'll die this summer, because I'll be too stubborn to die while Everett's away.' I didn't pay too much attention, because this was just the kind of thing she *would* say. But she did die just two months afterwards, the 22nd of August.

"But she was determined. 'Well, we'll hold on some long,' she said, 'we'll do something even if it'll lose the car' – this was when we still had that little car – 'we'll hold on if he's away or not.'

"So this was the feeling, you see. Even if he had been gone the nine months, I knew that I would have had what help people were able to give. Nobody was able to give much help, really, though, because nobody had anything left to give."

But support was beginning to flow from across the country. Even before the jailings, BC fishermen and shoreworker locals of the UFAWU were sending what they could from their own budgets. The BC Federation of Telephone Workers sent $500, a large contribution. The University of BC Employees Union sent $200 and a message of support; the Halifax School Maintenance Union sent $100 and a pledge of further support; the North Vancouver Civic Employees sent $25, the Burnaby local of the Oil, Chemical and Atomic Workers sent $75. From Toronto came $250, a gift of the United Electrical Workers. "It is a disgrace that companies anywhere in Canada can deny this right [of union recognition] to workers," wrote UE National Secretary George Harris, "Please be assured of our full support."

Walk the picket lines these hot summer days. Talk to the men and women and children marching up and down with placards on their backs: SUPPORT THE FISHERMEN. ON STRIKE.

RECOGNIZE UFAWU UNION. NO INJUNCTIONS IN LABOUR DISPUTES. A big man with a face the colour of a smoked ham strikes a match on his thumbnail, lights his friend's cigarette, then his own. A couple of lithe kids, their long hair rippling in the little breeze up from the harbour, display signs indicating their solidarity with the working-class movement around the world. They have never worked a day in their lives, and it is easy to make fun of them as the guilt-ridden children of the middle class, for the spirit of the 1960s is not yet dead: the Sir George Williams computer fracas and the Chicago convention of the Democratic Party were only two years ago; the Kent State killings are current news.

But don't knock these kids. All over the continent student leaders are calling for a "worker-student alliance," only to find that workers don't like them, don't trust them, view their hand of fellowship with suspicion. These kids in eastern Nova Scotia have actually forged such an alliance; they are walking picket lines, selling fish, babysitting, writing leaflets and press releases, putting the education of privilege to work against the very institution of privilege. Some of them are naive, some of them are doctrinaire, some of them will turn out to be bond salesmen after all, perhaps. Some will turn out to be sinewy lifelong leftists. But right now they are in full flush of their youth and conviction. They are devoted, and they are beautiful.

Walk into a kitchen, sit on the chair beside the oilcloth-covered table while the oil stove sits silent in the background, the men and women seeking the cool, not the warmth, pulling on bottles of Schooner and Moosehead beer, talking excitedly about what's happening across the province. The miners are out. The steelworkers are going out. Will they *really* call a general strike? Did you hear what Akerman said? Yeah, even Regan says if he were Premier he'd call the legislature for a special session, give bargaining rights to the fishermen same's other workers. High time, too.

"I don't know much about a co-adventurer," a fisherman declares, "but I don't see how they can keep us from gettin' organized. The simple reason why is because they pay us a wage and we pay income tax, we pay unemployment insurance, we pay Canada Pension, so when the company turns around and says

Credit: *The Fisherman.*

we're co-adventurers, then my opinion of it is, they're bloody liars. 'Cause nobody that does those things is a co-adventurer, he's an employee. A co-adventurer in my opinion is a feller that goes out all by heself and starts exploring for something, like Christopher Columbus did."

Snatches of conversation:

"There were a lot of oil went ashore on the beaches from the *Arrow,* and there were a lot gathered up off the surface of the water, but there's still a lot around – and as far as I'm concerned that's one thing that still makes it hard for the shore fishermen – "

A woman's voice rises above the babble:

"That priest, huh! He says Homer Stevens' a Communist. Well the way things're going we'll *all* be Communists before we go to our graves, ain't that right, Ma? The way it looks to me, you stand up for your rights, why then you're a Communist. . . ."

". . . call a big meeting on just a few hours' notice," says a chunky farmer from Prince Edward Island, an officer of the National Farmers' Union who's come over with a load of potatoes. "But see, why we support the fishermen, we're in a similar setup, similar product, and we may need *them* some day to picket, or give us information, set up a boycott or what have you – "

And over by the sink, a man in his thirties, in a clean white shirt and twill pants, holds a beer in one hand and stabs at the air for emphasis with his other hand.

"We are *scared*," he announces, "that if they can beat *this* union, they're gonna come and say – to the Operating Engineers, which I'm in – we don't *wantcha.* And they're gonna go to the *Labourers* Union, they're gonna say, we don't *wantcha.* They'll go to the *Teamsters:* we don't *wantcha.* And there's *no* way we're gonna be able to do anything *about* it.

"We don't care about this union, *whatever* trouble it had before, the trouble they put in the paper here the other day – we don't *care* about that. What we're fightin' for, is the fishermen *want* this union, they *desire* this union, the same way as when we joined the union *we're* in at Gulf Oil. This is what *we're* scared of, and this is what we're backin' up."

"Right, b'y," says a friend of his, who is missing a finger. "If

93

the government says to Booth Fisheries, you can operate without a union, then every other company in the country's gonna say, We can't operate with our unions – go home, b'ys, go home, we'll hire somebody else. We'll import 'em from the Old Country."

"I'd like for them buggers in the gov'ment to try keepin' a family of kids on twenty dollars a week," laughs a young mother. "They wouldn't be long then, puttin' a new law through."

"They move fast enough when it's a big shot's money they're protectin'," her friend agrees. "Look how long it took old Stanfield there to put through the new telephone law."

"That's right, that's right. . . ."

The telephone law was one of those entertaining sideshows which occasionally enliven the public scene as one part of the corporate elite tramps on another part's toes, and government scurries about protecting its special friends. In the summer of 1966, Bell Telephone moved to take over Maritime Telephone and Telegraph, the Halifax based utility which provides most of Nova Scotia's phone service. Bell was both acquiring a profitable subsidiary and protecting a captive market for telephone equipment produced by its subsidiary, Northern Electric. A Nova Scotia firm supported by provincial money was trying to break into the MT&T market at the time. By September 11, 1966, Bell held 51 per cent of MT&T's common shares. On that day Premier Stanfield – who had not yet bitten the sour banana of national politics – convened a one-day sitting of the legislature for the sole purpose of passing a bill restricting all MT&T shareholders to 1,000 votes, regardless of the number of shares they held – thus effectively preventing Bell from exercising the powers of ownership. This extraordinary measure passed unanimously.

In 1970, a large body of Nova Scotia opinion was moved to wonder how the government could be so nimble when it was the money of the codfish aristocracy that was at stake, and so ponderous when the fishermen needed a similar end-run. The government protested – oh, shopworn Canadian excuse!! – that it was unclear whether fishermen fell into provincial or federal jurisdiction. That uncertainty, in fact, was what had caused Judge Green's commission of inquiry to be appointed by both the federal and provincial labour ministers.

Meanwhile, Judge Green soldiered on, a little asbestos corporal in the firestorm of wrath. Two days after Everett Richardson's sentence, Green told a group of fishermen testifying in Canso before his inquiry that certification of fishermen's unions was "inevitable" and would likely come about within a year. "You should have the right to be represented by any union you choose," Green remarked. In Halifax, Labour Minister McKeough said he himself "wouldn't be a bit surprised" if Green were right. Yes, he told a reporter, he agreed with Green that it was "fair and just" for the fishermen to be represented by the union of their choice.

But the firestorm still raged, the injunction was still flouted, and Everett was still in jail. In Halifax, a committee of church leaders called for a halt to all proceedings, picketing and other actions, until Judge Green completed his inquiry. The churchmen said they were moved "by the urgent need to reduce public tension and fear in connection with the rapidly developing conflict." They asked that all the contempt cases be adjourned, and that all the fishermen in prison be released on bail.

Meanwhile Homer Stevens held a meeting with Mario Dubé, president of the Cape Breton Building and Construction Trades Council, and emerged to call on the wildcatting thousands to go back to work.

"The spontaneous actions of trade unionists in the Strait area confirm the confidence of the striking fishermen in the labour movement in Nova Scotia," Stevens declared. "We are very sure the labour movement will help the fishermen win this strike." But he agreed with other labour leaders that the demonstration was enough. As Maurice McCarthy, vice-president of the Halifax and District Building Trades Council, said, "morally, workers supporting the fishermen are right. However, as union members they are legally wrong in not honouring their own contracts."

But the work force, though slow to rouse, was slow to cool down as well. Despite the pleas of their leaders, they stayed off. And on Everett Richardson's third day in jail, their massive protest had its effect. Leonard Pace, QC, a Liberal politico who was for the moment acting for the fishermen, went to court with Assistant Deputy Attorney-General Malachi Jones. The two jointly applied for bail for the fishermen already in prison, and asked that sentences and hearings for the remainder all be held over till October 27. The motion was granted. That night sixteen fishermen from Petit de Grat arrived in Halifax by bus, singing their heads off and joking. "Who are those guys?" asked a by-stander. "Those are the fishermen," someone said, "they're here to go to jail tomorrow." "Well, why the Christ they singing?" But they were singing because they knew perfectly well they weren't going to jail. With Everett Richardson's sentence, the court had over-reached itself; on Friday, June 26, their trials were also bound over to October 27, and a cheerful Homer Stevens led twenty-three released fishermen into a special Nova Scotia Federation of Labour meeting in New Glasgow later that day.

That gathering called for an immediate meeting with Premier G. I. Smith, announced a series of demonstrations, and established a defence fund to provide living expenses and finances for the fishermen who had to fight contempt charges. The Federation, declared its president, John Lynk, would "get the public information, and demonstrate the action that has been taken against the fishermen in their fight for free collective bargaining." But, as if conscious that these were hardly stirring proposals in a province with 6,000 workmen off the job, still seething over the jail sentences, Lynk added that "in no way is a general strike ruled out." The odds of one were "very strong if there is no action." Meanwhile, however, workmen should go back to their jobs.

Mario Dubé, down in Cape Breton, was disappointed over the result, and said his council would meet on the weekend to decide its own course of action. "I thought they were going to take some action right away," he complained, "but now we're at the same point as a week ago. I wouldn't blame the Cape Breton people to go on alone. They've gone on alone in the past and they've won."

J.K. Bell, secretary-treasurer of the labour federation and always one of the fishermen's stoutest supporters, advocated that the two fishing companies now be taken over by the province and run as crown corporations. He pointed to the ship-building subsidies and public wharves of which Booth had been the recipient, and to the $9 million in public funds advanced to Acadia. "You goddam right the province should take it over," cried a curly-headed Mulgrave fisherman. "The taxpayer got a helluva lot more money into it than the company does."

The day after the Federation meeting, Booth's ostensible deadline for settlement of the strike quietly passed without notice. But Father George Topshee, director of the once-feisty extension department at St. Francis Xavier University in Antigonish, did announce that his department had found another operator for the Booth plant who claimed to be able to produce at least three and perhaps as many as five or six draggers to assure a plentiful supply of fish. The new operator would not be a Nova Scotian, Topshee admitted, but at least the community could be assured that Booth's departure would not mean the end of a vital local industry.

In Canso, the town council had voted $100 a month to each family affected by the strike.

"At the meeting," says Everett, "there was quite a few there supporting the women and there was quite a few setting in the back that was there for to condemn the welfare for the fishermen. But the mayor opened the meeting and brought up the case, what the meeting was called for – and one feller did get up and wanted to say something, but he wouldn't leave him say it at that time. Anyway, they passed it that not only the fishermen would get welfare but anyone that was in town that needed welfare would get it."

"Pushed right through, right quick," Jean puts in.

"But then, after the mayor and the council did pass this here, then the welfare officer got up and he still opposed the thing."

"He said," mimicks Jean, "Well, I might have to obey, but I still don't support your decision."

Instead of writing cheques, the welfare officer became unavailable. Ron Parsons led a delegation of fishermen's wives to apply for welfare benefits. Still no cheques were issued. So Parsons and the women occupied the Canso Town Hall.

"When the women went down there fighting, there was no one in town," Everett explains. "They put up such a kick that they did make the mayor promise to call a council meeting with the welfare officer. The women were prepared to stay in jail that night."

"We were," Jean grins. "The bunch of us nearly got arrested. It was touch and go there for a while."

Judge Green now apparently decided he could mediate after all; he wired the union and the companies, asking them to meet with him on July 2. Sensing its strength, the union made it clear it would demand that the injunction be lifted, that Booth return to Petit de Grat the three trawlers it had ordered to its plant in Fortune, Newfoundland, at the outset of the strike, and that the companies at once recognize the union and begin contract negotiations, with a signed agreement before the men returned to the boats. The companies continued to insist they could not recognize such an irresponsible, unreliable union; Booth repeated that it was not bluffing about closing the plant: its confidential employees, fairly senior management, would be laid off July 1.

Meanwhile the marchers kept up the picket line.

"Now the women are a great help," one of the men told a visitor. "With their mashed potatoes and their eggs, they're doin' great."

Mashed potatoes and eggs? What was this, a picnic?

"Don't jostle me, my dear," said one. "Look what I got in me pocket." She held it open, revealing juicy tomatoes and ripe eggs. "Never know when you might want to throw them."

"Hey," said her friend, "you hear about what Grace Kelly learned when she married Prince Rainier?"

"Wha'd she learn?"

"Not all rulers got twelve inches."

July was a curiously inconclusive, irritable month. By now the men had been out for three months, and their strike was the hottest issue in the province. Yet nothing happened. The companies met with representatives of the government and the Federation of Labour on July 2 and 9; when Stevens pointed out that one of the two parties to the dispute – the union – was not being included in the talks and demanded that union officers be present at a meeting a week later, the companies refused to meet. They would, they said, meet with their own trawlermen, but not with "West Coast officials" of the union. "I don't foresee a very quick solution," said a downhearted Labour Minister, Dr. Tom McKeough, who had been presiding over the talks. "The talks have ceased for the time being, though I'm keeping a line of approach open to both sides."

On July 20, claiming it had "documented evidence" of a

planned Booth pull-out (the confidential employees had been given another two weeks of employment till July 18) and citing "persistent and growing" reports that Acadia planned similar action, the union called on the provincial and federal governments to take over the plants. The ship-building subsidies given both companies, and Acadia's heavy debt to the province, gave the governments a great deal of potential leverage. The whole tone of the union's messages at this point was confident, almost peremptory; it clearly believed that it had the backing of the overpowering majority of Nova Scotians and that the governments would have to respond.

At a press conference, Homer Stevens reported that "financial support from unions is still coming in, and even increasing. Our members are digging in for a longer strike to win basic human rights and a decent contract. However, the issues are so clear that no one in government can avoid them. If the cabinets don't wish to act alone, they should call emergency sessions at the provincial level, and if necessary at the federal level, to clear the decks for action."

Union support was certainly strong. Three days earlier Gerry Sharpe, president of the pulp and paper local at Port Hawkesbury, had presented a donation collected from the paper workers on the job. "I'm here," Sharpe told the fishermen's joint council from the three ports, "to express our moral and financial support." He handed over a cheque for $5,816.80. It was, said one observer, "the kind of support that makes the fish companies blink."

By calling for the plants to be taken over, the union was countering the companies' most potent threat in chronically underemployed Nova Scotia: the threat to pull out. Booth set another deadline, this one for August 21. But the threats rang curiously hollow. After three and a half months, people were beginning to think that only the departure of the companies *could* end the strike. The companies' denunciations of the "outside" union were beginning to recoil upon them too. British Columbia, however far away, is still part of Canada. Chicago and Hull are not. "Sure, there's outsiders manipulating Nova Scotians," said one old coal miner. "But that ain't the *union.*"

"The companies are trying to starve us out," said Mulgrave

fisherman Ray Cooper, "but they're not doin' a very good job on it. Looks like we'll starve out the companies instead."

His fellow fisherman, Reg Carter, was less restrained. "Let them pull out!" cried Carter. "The government got to take it over. Why should the people of Nova Scotia turn around and kiss England's arse? Let them get out and good riddance to them!"

Not everyone agreed. In Petit de Grat, Father Arsenault was losing his confidence. Homer Stevens bothered him – Stevens was, he felt, *too* capable a leader, a man to whom power would naturally gravitate. Four months was getting a bit long. And Booth's threats to pull out worried him.

That July, Homer Stevens' wife visited the strike area. Grace Stevens found the strikers "an inspiration," and she thought the Nova Scotia women were functioning more like a real union auxiliary than their experienced counterparts in BC – walking the picket lines, drumming up support, taking their children and going to address other unionists. And she was appalled at some of the effects of months without money.

"I know of a woman who was taken to hospital because she couldn't afford her regularly prescribed drugs," Mrs. Stevens wrote to *The Fisherman*. "Then there was the fisherman whose phone was about to be taken out for non-payment when a picket line was hurriedly formed and the telephone employee, a union member himself, respected the line and left."

Fishermen's wives, remembering that summer, recall not the big public events but the hard work and the little personal touches. In Mulgrave, Eric Fitzpatrick's wife, Gail, was putting in twenty-hour days, picketing and collecting money, baking bread and pies and cakes for sale in a nearby store until her health gave out and the doctor ordered her to rest. Big bluff Eric, a good-natured Newfoundlander, pitched in around the house – somewhat clumsily at times – helping with the kids and the housework. Union men and women came and went through their tired little rented bungalow. One time Homer Stevens and Glen McEachern, the UFAWU business agent, were coming for supper. The Fitzpatricks had $20 a week plus the proceeds of Gail's baking to live on; they have six children; there was nothing in the fridge to eat when Gail went out to work. When she came back, "Homer and Glen had filled the fridge." Her face lights up, and in the rhythmic accents of her native Arichat she says, "I think it was the most wonderful thing that ever happened to me."

On July 27, the conflict heated up again.

ULTIMATUM: WORK OR FACE CLOSURE

screamed the big red headline in the *Chronicle-Herald*. The story by Linden MacIntyre, announced that Booth Fisheries would soon begin publishing paid advertisements "tracing the dispute since its inception, Booth's position in the controversy, and a final warning that it will leave Nova Scotia if the strike is not ended." MacIntyre pointed out the firing of Booth's employees July 18, and said company officials had made it clear that the shutdown had already begun. He noted in passing that the fishermen were still gaining support, and that the previous Saturday had seen forty members of the Steelworkers from Sydney marching in the fishing ports and leaving behind them a cheque for $2,000. Steelworkers' president Winston Ruck promised considerably more help, remarking that the $2,000 had been "picked up" with little or no organized effort.

"It was a pleasure for us to be in the midst of these people," Ruck told MacIntyre. "This strike should be commended by everybody who is interested in justice being done."

The Nova Scotia Federation of Labour secretary-treasurer, J. K. Bell, responded that "Booth is being enticed out of Nova Scotia by a neighbouring province." The new Booth offensive "doesn't come as any surprise; it's part and parcel of Booth's program." And he went on the attack himself. If Booth wanted to play such games, he said, "they may find that some of their plants in other parts of Canada and the United States will be picketed." In fact, there had already been some spontaneous picketing at the company's premises in Toronto.

Bell also foresaw a possible boycott. "A boycott of their products could result in another situation like the California grapes episode," and he threatened that similar actions could be taken against other companies which were helping Booth. He pointed out that Booth's only real market was its parent, Consolidated Foods, and that to supply an adequate amount of fish the company actually bought more fish than it produced.

The threat of closure struck Bell as essentially irrelevant. Acadia was threatening to close the Mulgrave plant; he remembered, however, that the company had wanted to do that at the time they opened the new plant in Canso, but agreed not to do so under prodding from the province. "But it's no secret that Acadia is trying to unload its Mulgrave plant," Bell concluded. And he clearly didn't think the strike had much to do with it.

Judge Nathan Green was still inquiring, blaming the delay in his report on "the occurrence of meetings which have been held between government officials and the Nova Scotia Federation of Labour." But he was planning final hearings at the Halifax court house in mid-August, and he hoped to present his report by early September.

The politicians were lying low. The prevailing view in the Nova Scotia cabinet was that the Green inquiry would take the heat off, and that once Green brought down his report would be soon enough to make a move. Labour Minister McKeough dissented, arguing that the dispute was serious enough and bitter enough that it could not be royal-commissioned away. Education Minister Gerry Doucet, whose Richmond riding included Petit de Grat, sided with McKeough. Doucet was an able Acadian lawyer still in his twenties, and because of his public silence on the strike he was thought to be in trouble in his own riding.

Liberal leader Gerry Regan's concern could be measured by a July 29 speech to the Sydney Rotary Club on the subject of labour-management relations in which he managed not to mention the fishermen at all. Regan's most memorable comment had been a wintry expression of distaste after Everett Richardson's sentence: the government, he said, was "paying too much attention to legal technicalities in contradistinction to social realities."

By contrast, NDP leader Jeremy Akerman was making enormous political gains through his unwavering support for the strikers. On July 27, Akerman roasted National Sea Products as "the real villain" of the strike. National Sea had been active behind the scenes, said Akerman, "because it is scared to let the UFAWU get a foothold in Nova Scotia. How closely behind the backs of Premier Smith and his government is National Sea standing? Is National Sea more powerful than the Nova Scotia government?" Meanwhile the Halifax constituency association of the NDP damned the "irresponsible corporate behaviour of the companies" and pledged to send the fishermen $300 a month for the duration of the strike.

But the big noise in late July was the Booth advertisements, published in conjunction with the *Chronicle-Herald's* banner headlines on July 28 – 31 – and published in many other papers as well. Headed

A FISH STORY THAT IS NOT A "FISH STORY"

they declared Booth "a Canadian company since 1909." Here was news indeed. But no: "Booth Fisheries had been operating in Canada since 1909. So, although it is American-owned, it has a longer history than many Canadian-owned companies." Nothing further was said on the point. The company argued that it had been of benefit to the community, building a plant and ships worth $2,250,000, paying annual wages of $1.5 million. "There was never a hint of any problem until Homer Stevens . . . headed east from the West Coast with the self-appointed mission of organizing the fishermen as members of his union."

Now, said Booth, we are "not anti-union." But the fishermen couldn't be unionized: they weren't employees; they were co-adventurers. Nevertheless, Booth would accept any "responsible" fishermen's union – but an investigation of the UFAWU "proved to Booth beyond any doubt that this Union was irresponsible, unreliable, and contemptuous of Canadian law – (involved in 34 labour disputes and strikes in 20 years, expelled from the Canadian Labour Congress, Stevens sentenced to one year in prison for contempt of court, etc., etc.)" So Booth decided "it could not in good conscience negotiate with a union having such a record."

And the union "has not changed its ways." The proof? Its irresponsibility was shown in refusing to allow maintenance men into the plants, which had meant "serious deterioration" of equipment. Its unreliability was revealed when it agreed to let Booth meet with some of its own trawlermen in the presence of the Minister of Labour and representatives of the Federation of Labour, but "without any West Coast representatives of the union." Came the meeting, and "Mr. Stevens insisted that he and other non-fishermen union officials be in attendance, plus fishermen's wives, representatives of a youth group, and the president of a farmers' union. Few, if any, Booth fishermen were there. Booth, understandably, refused to meet with such a group. Mr. Stevens gave a statement to the press, stating that the Company refused to meet the fishermen . . . whereas it was he who had broken the agreement."

Irresponsible, unreliable – and contemptuous of Canadian law. "The Union's contempt of law was shown in the recent past by its refusal to obey an order from the Supreme Court of Nova Scotia."

In its second advertisement, Booth took up several specific accusations. Did the company show little regard for the health and safety of its fishermen? No: "Booth ships are inspected annually by the Canadian Steamship Inspection Service and comply with all their safety standards." (These inspections are required by law, and cover only the basic seaworthiness of the ship itself, not working conditions aboard.) But "Booth goes even further and has its insurance company make a second annual inspection at Booth expense. . . . Because of these precautions, Booth can state unequivocally that there are no safer fishing trawlers in operation on the East Coast of Canada." Booth has every man covered by Workmen's Compensation, and "pays for a $10,000 life insurance policy for each and every crew member." The ships have radio-telephone and when a crewman is ill or injured, action is taken at once either to take him off by helicopter or another ship, or by putting back into port. Booth puts "the life and welfare of the fisherman before everything else for they realize that ships can be replaced, but human lives cannot."

The union accuses the company of stealing fish from the men. Booth denies it. "The company insists that a crew member or a representative appointed and paid by the crew be in attendance at all times to verify the weight of landed fish."

The union says the company treats its men like slaves. Booth gives a corporate chuckle: they "can only assure you good people that they neither 'shanghai' men nor do they shackle them to the oars. We guarantee that all our fishermen become crew members of their own free choice." The ad then cites the pay of its crewmen as follows:

| Six Captains | averaged $16,200.00 each |
| Six Mates | averaged 9,490.00 each |

Six Chiefs	averaged	9,490.00 each
Six 2nd Engineers	averaged	8,059.00 each
Six Cooks	averaged	6,964.00 each
Six Bosuns	averaged	6,964.00 each
Twelve Icers	averaged	5,764.00 each
24 remaining crew members	averaged	5,504.00 each

These earnings are for eleven months work as each ship spends three weeks in annual refit each summer and ties up for at least a week at Christmas. SLAVE WAGES?"

No, not slave wages – and, said the fishermen, not accurate ones, either. These are gross figures, from which the company makes deductions. And the men who earn these wages work over 5,000 hours a year. For the junior men, that's a rate of about a dollar an hour – on the basis of Booth's own figures.

In the third ad, Booth took on Stevens' point about the public money involved in the fishing operations – a matter in which Booth was far less deeply engaged than Acadia. The subsidies for the draggers, Booth wrote, were paid "entirely to George T. Davie Co., not to Booth Fisheries" because it was Davie's yard which built the draggers.

Homer Stevens replied that the subsidy is recorded in Ottawa as being granted to Booth, not to Davie. But the point is academic; the fact of the matter is that public subsidies *were* paid on five of Booth's six draggers, and that Booth was therefore able to buy them at a far lower price than their actual cost. The point of the subsidies, of course, was to make Canadian shipyards competitive with their counterparts in Europe and Asia, and they may represent a perfectly defensible policy. But they did confer direct benefit on Booth.

On other subsidies, Booth declared that its plant "has not one cent of either provincial or federal government subsidies or monies in it. Nor did Booth borrow any portion of the $1,250,000 [the cost of the Petit de Grat plant] from either government." The company goes on to admit the federal government did build the plant a wharf and rented two-thirds of its surface to Booth – at a rental Booth never specified. And it built a $70,000 water system which Booth was paying off at $265 a month. "Needless to say, Booth has honoured this commitment through to the present date."

In its fourth and final ad, Booth took issue with Homer Stevens for accusing the company of failing to meet its moral responsibilities in the community. Professing to be unsure what Stevens meant, the company outlined what it thought its responsibilities were: "to do all in its power to operate a *viable* fish processing industry." The plant had been viable for twenty years because of "the close co-operation and team work the Company has enjoyed with both its plant employees and fishermen." The ad continued in boldface type:

It is Booth's firm conviction that it could no longer count on the co-operation of its fishermen, if they were subject to the control of Mr. Stevens and his West Coast Union. Rather than attempt such an operation which, in our opinion, is predestined for eventual failure, Booth would rather retire from Petit, thus leaving the way open for some more optimistic operator to take over.

Referring both to Father Topshee's proposals and to the increasing pressure for outright government takeover, Booth elected to "publicly announce its willingness to comply with either of these recommendations and will accept a fair market value for its shore properties." Finally, the company announced that it had indeed "given to the Provincial government of Nova Scotia its formal notice of closure which becomes effective in the very near future. The Company most sincerely regrets having been forced to take this action for it" – and here the ad switches again to boldface –

had believed that their twenty years of operating at Petit had made a definite contribution, not only to the immediate area, but to the province as a whole. If the Company is incorrect in this assumption, its retirement from business in Petit de Grat is the best course of action for all involved.

As the last of Booth's advertisements appeared, the executive of the Nova Scotia Federation of Labour was meeting in Halifax to plan its strategy, a strategy which revealed once again the ambiguous response of the Federation to the fishermen's strike. On the one hand, natural union sympathies lay with the strikers, and the tactics used against them – notably the injunctions and contempt

106

convictions – had implications for the entire labour movement. The Federation was also being pushed by many of its 55,000 members who had already shown themselves perfectly capable of independent action.

On the other hand, the general CLC attitude to the UFAWU – expressed by Jean Beaudry's comment that because the UFAWU was not in the CLC, it was "not entitled to the services of the Congress" – tended to restrain the Federation's enthusiasm. At times it almost seemed to resent being forced to throw its weight behind a union whose militancy constituted a standing challenge to the Federation's whole view of the labour movement. In a simple two-way fight, however, the Federation had no real choice.

So Federation president John Lynk conceded grudgingly that a general strike was "still under active consideration," something that would become "a high priority measure" if all other measures failed "within a short period of time." The five points of the Federation's current attack, however, fell short of any militant action.

The Federation proposed that the seven regional labour councils hold demonstrations "to inform the general public of the situation up to the present time." It called for a stepped-up financial appeal among unionists, and a more active involvement by the provincial government directed towards forcing the companies to recognize the union. It called for a special session of the legislature to bring the fishermen under the Trade Union Act, and if all else failed, it called for the nationalization of the fish plants.

The striking feature of these proposals is their dull vagueness. Demonstrations and financial appeals were, by now, old hat; essential though they were, they led nowhere. The other three proposals called for government action – but they included no timetable and offered no clear indication of what the Federation would do if the government failed to act.

The flabbiness of the Federation's approach may well have been crucial. Lynk pointed out that a great many unions were already on strike, and that the coal mines had just shut down for their annual two-week vacation break; a general strike might have drawn a ho-hum response from the public. "You know," said one observer, "the reaction might be, so what? They're all on strike anyway."

107

Perhaps so. And yet the Federation itself expressed concern that the 700 shoreworkers were nearly out of unemployment insurance benefits; once those ran out, their willingness to support the strike would be bound to weaken. Even among the fishermen, a certain number had by now drifted off to work on the Great Lakes' boats or in some other industry. The strike had gone on for four months, and men with families can't live indefinitely on $20 a week.

Suppose that the Federation had said, simply, that if the companies had not recognized the union by August 15, the provincial government would be expected to call a special sitting of the legislature for August 20. If the government failed to do so, the Federation would call a general strike and continue it until the legislature was called. Given the mass support for the strikers, which was by now at its peak, the Federation could almost certainly have made such a threat stick, and the government would have been hard pressed to resist such pressure.

But the Federation mounted no such pressure, and the moment passed.

On August 2, Booth confirmed that it was legally entitled to leave Nova Scotia August 20, having given the required ninety days' notice to the provincial government in mid-May. "It looks like we'll be retiring after our notice is up," said Charles Gordon, who also said he had had no indication of any interest by the province in taking over the plant. The same day's news revealed details of Father Topshee's plan to end the strike, which he was circulating to the CLC, the Nova Scotia Federation of Labour, Booth, Acadia, the Atlantic Provinces Economic Council, and the Dalhousie University Institute of Public Affairs, among others. Judge Green was said to have asked Topshee to present his plan at the final hearing of his inquiry, scheduled for August 13.

Essentially the plan called for a completely new union to take over all the fisheries contracts for a period of one year – a union which had no present involvement and no long-term interest in the industry, such as the United Mine Workers or the Steelworkers. During that year all interested unions would be given a chance to "bid" for the contracts, and the union chosen by the majority of the workers would assume overall jurisdiction both for fishermen and shoreworkers right through the Nova Scotia fishing industry.

The same day, Donnie Cadegan announced the permanent closure of Acadia's Mulgrave plant.

"It is impossible to re-open the Mulgrave plant," said Cadegan. He blamed the problem on the union, which he accused of preventing maintenance personnel from entering the plant since the beginning of the strike. Part of the roof had caved in, pouring water into the compressor room and ruining two large motors. "It is an old plant that has to be maintained daily," Cadegan explained, "and we have not been in the Mulgrave plant since April to do any maintenance. When Homer Stevens and his United Fishermen and Allied Workers Union tied up the plant, I warned them there was a danger it would not re-open." Acadia had originally intended to close the plant when its new Canso plant was opened, but "a decision was made late in 1969 to extend its life expectancy. At that time, a plan of rehabilitation was put into effect to bring the plant back up to Canada Inspection Regulations which would enable it to carry on. At the same time a decision was made to increase production by stationing two extra trawlers at the Mulgrave plant. This would have given us six trawlers." He said the company had chartered the additional trawlers and had had one fishing; the second would have been in the water by the beginning of May after a refit.

Could the plant be opened by another operator? Cadegan thought not: any such operator would be "bucking high labour costs" because of the industrial activity just across the Canso Causeway in Port Hawkesbury. All that could be done was to move the usable equipment and the trawlers to Canso. Cadegan said the company had had some feelers about buying the plant, none of which had "anything to do with fishing, but something else in the industrial line."

His conclusion? "Fishing is finished in Mulgrave," Cadegan declared.

But the fishermen's support continued. In the Cape Breton fishing village of Main-à-Dieu, a group of sympathizers "put up a little notice at the wharf asking for dollars for the strikers and in no time at all we had $60," according to T.H. Lathigee, a former Cape Breton County councillor. He said the men were outraged at the contempt sentences and "if we didn't have to make the most of our fishing season right here, a lot of us would be up there on the picket lines with those men."

On August 4, the picket line in Canso swelled to 250 people. There had been some pushing and scuffling, and some hard words exchanged with management. But the chief problem was that newcomers were going into the plant and nobody knew what they were doing; in addition, some of them had made deliberately provocative remarks about the union to the picketers.

The mass picketing worked. The strangers stopped coming, and by the end of the week things were back to normal. Rumours about violence in Canso flickered around the province, drawing statements from the mayor and the local RCMP. The Mounties reported "several stone throwing incidents," but nothing very significant. "Nothing serious," said mayor Hanlon, "just some of the boys trying to get in the plant."

"Well, the women were savage sometimes," Linda Gurney said a year later. "One time Claude Bennett – he was a supervisor – he hurt Gert Richardson's hand by pulling it through the wire fence. So the next time he came out we whipped him with pieces of cod line with knots tied in them, and I grabbed his back pockets and just *pulled*. Well, the whole back came off his pants." She gives a peal of laughter. "I can still see it! He was wearing blue boxer shorts with yellow butterflies on them."

On August 5, the first of the demonstrations called for by the provincial Federation took place in Port Hawkesbury. Several hundred fishermen and unionists, along with their wives and children, marched through the town singing "Solidarity Forever" and "We Shall Overcome," concluding at a rally addressed by Leo McKay, executive secretary of the Federation; Homer Stevens; Will Offley of the New Democratic Youth; and Charlie Joe Gallant, the retired coal miner and NDP candidate who was challenging Education Minister Doucet in the upcoming provincial election, with the slogan "No Fish in the Net: No Vote for Doucet."

The Federation, McKay told the rally, was "100 per cent behind the striking fishermen," and hoped similar demonstrations would "blossom out across the province. When they are over, if the government isn't ready to call the House into session and pass legislation giving you the rights that other trade unionists have, further drastic measures will have to be taken."

They cheered – Everett and Jean Richardson and Linda Gurney among them. Everett's name was by now a household word in Nova Scotia: his sentence, more than any other single thing, had brought the fish strike to the centre of the province's life. On the way home, at the rotary by the Canso Causeway, Everett "just let me attention slip a moment" and ran broadside into a semi-trailer, demolishing their car and sending the two women to hospital in Antigonish. Everett was uninjured. Jean and Linda were treated for cuts and bruises and released after a brief stay. "It didn't amount to much," Jean remembered a year afterwards, "but it did mean that we missed some of the big demonstrations; I had to lie here by the window and watch the cars driving off. And we still don't have a car."

"It was only a little Envoy," sighed Everett. "But it was good for to get around in, you know."

The next day, the Cape Breton Labour Council announced that it would call for a general strike of Cape Breton's 15,000 unionists on August 21 if the companies had not by then agreed to negotiate and the government still had not acted. It called upon other labour councils across the province to join in a mass walkout. That evening, Homer Stevens appeared on the Sydney television station CJCB. Did he agree, asked the interviewer, that a general strike would have great ramifications?

"The ramifications for labour if they *don't* act are greater," replied Stevens. The governments, he said, could quickly break the deadlock, and should do so. "I think the labour movement is hoping that will happen; at the same time, the labour movement has indicated tonight in that meeting they are prepared if necessary to force the governments to live up to their responsibilities."

Just where did the provincial government stand?

"I think most of the people of Nova Scotia would really like to know where they stand," said Stevens. When the union had asked for a provincial takeover, "they said, We'll refer this back to Judge Green – who after all is there acting on behalf of two governments. We don't think there's need, really, for further investigation or inquiry. It's really time for the government to be active, and right now they seem to be sitting holding back, perhaps trying to pass the buck to the federal government, who in turn are passing it back to them."

Asked to explain the co-adventurer business, Stevens said, "It could have been applied to fishing in its infancy. Some fishermen may have owned the boats and others may have gone as crew members, and they joined in sharing all the costs. The situation is so different today that it has no resemblance to the early pioneers of the industry. The boats and gear in the main are owned by the companies. All the marketing is controlled by the companies. They not only have the processing facilities, but they have the marketing agencies, the distribution facilities and so on. They're teamed up with big food manufacturers and distributors all over North America and all over the world.

"So where does the poor fisherman sit in this? Whether he's making $2,000 or $3,000 a year, whether he's making $10,000 or $15,000 a year, he's still in the position where he is really at the mercy of the fishing companies. Unless he has bargaining rights, that earning can be removed from him any time the company says, 'Well, we either don't want to take your production any more,' or, 'You're fired off our boats and you can go look for a job someplace else.'"

And what about his own politics?

"I believe that every man has the right to his political opinion or his or her religion or anything else. I don't ask Cadegan or Lewis or any of these other people what their politics are. They might be the worst type of right-wing Conservative or the worst type of right-wing Liberal – that's their business. But these people with the old idea that they are going to run the show forever, without the working man having a voice in it – I think they're on their way out, and I think they better wake up and smell the coffee. If they carry on the way they're going, pretty soon the working people of this country are just going to say, 'Look Acadia, Booth, get the heck back to where you were. If you can't treat us as human beings, go back where you started from.' They're going to say that to a lot of people and we're going to take this country over, running the factories and the mines and the mills and the fishing industry the way we want it, the way we the people of Canada want it. We can feed hungry nations, we can feed our own people, we can have the highest standard of living – why should we be stopped from that?"

Booth Fisheries reproduced a transcript of the interview, marking the last passage for special attention.

Meanwhile an exchange between the *Chronicle-Herald's* Harold Shea and Donnie Cadegan reveals the background to the kind of coverage the fishermen complain about.

"Dear Mr. Cadegan," wrote Shea on August 5, "As per our conversation of Tuesday night I am enclosing a copy of the news story which resulted therefrom. It is my understanding that you wish to check it for accuracy prior to publication, to ensure it is an accurate digest of what you said in the interview.

"May I suggest you telephone me Thursday at 426-3098 . . .

"May I thank you for your courtesy."

The resulting story was headlined:

NO 'VIABLE OPERATION' WITH STEVENS, UFAWU.

It reported Cadegan's opinion that 60 per cent of the Acadia trawlermen were no longer involved in the strike, having left the area or taken other jobs. The strike, said Cadegan, was being carried on by inshore fishermen "who were not involved in the strike in the first place. What they expect to gain is not clear." And he announced that Acadia would follow Booth's lead in publishing a series of advertisements "to put forward our side of the story."

"Acadia is prepared to bargain with our trawler fishermen at any time, outside the UFAWU," Cadegan said. "We don't think we can run a viable operation with the UFAWU and Mr. Stevens as its leader."

Cadegan thought the union was flagging. "As crews came ashore," he said, "they were pressured to sign union cards by members of the union, but the majority of these people have left the area and are no longer involved. Of the 143 men, only 35 – 40 per cent are left picketing. Where are the rest? They are working for other fish companies in the Atlantic provinces and for lake shippers in central Canada, or have jobs elsewhere. Are they still paying 10 per cent of their wages to the union?"

As for the inshore fishermen, without whom Cadegan claimed the strike could not continue, "Acadia's Canso plant has always purchased fish from the inshore fishermen, but their catch is seasonal and relatively small, and of inconsistent quality. Booth

Fisheries and Acadia's Mulgrave plant have not bought inshore fish for many years, and we would be happy to have someone else purchase their fish as we are moving our four Mulgrave trawlers to the Canso plant."

But when I talked with him a year later, Cadegan claimed he had offered $1,000 cash to every fisherman who would build a new boat forty feet in length or more. "No strings attached!" he cried. "If I could get 10,000 pounds a day of inshore fish instead of 5,000 that's one less trawler I have to build."

"Sure!" laughed Fuss Richardson, Everett's cousin, a burly ex-fisherman who then operated a garage in Canso. "Sure! This is what hurt Cadegan so bad, they lost the inshore fish! Yet I've worked at that plant down there, and the plant manager before Cadegan was a personal friend of mine. He came here and I drank with him and everything. Now to the day that man left, he always insisted that they wanted nothing to do with the shore boats, nothing whatsoever. Their fish was of no value to them at all. But then the whole thing comes out of the bag – Cadegan tried the same thing, just trying to keep the price down, that's all it was. When the fish weren't comin' in, then they knew how bad they needed the shore fish. That was after the strike, when the two new buyers come into town and nobody sold to the company. The plant workers, now, they benefited a day and a half, two days a week off of shore fish."

Acadia's first advertisement appeared on August 12, headed
A STATEMENT BY ACADIA FISHERIES.
"Acadia Fisheries is a small company," it began, "owned by an old English family business, still run by one family. In Mulgrave and Canso, Acadia Fisheries is in the hands of good Canadian citizens with a deep respect for Canadian law and order and concern for the welfare of the communities they live in." It didn't want a strike, the company said. "To settle the ILLEGAL fishermen's strike, Acadia is being asked to recognize – not legally but VOLUNTARILY – the United Fishermen and Allied Workers' Union. This union organized the strike. It is an ILLEGAL strike. The picketing is ILLEGAL."

"Why is this strike ILLEGAL?" the company demanded. "Because fishermen are NOT EMPLOYEES. Acadia does not hire or fire fishermen. By law and in fact, fishermen are either completely free and independent or are 'co-adventurers' or partners sharing the earnings of each voyage."

And why was the picketing "ILLEGAL"?

"Because the Supreme Court of Nova Scotia found it to be so and ordered it to cease." The article went on to condemn the union's record, particularly the 1967 trawl strike in Prince Rupert as a consequence of which Stevens had gone to jail, and in the aftermath of which the Supreme Court of British Columbia had just the previous week found the union liable for damages of over $100,000. Acadia's advertisement quoted the court as saying that, "the irresponsible and widespread misuse of the terms 'unfair' and 'hot' in relation to these vessels and their owners and cargoes, knowing the connotations such terms have for the legitimate trade unionist and how they would mislead the undiscriminating, was quite without justification."

"In our opinion" Acadia continued, "this is a bad record and this Union is not good enough for the fishermen of Nova Scotia. We are a small company and our voice does not carry far, but we firmly believe that it would be impossible to operate a viable fishing industry if this Union represents the fishermen."

"Ours is NOT a fight against unionism," Acadia concluded, "it is a stand against ILLEGAL ACTIONS and IRRESPONSIBLE UNION LEADERSHIP."

Its second advertisement compared Acadia's own record with that of the union. Not surprisingly, it concluded that Acadia really had done very well by Nova Scotia: it had "invested its capital and carried on operations in job starved areas for eighteen years WITH NO SUBSIDIES," it had met an annual payroll of $1,800,000 and paid over $2,000,000 annually for fish; it had had good labour relations, built and operated a new plant with "provincial government LOANS – NOT GIFTS, NOT SUBSIDIES, and had "voluntarily operated a second shift at Mulgrave, at great financial loss to provide employment for Canso employees when the old Canso plant was burned down."

And the union?

The union had "apparently closed Booth's Petit de Grat plant permanently, closed Acadia's Canso plant and placed its future in jeopardy, put 800 plant workers out of work in three communities, put 250 trawler fishermen out of work or forced them to seek work elsewhere, put 140 inshore fishermen out of work in Canso area, permanently closed Acadia's Mulgrave operation.

"We leave the judgement to the fair minded people of Nova Scotia," Acadia concluded.

That same day Premier Smith announced another inquiry – this one into the proposed closure of the plants in Mulgrave and Petit de Grat. Emerging after an all-day Cabinet meeting, Smith said the commissioner, as yet unnamed, "can and will elicit all the facts that are relevant to the proposed closing of both plants." The inquiry would be set up under the Industrial Closing Act, and would have the right to summon witnesses and documents, and to take evidence under oath.

And that same day, Attorney-General Donahoe made his long-awaited move. He asked the provincial Supreme Court to determine whether the strike fell within federal or provincial jurisdiction.

"Some people are screaming for the government to stop the strike at Canso," commented an unnamed official, "but what can you legally do if you aren't sure your laws are valid?" Donahoe himself maintained that the government had indeed taken an active role in the strike by naming Judge Green to conduct his inquiry, but "it now appears that it may be a solution can be reached only by legislation." His own opinion that the strike was a federal responsibility was borne out, he felt, by the fact that the federal Minister of Labour, Bryce Mackasey, had appointed Green – an odd conclusion, since the government of Nova Scotia had also made the same appointment, on the basis of which Donahoe was claiming it had not shirked its responsibilities. But no doubt these matters are clearer to lawyers.

By now the strike was a major preoccupation of the provincial cabinet; its day-long meeting had been mostly taken up with the whole mess in Canso Strait. The fishermen saw the new legal manoeuvre simply as a delaying tactic. The province, labour people pointed out, could just as easily establish its jurisdiction or lack of it by passing a law and then waiting for someone to challenge it. Would Acadia Fisheries, $9 million in debt and behind on its payments, really be willing to do so? Would the federal government be particularly eager to open that can of worms? If Booth were actually about to withdraw, would it bother? And if it weren't, would it really wish to take on public opinion, the labour movement, and the government of the province?

"It's just another stall," shrugged Homer Stevens.

INTERLUDE
Mid-Term Break

"I'm so tired, I haven't slept a wink;
I'm so tired, my mind is on the blink.
I wonder should I get up and fix myself a drink
No, no, no."

The Beatles, *I'm So Tired*

Holy Lord dyin' Jesus Christ!

Cherished reader, if you are bored by now I don't blame you. The summer went on like the dull pain of a toothache: meetings and statements, resolutions and pamphlets, as though the sharp and urgent cry of the fishermen for justice had somehow been absorbed by bureaucrats. We are waiting, waiting, waiting for something decisive to happen. It doesn't. The governments mutter about jurisdiction. The Federation growls but never bites. We wait. Reams of turgid prose roll off the presses. Heavy editorials flop onto the news-stands. We wait. Cabinet ministers issue judicious, vague statements. Clergymen pray ineffectually on both sides. We wait. Inquiries lumber forward. The fishermen work at sustaining their support. MLA's dither and equivocate. We wait.

And Everett? Everett waited too, working hard at his committee jobs, keeping the books, staying off the picket line. He had taken his lumps once, he wasn't looking for special problems.

Jean and Linda took his place on the picket line.

If this were a novel I could wave a hand and abolish the tedium. But it's not a novel: these are real people, real events. Booth and Acadia published a series of boring and shoddy ads, and I can't make them readable. I can't even ignore them. They were the companies' major statements on the issues of the strike, and if I cut them too severely you would suspect me of unfair bias. I *am* biased, but I hope I'm not unfair. In general I'm sympathetic to workers, not to multi-national corporations, and I think their account of the strike and its causes is a load of horseshit. But I've given it to you as completely and as fairly as I can. You can judge it for yourself.

In a way, it's *important* that you and I endure together the irritations, the frustrations and the ennui of that long, inconclusive summer. We're following a strike, and strikes have periods like that. In fact, after being involved in a number of protest movements myself, I don't think those periods are accidental. One of the chief weapons of the Establishment is endurance. The bastards can't out-wit us, but they can generally out-wait us.

The days grind by, like sandpaper. We're low on food, the phone is cut off, the power commission is sending dunning letters. We're tired of being embarrassed whenever we meet our landlord, we'd like a pair of trousers, the washer is broken and we can't afford to fix it. There's no guarantee that we're even going to win. What's the point? Why go on straining heart and mind and muscle for a dubious result?

Donnie Cadegan and Earl Lewis are still drawing their salaries. In Hull and Chicago our most strenuous efforts are considered a minor local irregularity, nothing more. The province allows Acadia extra leeway on its loan payments, recognizing that it faces certain unfortunate difficulties. The town of Canso can't collect its taxes, but it doesn't press its case against the town's economic mainspring.

The sandpaper days are wearing us away, feather-edging our will, thinning out our resolve, skimming off our substance.

We wait.

If we express our frustration, the press will thunder at us for violence and irresponsibility. If we take it out on one another, our unity will dissolve and we'll drift back to the boats, one at a time. We've shown our courage, now we have to show our patience and endurance. It ain't easy, by the Christ.

Anyone can see the heroism of an Everett Richardson, standing before the power of the judicial system, and daring it to do its worst. But we're seeing another kind of heroism, a more subtle and less obvious kind, as the tiresome summer creeps forward. We're seeing new skills of self-discipline, will, and forbearance.

You're bored, cherished reader, and so am I. And so were the fishermen for whom there was no mid-term break, no relief, no clarity.

Stand by Everett and Jean, and struggle through that endless summer. I promise you something livelier in the next interlude.

UNIVERSITY
Not a Contract
to Write Home About

"If the scabs get in the way we're gonna roll right over them;
If the goons get in the way we're gonna roll right over them;
If the cops get in the way we're gonna roll right over them;
We're gonna roll the union on."

– labour song

On August 10, another massive march of fishermen and their supporters crossed the Canso Causeway – "probably just a preview of huge marches to come if the fishermen do not win the strike soon," noted Linden MacIntyre. The Cape Breton Labour Council, counting down to its August 21 general strike, had called a mass rally for the following Friday, in Sydney, asking all trade unionists on the Island to turn out, and inviting Gerry Regan, Jeremy Akerman and Labour Minister McKeough to join them. The labour councils of Truro and New Glasgow were meeting to plan a joint demonstration. Halifax was expected to follow suit. The hot, frustrating summer was growing hotter.

Acadia's ads continued. One such ad devoted itself to a personal attack on Homer Stevens, citing material from the 1967 Prince Rupert strike.

ANGRY WIVES MARCH ON FISH UNION,
said one headline printed in an ad, and Acadia also reprinted a letter to the editor, apparently from the Vancouver *Sun*, accusing Stevens of advocating opening Canadian waters to Russian fishermen, trading with Russia and China, and "Union with the USSR rather than the USA." The letter was signed by Mrs. Milton Bush. "Who is Mrs. Bush?" asked a pamphlet issued by Sydney steelworkers. "No doubt the intention is to depict Mrs. Bush as an 'angry wife' of a UFAWU fisherman. The truth is that Mrs. Bush is the wife of a vessel owner and one of the most militant anti-UFAWU people in Prince Rupert."

"What the ad completely overlooks," said the steelworkers, "is the fact that Homer Stevens was elected year after year by the

West Coast fishermen who know his record far better than does Cadegan." Cadegan's own competence was repeatedly questioned by the strikers; even today some of them refer to him as "that fish-plant undertaker." "We suggest," said the steelworkers, "that, to keep the record straight, Mr. Cadegan counterpose his own record to that of Stevens. What did the Cadegans contribute to the fishing industry? How many times did they go bankrupt and, to bring the record up to date, what kind of management did Cadegan give to Acadia Fisheries?"

One of Port Hawkesbury's oldest businessmen – A.J. Langley, Senior, eighty-two years old and the father of the town's mayor – was asking the same question. On August 11, Nova Scotians learned that Port Hawkesbury Shipyards Ltd. had gone into receivership, with debts of more than $540,000. The shipyard, incorporated over a century earlier as the Strait of Canso Marine Railway Company Ltd., was a subsidiary of Acadia Fisheries, who blamed the bankruptcy in part on the fish strike. The company had relied heavily on refitting work for Booth and Acadia draggers.

But Langley, who owned the company from 1923 until he sold it to Acadia in 1962, questioned whether the strike had much to do with the bankruptcy. "I didn't depend too much on the fish plants," Langley scoffed, "and I never paid less than seven per cent annual dividend – sometimes as much as ten per cent – to the shareholders." Most of his business, he recalled, had come from the coasting trade and from government.

"I gave it up because my health was gone and there wasn't much chance for me recovering. But now I'm back in shape and working twelve hours a day. I'm seriously thinking of buying it back."

Meanwhile, Father Topshee's plan was foundering. Why should the Brotherhood or the Seafood Workers – who already represented many of the trawlermen and most of the shoreworkers, respectively – give up their membership to an industry-wide trusteeship, and risk losing their members permanently? The CLC unions objected that Topshee's scheme would give the non-affiliated UFAWU the same status as they themselves held. Every local faced the possibility of eventually belonging to a union it didn't want. Every union currently in the industry had to contemplate the possibility of being frozen out of it. And the union to which the CLC had given jurisdiction in the fishing industry, the Canadian Food and Allied Workers, had virtually no members in Nova Scotia and stood no better chance than anyone else of ultimately capturing the industry-wide membership.

"Amalgamating unions is as tough as amalgamating municipalities," one union officer explained. "Everybody's in favour of it – for the other guy." Another insider drew another analogy. "The ecumenical movement is a great idea, but it's no solution for Northern Ireland."

As company and union men gathered in Halifax for Green's hearing, the *Chronicle-Herald* made perhaps its most blatantly partisan intrusion in the whole strike.

B.C. UNION LACKS TOP CLC BLESSING

its red headline blared on August 13. A subhead explained, "Communist leadership is factor." The story, filed by Eric Dennis in Ottawa, was nothing more than a rehash of the May meeting of the CLC at which the fishermen had once again been refused re-admission. The story didn't even support the subhead: "Key figures in the United Fishermen's organization are still ideologically suspect by the Congress, but the main reason advanced for refusing affiliation as a separate body is that there should be fewer rather than more unions among organized labor in Canada for the good of the movement." The only new ingredient in the story was a remarkably non-committal interview with CLC executive vice-president Joe Morris, who said he was trying to arrange a merger between the CFAW and the fishermen, and who was pleased by the province's referral of the question of jurisdiction to the provincial Supreme Court.

In another column, another subhead said, "Settle strike easy." Under the byline of Jim Robson, the story began: " 'If Homer Stevens and the United Fishermen and Allied Workers' Union left the province the strike would be over tomorrow,' says Acadia Fisheries general manager A.L. Cadegan. 'This,' he said, 'would be the simplest way to end the fishermen's strike.' "

No doubt.

Cadegan, in town to give his testimony, posed the possibility of an "impasse in the strike which could last five years," because "Acadia is not budging an inch." He also took the occasion to challenge the union's charges of low pay and poor working conditions on the trawlers. "Most of the trawlermen, even the good ones, will not fish all year around," said Cadegan. He claimed that during 1968-69, Acadia's trawlers made an average of twenty-seven trips during their eleven months of operation, and no trawler made fewer than twenty-one trips. But "52 per cent of Acadia's 143 trawler fishermen sailed on four trips or less and 74 per cent sailed on ten trips or less. Then people say they don't make a living. Well, how can they, if they don't make the trips and work?"

The least a trawlerman could make during a full season, if he took all the trips, would be $4,700 on a side trawler and $5,300 on a stern trawler. And those were the figures for deckhands. "The deckhands are at the bottom of the scale," said Cadegan. Everyone else earned more.

But Cadegan wasn't worried: the fishermen of Canso, he said, didn't support Homer Stevens. For example, only a few Canso men joined the Canso Causeway march the previous week. "Stevens used the excuse that the men couldn't get transportation from Canso," Cadegan scoffed.

The next day Merlin Nunn, counsel for Acadia, told Judge Green that the traditional co-adventurer approach had worked well, in the company's opinion. Acadia received 70 per cent of the catch and the crew 30 per cent; the crew paid for its own food, and the company paid everything else. Food cost about $750 per man per year, and he gave the net earnings of crewmen as $3,950 on side trawlers and $4,550 on stern trawlers. (Cadegan's figures, apparently, had been gross income.) Some fishermen didn't make more than $1,000 a year, Nunn said, but they were "transients" rather than regular crewmen.

It's worth pausing for a moment to contemplate what is actually being said here. If a man on a side trawler gets $3,950, he must then pay income tax, Canada Pension, and Unemployment Insurance. With luck, he might take home $3,600, or $300 a month, which represents 60¢ to 70¢ an hour – about half the Ontario minimum wage at the time.

Country cunning might enable such a fisherman to survive. The family would grow a garden, raise a pig, eat a good deal of fish. He'd shoot a deer, do his own house repairs and forgo such luxuries as toilets, washing machines, and central heating. He'd make good use of the eighty-four days a year he was not at sea.

But whenever he *did* have to buy something, he'd pay the highest prices in Canada. He'd be too poor to be eligible for an NHA mortgage. He'd pay an extra dime a gallon for gas, an extra nickel or so for fuel oil. Nova Scotia's power rates are Canada's steepest. Cars cost $400 or $500 more than in Ontario. In the winter, fresh fruit and vegetables in rural Nova Scotia are indifferent in quality and outrageously expensive. Sales tax and income tax are among the country's heaviest.

In 1968, the Economic Council of Canada juggled 1961 census figures and announced that two people living on $3,500 a year were impoverished. In November 1969, the Canadian Labour Congress reported that inflation meant an urban family of four needed a minimum income of $11,000 a year. In August 1970, Booth and Acadia were claiming that $3,600 a year was enough money for family men doing the backbreaking work of mid-winter trawling.

We're using Acadia's own figures, remember, based on the co-adventurer arrangement which Merlin Nunn said had "worked successfully." For whom?

Booth Fisheries was represented at the Green hearing by W. H. Jost, which casts an interesting light on relationships within the industry, for Jost, one recalls, was also a director of Acadia Fisheries. He told Green that the union "has shown contempt for the rights of others and the rights of law." To recognize the union would disrupt the fishing industry in Petit de Grat.

Jost outlined Booth's "lay arrangement," as it's known: 63 per cent to Booth, 37 per cent to the crew. Crew members were paid $6 a day when the trawler was tied up because of the company's failure to operate it. Engineers got $10 a day in that case. Jost repeated the company's claim that the union's refusal to allow maintenance workers into the plant had damaged it, possibly irreparably. The dispute, he concluded, had reached the point where either Booth or the union had to withdraw.

Homer Stevens appeared for the union, and he laid the blame for the continuance of the strike at the feet of the government. Either the fishermen should be given the normal rights of workers to organize, or the governments should take over the plants themselves.

Judge Green said he recognized the urgency of the matter, and promised a report as soon as possible. The next day, after the hearing had ostensibly closed, Green accepted a further brief from all the fishing companies in the province. Even National Sea Products, which had voluntarily recognized the Brotherhood, joined its sister companies in one final effort to assure the Judge that fishermen were not employees, but co-adventurers who could not properly be unionized.

The union – with the help of the NDY and others – now replied to the company advertisements with a pamphlet.

Among other points, the union reminded readers that Booth and Acadia had flatly refused to meet with the union or with mediators, and had refused Labour Minister McKeough's suggestion in mid-July that a vote of the trawlermen be held, with union recognition to follow if the majority of the trawlermen voted for it.

On the question of maintenance, the union reported that

> from the beginning of the strike, the UFAWU pickets permitted the following persons to enter the plant: manager, office manager, assistant office manager, clerk-typist, powerhouse engineers (refrigeration) and three watchmen with experience at other jobs. On July 8, four additional men including the marine superintendent, a carpenter, and two welder-engineers had been allowed inside to repair a water system.
>
> During the course of the strike, the company decided to stop sending some of these people in. But on July 9 they requested through the Minister of Labour that more workers be allowed inside to conduct a maintenance survey and clear up year end office business. They refused to attend the meeting at Province House on the 14th to hear the Union's reply to their own request, a reply considered reasonable by the Minister and the N.S. Federation of Labour.

On the question of earnings, the union pamphlet compared Booth's figures with the actual income tax statements of the fishermen. The differences: instead of $9,490, mates made $7,882. Icers made $4,651 as opposed to Booth's claim of $5,784. Deckhands made not $5,504 but $3,600. To place their figures in context, the union men cited government surveys in the Newfoundland fishery, which reported incomes very close to those from the tax statements.

The union also cited a report by the Atlantic Development Board predicting

> a quickening of the trend from inshore to deep water fishing. Arising from this will be a substantial reduction in employment opportunities in the inshore fishery with only the partial compensation of increased manpower needs in the offshore fishery.

The ADB also forecast consolidation of fish plants into a few large operations serving the offshore fleet, rather than the traditional small plants buying from inshore fishermen. Pointing out that the ADB had worked closely with the fishing industry in preparing the report, the union drew the obvious conclusion: the Mulgrave and Petit de Grat closures were part of a long-term strategy in the industry, and had nothing essentially to do with the strike.

As for working conditions, the pamphlet drew the following remarks from the testimony before the Green commission:

> I lost three fingers last year, and they didn't even have nothing to wrap them up in on the boat when it happened. They didn't even have a first aid kit on board.

> How come we are forced to go out in boats that aren't even fit to go out in? What about going to sea in boats that have the bilge pumps either broken down or all plugged up with dirt and won't pump water anyway? What are you supposed to do? You've got to go because you've got no choice but to go because if you didn't go then they'd blacklist you.

> You only get compensation if you get hurt and if you get sick you get nothing.

> When I was ordering groceries for those draggers to feed those men . . . you can't go where you like to buy those groceries but you have to go where the companies tell you to go. Why can't a man go and buy his groceries where he wants to, when the men are paying for the grub?

We were laying off Cape North and this man was laying in pain and he asked the skipper to bring him into Sydney which is not too far from Cape North and the skipper said he couldn't bring him in because he might get fired by the company.

Cadegan vigorously denies such charges. The food, for instance, he claims is bought wherever the cook wants to buy it – but too often the cooks themselves are on the take, and are persuaded to use one store rather than another because of kickbacks. "The cook and the skipper got a rake-off!" Cadegan told me. "A bottle of rum, a couple of cartons of cigarettes. I don't know why they'd do that, either. The cooks got $7 a day and a full share of the catch – now that's fucking good money."

As for Gerald Collins and his fingers – "First aid kits were *always* on board. And you know, lots of men have complained of sickness and just used it as a way to get in. It's up to the skipper and the trawler manager to see that they're up to snuff. We wanted to train one man in each trawler for first aid, too. You know, the company certainly wasn't perfect – but we weren't as bad as we're painted.

"Gerald Collins [who had lost his three fingers] got a damn good settlement on that accident, too. He got $80 a week compensation, and then a lump sum over $10,000. I've got the figures." He rummages around some files, comes up with the amount. "Here it is – he got $12,258 all told. We made *numerous* trips to various ports with men who were sick. Hell, one time we took a man off with a helicopter."

Green's final hearing was hardly over when the fishermen had to jump in their cars and race to Sydney, 265 miles away, for the mass rally held by the Cape Breton Labour Council the next day. A hundred people, fishermen and their families, led a huge motorcade through downtown Sydney, winding up at the Steelworkers' Hall, where they were addressed by McKeough, Regan, Akerman, Anglican Canon Mel French, John Lynk, Winston Ruck, and Homer Stevens. Most of the speakers won cheers and applause. McKeough and Regan drew catcalls and heckling.

The government, McKeough insisted, was doing everything it

could do. It wouldn't have been right to intrude earlier; now the issue was certification, and the first step in that direction was to refer the question of jurisdiction to the courts. Loud boos. McKeough laughed them off. The second question was the right of the fishermen to choose their own union – "and as far as my department is concerned, there is no question that the workers must have the right to the union of their own choice."

As for the red-baiting directed towards Homer Stevens, McKeough said his department wanted nothing to do with anyone using that tactic. Nova Scotia's Human Rights Act gave everyone the right to whatever politics or religion he chose. That was a popular sentiment in Sydney that night: Regan said the same thing, and Canon French called the red-baiting a carryover of McCarthyism from the 'fifties. But McKeough had nothing new to offer, and "the storied good humour of the strikers was obviously growing thin," as the *Highlander* reported. McKeough announced he was cutting his remarks short, although he had other things to say, and sat down.

Regan joined McKeough in calling for the Labour Council to abandon its plan for a general strike a week hence, but he also criticized the government for sending the jurisdiction question to the courts; it should have been submitted jointly by the two senior governments to the federal Supreme Court, where it would no doubt have to go anyway before any final answer would emerge. He agreed with critics who said any ruling in Nova Scotia was bound to be appealed, causing a further ten months or more delay. Why hadn't he brought in legislation himself? Regan was asked. He said the Opposition couldn't bring in legislation, but the Liberals had at least brought the matter up in the House, which no other party had done since the Fishermen's Federation Act of 1947. (He didn't point out that it had been Liberals who passed the contentious act in the first place.)

Akerman said the matter was simple: repeal the Fishermen's Federation Act and amend the Trade Union Act to cover fishermen. If the province could legislate for fishermen in 1947, it could do so in 1970. McKeough retorted that it was easy for Akerman to make things look simple, but the matter was actually very complex. Regan agreed. But Akerman went on to deliver a thundering speech which brought him a roaring ovation.

When governments can be so indifferent to the aspirations of working people, when the courts can be so abused, and when foreign corporations can play the robber baron in our community, it is without question time for labour to unite and take decisive action. If it takes a general strike, then a general strike is what we should have. The hottest fires in hell are reserved for those who remain neutral in a time of crisis such as this.

Homer Stevens told the rally that the government knew perfectly well that fishermen are employees, but that anyone who still didn't believe it could simply go for a trip on a trawler and see for himself. John Lynk defended McKeough, saying that the Minister and his department had done everything that they had been asked to do by the Federation. As the *Highlander* remarked, that "provided an interesting insight into relations between the Federation and the Labour Department." Canon French advocated a general strike, and Lynk once again said it hadn't been ruled out.

Winston Ruck said Local 1064 of the Steelworkers would strongly support a general strike. "After four and a half months of strike, the need for united action in support of the fishermen is clear," Ruck declared. "The fishermen *can't* lose this battle. We can't *let* them lose this battle. Because if they lose, we all lose."

But not everything was going the union's way. The day of the rally, Father A. P. Poirier of Arichat appeared on the Sydney radio station CJCB's "Talkback" program and argued that the area would be well rid of Homer Stevens and his union. He condemned Stevens as a Communist – though he admitted under questioning that most of his information came from Booth Fisheries – and said that "bread and butter" was more important than "cheap propaganda." But the fishermen surely wanted the union? Fishermen, said Poirier, are unskilled workers; it wouldn't be hard to replace any who refused to see the light and quit the UFAWU.

But the real jolt came from Petit de Grat, from the president of the Canadian Seafood Workers, a member of a local "Committee of Concern" set up to attempt to keep Booth in operation. The committee conducted a poll of Booth workers (including management) in the parish hall. "Should Booth leave Petit de

Grat?" it asked. The vote was 269 to 1 against Booth's departure.

Albert Martell, the president of Local 109, interpreted the vote as a demand that the UFAWU get out. He claimed, along with other members of his committee, to have polled the "forty to fifty" fishermen still in town. On the day of the rally, he fired off a telegram to everyone involved: to the Premier, the Leader of the Opposition, to local MP Allan MacEachen and local MLA Gerald Doucet, to McKeough, to John Lynk, to J. K. Bell and to Judge Green.

> Local 109 [Canadian Seafood Workers' Union] is in danger of losing its bargaining rights and seniority if Booth [Booth Fisheries Canadian Co. Ltd.] doesn't reopen shortly. Local 109 demands positive action be taken by the government of Nova Scotia and the federation of labor to remove Homer Stevens and his co-workers from our province of Nova Scotia.
>
> Overwhelming majority of Booth Employees local 109, Canadian Seafood Workers' Union, voted yes for Booth to remain in Petit de Grat. Of the remaining striking fishermen of Petit de Grat, 90 per cent are in favor of joining another union affiliated with the Canadian Labor Congress. The 90 per cent striking fishermen are in fear of reprisals due to threats made by Homer Stevens and his co-workers. Local 109, CLC, and 90 per cent of the striking fishermen of Petit de Grat are asking for support from all unions affiliated with the CLC in helping to settle the dispute.

A spokesman for the committee, Clem Benoit, told Linden MacIntyre that about thirty-six of the fishermen were "for getting rid of Homer Stevens" and revealed plans for a mass meeting or a march of concern to save the fish plant. "We were in support of the strike at the start," said Albert Martell, "but it's been dragging on for five months. Now we're in danger of losing the only industry we have."

Stevens denounced the whole affair as a Booth ploy, a charge given some credibility by Clem Benoit's position as production manager of the Booth plant – though Benoit denied that Booth had anything to do with the telegram. "It sounds like a desperate attempt by the company to break the union," Stevens suggested. Roy Keefe, president of the Seafood Workers, said in Canso that

"The strike has gone on long enough; something has to be done."
But he himself had been a strong supporter of the fishermen
from the outset, and faced with Martell's initiative he simply
said, "I'm keeping neutral."

The next day the UFAWU struck back, charging conspiracy
between the companies, the *Chronicle-Herald* and the Cape Breton *Post,* Father Poirier and "people they control or influence."
It argued that the vote was not understood by the voters to be
anti-UFAWU, but only pro-Booth. Union members had not voted
and had not been allowed into meetings of the Committee of
Concern. They had not authorized Martell's telegram and were
not afraid of anyone including their own union. And the telegram had been sent without a meeting of Local 109 being called
to authorize it.

The tone of the union press release is bitter: the papers, especially the Halifax daily,

> try to smear the fishermen and exonerate the company
> inspired conspiracy with the usual blaring headlines, half-
> truths, inuendo, (sic) falsehoods and the editorializing of arti-
> cles and news stories in the slanted manner of Time magazine.
> [Father Poirier] has come out squarely in favour of Booth's
> dictatorial policies all the way from refusing to recognize that
> trawl fishermen have the right to a union or leaders of their
> choice, to an open call for replacement of Petit de Grat fisher-
> men with strikebreakers imported from Newfoundland and
> other parts of Canada. UFAWU members believe this man will
> fail because condoning or calling for such open strikebreaking
> is neither in accordance with Christian principles, nor does it
> truely (sic) reflect the conscience of the Roman Catholic
> church, the clergy, its following or people who believe in free-
> dom and justice, as well as a better role for their clergy.

The union announced further plans: a rally in Halifax the following Wednesday, with an accompanying fish sale (a sale in
town the previous week had raised over $800); a street parade in
Halifax; and vigorous support for the general strike due the following Friday, August 21.

The union fishermen were clearly stung by what they saw as
simple betrayal in Petit de Grat. Despite his mutterings about

threats, Martell admitted to the Cape Breton *Post* that he himself had encountered no violence and had received no personal threats. In a lusty counter-attack on Father Poirier, Father Morley and his fellow priest at Bras d'Or, Father Joseph Muise, expressed shock and dismay. Writing in the parish bulletin, Father Muise declared that

> A whole movement should not be condemned because one man is said to be a Communist, as is happening with the Fishermen of Nova Scotia. The Steelworkers' Union and the UMW Mine Unions had their share of Communists when they were in the organizational stage of their history. Yet, everybody with a sense of fairness has to admit that these unions have done a great deal for the betterment of steelworkers and miners, and their families . . . The right to organize and the principle of unionism cannot be denied by right thinking Christians.

Father Morley said he "would be honored to be the author of everything Mr. Stevens is doing in the Strait area and of everything I have heard him speak. Regarding Mr. Stevens' statement on the role of the Catholic clergy in this strike, I must say, regretfully, that he is absolutely right. . . . Father Poirier's willingness to invite crews from out of the Province to take over the striking fishermen's boats is strange and incredible doctrine to be propounding in 1970."

He had attended union meetings in Canso and Petit de Grat and several times visited the union hall in Mulgrave, said Morley, and "I heard no propaganda, cheap or otherwise. The conduct of Mr. Stevens was always exemplary and certainly no union man could fault the values he expressed. I was proud to see the fishermen and their wives sharing so fully in the union meeting, their views being sought and their voices being respectfully heard, probably for the first time in their lives."

And Morley mused sadly on democracy in the crunch. "We talk about accepting the union of their choice, but we won't accept that it is this particular Union, the UFAW and this particular leader, Mr. Stevens, that the fishermen have chosen. And rather than accept that, we – churchmen, the government, the press – deny our principles. This was the Union that first went to these fishermen and from all I have been able to see and hear, the men have chosen this union as completely and definitely as it is possible to choose a union. It's the union of their choice. That is the unassailable fact of this strike. If Church and Government and the daily press were honest, then they would accept that fact with whatever implications it may embody."

But no. On Monday, the 17th, the *Chronicle-Herald* again startled followers of the strike with a banner headline:

TRAWLERMEN DISCLOSE PLANS TO QUIT UFAWU

Linden MacIntyre reported that "a rump group of about twenty trawlermen" in Petit de Grat were prepared to drop the union if the strike had not ended by August 20. "A spokesman for the dissident trawlermen said yesterday: 'Five months is enough to turn anyone sour.' " The men were considering forming a union of their own, and "officials of Local 109 said they will back the trawlermen all the way, providing the new union is affiliated with the Canadian Labour Congress."

MacIntyre reported that one fisherman with five children said he hadn't earned a penny in two months; he had been fishing on his own during the strike, but the union had put a stop to moonlighting and had told fish buyers not to buy from striking trawlermen. Another trawlerman, this one unmarried, said "Personally I could hold out till Christmas, but there are lots of others who are going to be in trouble." He reckoned 60 to 70 per cent of the Booth trawlermen were ready to quit the union. "If nothing happens by the 20th, we're going to drop out and go for another union. I will not go back to work without a union; I'm afraid the company might want revenge for the strike." MacIntyre quoted a former Booth chief engineer, Arthur Sampson, as saying he would stick with his new job as a carpenter. He was "not interested in going back to sea" because he didn't want anything to do with any fishermen's union: he had a grudge against the UFAWU because some of its members had threatened him in Newfoundland early in the strike.

Certainly the strain was beginning to tell. Go to a meeting in Petit de Grat this hot August evening. The salt air is heavy with heat and the reek of seaweed on the warm beach, the surface of the harbour glitters like crushed foil. In the hall, crowded with Acadian fishermen, their wives and other supporters, Homer Stevens is having some difficulty maintaining his fabled patience.

"There were Canso fishermen," he's saying, "that had the gear and could have kept on fishing and did want to keep on. But the other men said, 'If they keep on fishing we're gonna break our own strike' – and those were the ones that carried the majority. I believe that they were right, that you can't be on strike against a company on the basis of prices and then go out and fish for another company for *half* of those prices, and still consider yourself as being on strike. What kind of a strike is that?"

It's an angry meeting, full of shouting and disruption. Stevens faces plenty of vocal opposition – and has plenty of equally vocal support. What about men going to work on the Great Lakes' boats?

"I've got a list here of people who were suspected of being on the Great Lakes," says Stevens. "I thought it came from this local. Is that right?"

"Right!" shouts a fisherman.

"Okay," says Homer, "now those names have been phoned to the Seafarers' Union in Montreal, and we've asked that if they found them working on Great Lakes' boats, that they take steps to see that they get off those boats."

"They're genuine scabs whichever way you look at 'em," comes a voice from the floor.

"Not only on the Lakes," cries a young fishermen, "There's some of 'em in Port Hawkesbury here, what we gonna do about that?"

"I don't know how you can stop them from fishin'," a woman protests. "Now that's the greediest thing you ever did."

"It's a strike!" declares a fisherman, twisting in his chair. "They're breakin' the strike!"

"Well, can you live like this forever, on beans?" replies the woman.

The meeting dissolves in charges and counter-charges, loud arguments erupting in every corner of the room. "Order, now, order!" shouts the chairman. Things subside. It goes to a vote. The meeting votes that all outside work be stopped so that the full energies of the strikers can be brought to bear on the struggle.

"You have the right to make a motion in this meeting that the strike be called off," Homer says to the woman who's been leading the opposition. "You can make that motion any time. But remember that the company's got nothing but your disunity to win on. If you're united, if you stick together, they *can't* win. They *can't* win! Because people all over this province are saying, the fishermen have got to win this strike, we're not gonna let 'em lose it! And the company knows that! That's why they put in these ads.

"All I'm sayin' is keep your eye on that overall ball and work together. I've talked so goddam much, I've talked twice as much as the sister who criticized – but I hope you'll forgive me for being just a little bit hot sometimes. I got my temper too. But I think your membership and your executive should sit down and talk about all this, because she's brought forward some things that we've got to think a bit more about."

Meanwhile, the Seafood Workers' president angrily defended the pro-Booth vote and his own subsequent actions. "This vote was by secret ballot, with a sealed ballot box, and with a presiding officer in attendance at all times. He was accompanied by the president of the local and by the secretary-treasurer. An RCMP officer was in the hall to make sure that everything was legal," the local said in a statement. Albert Martell explained that only Booth employees were allowed to vote, and 273 did so, of whom twenty-eight were management. It was not, he protested, a company tactic; it was organized by a committee made up of fish plant workers, one citizen and the parish priest.

Earl Lewis, the Booth manager, was naturally delighted. "This outburst by our employees," he said, "is the result of their realizing that the strike has gone on long enough and that Booth was correct in their appraisal of the UFAWU and Homer Stevens."

What next? Martell didn't know. The Seafood Workers didn't plan to crash the picket lines, and felt that "the government will look after us now. I feel we should also appeal to affiliates of the Nova Scotia Federation of Labor for help. They should give us their support," he said. "We want to confirm that Roy Keefe had nothing to do with this vote, but we also remind Mr. Keefe that he is obliged to support members of his locals."

What accounted for the sudden change in the shoreworkers? Martell said that plant workers simply grew sick of the strike and the prolonged loss of income. The union local's funds were nearly gone, members had lost group life and sickness insurance, many were running out of unemployment insurance benefits.

The *Highlander* read it differently: "it seems that Albert Martell and an undetermined number of others have simply lost heart as the conflict came down to the short strokes." Editorially, it deplored the inevitable bitterness and hatred that "will last for generations" as a consequence of Local 109's defection. "The real question will not be settled that way, however; all that will be settled will be that some people measured the trawlermen's right of association and judged it too expensive for themselves."

Short strokes indeed: by now, every day brought at least one new development in the conflict. On Tuesday, August 18, Father Poirier defended himself against his critics. "The role of the church and the clergy today is to protect the poor against any form of exploitation, either by management or by labour," he said. "They say I'm un-Christian. If trying to feed the hungry is un-Christian, then Christ was un-Christian." Poirier alluded to the fighting record of the priests in Antigonish Diocese, who had been a driving force behind the organization of co-ops and credit unions during the Depression. He pointed to his record as parish priest in Canso itself as well as nearby Little Dover, where he had himself been in charge of a fishermen's co-op. He was not, he said, against unions; they were perhaps more necessary than ever. "What union leaders and the workers must be on their guard against is the labour racketeer who seems to be more interested in himself than in the welfare of the worker and the community."

Short strokes: on Wednesday, August 19, another rally in Halifax heard Father Bob Lauder, parish priest of Ketch Harbour and director of Catholic Social Services, declare that church leaders of all denominations are "crying out for justice for the fishermen." Ron Parsons told the crowd that he had received a number of threats, including a promise to burn down his house. As a result, the union fishermen were mounting a guard at the premises. J.K. Bell told the rally that the provincial government was "a hypocritical lackey of big business," and Mrs. Laura Samson of Petit de Grat, a fisherman's wife, reported that the women of the community were "standing beside our husbands in their fight for a union of their choice." The NDY distributed a leaflet calling for people in the Halifax area to join the Cape Bretoners in the general strike now only two days off.

But Halifax, unlike Sydney, is not a union town, and Canso Strait is 200 miles away. *The 4th Estate* also called on organized labour to do something serious about the fishermen, suggesting a province-wide general strike – and reported that Leo McKay, of the Federation of Labour, had been looking into the *Chronicle-Herald* reports of fishermen thinking of leaving the UFAWU. "We just haven't been able to find any evidence of this at all," said McKay. Ron Parsons told the paper that "we have tried to find out who the Halifax daily papers might be referring to but we can't find anybody who knows." Parsons also reported trouble getting welfare benefits for the strikers and their families. "People here are hungry and the provincial government is working through the municipalities to make it particularly tough for them to get welfare. This is a cowardly way to try to break the strike."

Parsons himself was under continuing fire for his outspoken support for the fishermen. F.C. Burton, a director of Acadia, had written Bishop Davis to complain about Parsons, implying that Parsons had no right to take such a stand and referring to Parsons' various statements as "galling and disgraceful." He concluded by saying that "If the church and the federal and provincial governments support this union, then the strike is over and Acadia will accept it. Of our own volition, however, the company regrets very much that it cannot in all conscience and alone take the responsibility of introducing such a union to Nova Scotia."

Short strokes: on Thursday, August 20, the day before the Cape Breton general strike, Halifax city officials were looking into the possibility of laying charges against the fishermen for their fish sales. The reason: they had no vendors' permits and their equipment had not passed health regulations. The fishermen were using wooden boxes for their fish; the health regulations call for stainless steel with special drainage. The sale, said a city legal officer, was "definitely contrary to the law. There may well be prosecutions." Sales were said to be light: Steve Hart, an NDY member, said his location had sold about fifteen pounds of cod in the first two hours. "If we had haddock here we could make thousands of dollars," he said, "but we just can't get it." Only cod – and, in Dartmouth, mackerel – were on sale. The police? Hart shrugged. "If they were going to take any action they would have moved by now."

But the big news of the day was Judge Green's surprise presentation of his report. And its immediate effect – its *intended* effect, said the cynics – was to cancel next day's general strike.

The report itself was no surprise to anyone who had read the interim report published the previous May. Green reviewed his own terms of reference and the general arrangements and nature of the companies and their relations with the trawlermen. He outlined the various hearings he had held.

> The early meetings and the public meetings do disclose that there is and has been for some time a general sense of dissatisfaction and frustration with the 'working conditions,' which includes the remuneration received by the fishermen for their efforts. The Commission urged the fishermen . . . to elaborate and clarify these general 'charges.' Regrettably, this was not done.

Green did not explain this point further; but it does not sit easily beside passages from the testimony quoted in the fishermen's own literature.

> The Commission sensed that there were many matters of complaint which were held back, one of the suggested reasons for this reluctance was the fear of reprisals. Indeed, the Commission sensed that there was a fear of reprisal not only from the Company but also from the Union. The term 'sensed' is used, as there was (sic) no specifics given at any of the hearings.
>
> Whatever allegations were made on fact and by innuendo have been met by the Companies in their submissions. . . . Despite these answers, the Commission did conclude that the fisherman-operator relationship between the Companies and the fishermen, despite the efforts enumerated by the Companies in their brief, is not good. [He had, Green said,] attempted to explore and determine the areas of grievance, [but the union was not willing to proceed without recognition.] I find that there has been, over the years, a growing disenchantment and

a worsening of the relationship between employer and employee, or, as the Companies would classify it, as between the Companies and the deep sea trawler fishermen as co-adventurers.

Whatever his uncertainties about the fishermen's actual grievances, Green noted that "it must be patently clear that if there was general satisfaction in the working conditions, the emphasis on 'recognition' *per se* would not be so determined." And he did note the existence of the blacklist:

> The Companies . . . held the economic fate of the fishermen in their hands; if a fisherman for one reason or another 'crossed' a Company, he might find himself not re-engaged for the next voyage, and each voyage was considered a separate venture . . . such a situation can readily lead to attitudes of fear and frustration.
>
> It does not take much imagination to understand and realize that many of the happenings which have occurred in this situation since March 30, 1970, could and would have been averted if the recommendations of the Commission had been followed.

Green remarked that he had advised Homer Stevens to apply to the Canada Labour Relations Board for certification, but "this recommendation was not acted on." Later in the report Green cited cases which led him to believe "that an application to the Canada Labour Relations Board would not be a meaningless exercise," though he also made it clear the outcome of the application could not be predicted with any certainty. He also expressed his own conviction that jurisdiction *did* rest with Canada, not with Nova Scotia, and that provincial legislation might well turn out to be simply another embittering complication in an already intractable conflict.

As to the status of fishermen, "It is not only difficult but seemingly impossible to conclude as a viable proposition that the relationship between the parties in these particular circumstances is that of co-adventurers." Perhaps other fishermen in other circumstances could be so described, but in Canso Strait, Green felt, the co-adventurer principle was an "unrealistic, outmoded idea, which has no relevance to this day and age in this type of operation. Indeed, the Companies involved in this matter have, by their willingness to grant voluntary recognition to any Union which is a member of the Canadian Labour Congress, recognized, though they may not have admitted the validity of, this proposition."

Even if the companies were willing to grant voluntary recognition, this would only be a stopgap. "In the final analysis it is not good enough for fishermen to depend on voluntary recognition to give them a bargaining position. A properly certified union can and will remove many of the deep-seated problems and bring mutual benefits to all concerned." In the meantime, however, the companies were within their legal rights in withholding recognition.

"The course of conduct of the Union and its supporters is to ignore the rule of law and to use pressure to force the Companies to grant voluntary recognition to the Union. The use of force in any form can only be detrimental to all concerned."

This appears to mean that the union's pressure tactics actually constitute a use of force – and to equate ignoring the law with breaking it. Green says nothing more about it, overlooking the fact that the UFAWU had *always* relied on voluntary recognition; since fishermen had no bargaining rights, no other course was open to it; it had to regard the law as irrelevant or else go out of business.

The question of force, raised again and again during the strike, also needs to be clarified. A strike is a conflict in which real and important issues are at stake, and the fishermen of Nova Scotia are not a notably bland group. As Homer Stevens remarked, "the normal way in which fishermen settled arguments well into the third month of the strike was to challenge each other out at the ball park and settle it that way. There was all kinds of feuding going on, between families within the community and one community feuding with another." In this context, nobody can be surprised if the strikers on occasion offered to bash someone's head in. Nobody can be surprised, either, if the fishermen occasionally threatened those of their own members who muttered about breaking ranks on one point or another. Some of the talk about intimidation is no doubt true: a plant worker confronting thirty husky fishermen on a picket line might well feel intimidated without a word being spoken.

In the course of a long strike, then, no doubt there was some intimidation – though I have never been able to uncover much evidence of it. At the same time, most observers were struck by the absolute absence of violence even when the fishermen's patience was almost entirely exhausted. *Systematic* intimidation, intimidation as a union policy, as opposed to hotheaded outbursts by exasperated individuals, was never a feature of the strike.

And Judge Green's comment leads one to wonder how many people have regarded the strike itself as a use of force. The fishermen didn't see it that way, and neither do most philosophers of liberty. Ignoring the injunctions was certainly a form of classic civil disobedience as Gandhi developed it during his liberation struggle in India – but civil disobedience is a deliberately non-violent strategy, in which the participant knows in advance, and accepts in advance, that he will suffer the consequences of his action.

Nova Scotians were inclined, that summer, to follow the lead of Henry David Thoreau, whose comment on his own civil disobedience aptly sums up the mood of the fishermen. "As for adopting the ways which the state has provided for remedying the evil, I know of no such ways. They take too much time, and a man's life will be gone."

Green concluded by offering a "package deal," as he called it. "Any attempt to accept some [recommendations] and reject others can only lead to a continuation of differences," he warned, which would "abort any useful result of this inquiry."

Green proposed that the fishermen should select an *ad hoc* committee of four members from each of the three ports to represent them in negotiations with the companies "as a primary and interim measure." The companies should recognize these committees as qualified to negotiate for the fishermen until a union could be certified. The plants should re-open and the men "return to work without discrimination."

Both the Ministers of Labour should publicly undertake to pass legislation giving bargaining rights to fishermen as soon as the Supreme Court gave its finding on the question of jurisdiction. No matter what the court decided, the immediate result would be bargaining rights for fishermen, and a certified union would swiftly follow.

The report drew predictably mixed reviews. Broadly speaking, the companies, the government and their colleagues approved of Green's recommendations: the labour movement and its allies were disappointed. Homer Stevens' first reaction, as he emerged from meetings at Province House with Judge Green and others, was brusque. "Standing as it's written, I wouldn't have any part of it," he told reporters. He denied that he was under pressure to soften his position, and promised to have a fuller comment after consultations with the fishermen. The companies refused to meet in the same room as Stevens, and had their questions relayed by Labour Minister McKeough. Labour Federation president Lynk said "there are a few grey areas we want to clarify in our own minds" and felt his people needed "to give it more study." The *Chronicle-Herald* found the report "a sensible compromise" which "demands some give and take."

Liberal leader Regan was similarly cautious: "there's not a great deal in the report that's new, but the fact that such a proposal has been brought forward by a man of Judge Green's stature may indicate a path towards at least an interim settlement." But Jeremy Akerman denounced the report as "a colossal waste of time" and "a stalling tactic" which was "tailor-made to suit the government's position." He took the occasion to flay the government's "delay, deceit and complicity. All their commissions, investigations, and legal references seem designed to further draw out the situation to a point where the strikers are starved into submission."

That brought Akerman a scolding from Ed Johnston, regional director of organization for the CLC and a New Democrat himself. "Part of the problem here is that there are too many people speaking on labour's problems who aren't aware of what labour's problems are. Mr. Akerman should not be taking a stand on a labour issue when the unions themselves haven't expressed themselves."

In essence Green was proposing a compromise in a situation in which – like pregnancy – no compromise was possible. The men were striking for union recognition: Green's "compromise" meant they would go back to work without it. To the fishermen, that idea sounded more like capitulation than compromise. While new demonstrations were held in Sydney and Port

Hawkesbury, labour officials continued their deliberations in Halifax. Ed Johnston explained that the report was "a basis for an arrangement to bring the situation to a head, but if I were the head of the organization I'd want more guarantees."

What guarantees? Homer Stevens cast some light on that. The report said nothing about the inshore fishermen; on the matter of changes in the law, the federal government would not make any commitment, though the province might; and the composition of the *ad hoc* committees themselves could be arranged to exclude union members. Stevens was also concerned about possible damage suits, and about "what happens to the people who could go to jail." Nevertheless he would go to Canso Strait and "see if the report offers some basis on which the thing can be settled."

So Stevens left for the fishing ports. The fishing companies accepted the report, Regan endorsed it, and Local 109 of the Seafood Workers congratulated Regan. A week later, Labour Minister McKeough called on organized labour to force Homer Stevens to send his union's response. The government had been waiting over a week, McKeough protested, and had heard nothing from the union. "There must apparently be some division at arriving at a decision within the union itself," he remarked. "Information came to my attention about meetings in the area, but there is still no official way of knowing how many attended the meeting and what the decision was."

The decision, taken unanimously at all three ports, was in fact to reject the report – and Stevens had sent a wire to that effect to the Minister. McKeough was acutely embarrassed to discover that while he had been berating Stevens for the delay, CN-CP Telecommunications was actually responsible, having mislaid the wire in its Halifax office.

Stevens spelled out the union's reasoning in a long letter to McKeough amplifying the bare-bones telegram. The union members were obviously anxious to end the long dispute. He had been instructed, Stevens said, not only to reject the Green recommendations, but also to spell out the terms on which the fishermen *would* go back to work.

The members insisted that the rights of the inshore fishermen "must be equally guaranteed along with the rights and opportunities of trawler crew fishermen." The consolidation of the fishery into large offshore boats and centralized plants which the Atlantic Development Board had predicted threatened the inshoremen's very existence. "The inshore fishermen are being forced to the wall," said Homer Stevens, "in just about as vicious a way as the Enclosure Acts were used to take people off the land in Britain and stick them into factories and into the slums of London and Manchester." Most inshore fishermen, though technically independent boat-owners, can only sell their catch to one buyer; in Canso, for instance, Acadia Fisheries was the only game in town. Inshore fishermen also wanted the right to bargain for prices – and they had united behind the trawlermen. The trawlermen were not going to desert them, even though Green had made no recommendations about them, pointing out that they were not included in his terms of reference.* In fact, of course, the offshore and inshore men were often the same people: Everett Richardson had for years worked summers on the inshore boats and winters on the draggers.

The fishermen's second condition called for the two Ministers of Labour to commit themselves to immediate legislation once the result of the application to the courts became known. But the men agreed to form *ad hoc* committees, provided that the whole body of the fishermen should have the final say, and provided that the *ad hoc* committee should be advised by union officials and others. The re-opening of all three fish plants was to be one of the purposes of the negotiation; Booth was to return the three trawlers from Fortune to Petit de Grat; and there was to be no discrimination against the shoreworkers, the captains, or the union fishermen themselves.

The government and the companies were to drop all legal actions arising out of the strike. And finally, if the fishermen did not have collective bargaining rights and union recognition by the end of the following April, they were to have full freedom to go back on strike again.

The fishermen may have felt they had rejected the Green

*A debatable point: an inquiry into "the cessation of fishing" in the three ports and "any matters incidental or related" is surely broad enough to include inshore fishing if Green had wanted to do so.

report – but in reality, they had merely added some safeguards before accepting it.

"It is obvious that the fishermen are prepared to negotiate, subject to adequate safeguards, with the companies without insisting on voluntary recognition of the United Fishermen and Allied Workers' Union and without being represented in bargaining sessions by officers of the Union," Stevens continued. "It is also obvious the fishermen have neither abandoned nor repudiated their union. Nor have the fishermen decided to embark upon a course which opens the way for the companies to destroy their rights to belong to the union and to be properly represented by their union in the near future." The process of negotiation would be "to say the least, unusual and delicate, especially while neither government is prepared to assume full responsibility."

But the nub of the matter was clear: the fishermen were prepared to talk.

While the companies and the government digested these proposals, the stomachs of the fishermen's families were empty. "I went into one feller's place about then," says Edison Lumsden, "and all they had to eat was six slices of bread. They made a piece and a half of toast each for the feller and his wife, and one each for the three kids, and they had to send next door to borrow a can of milk."

The Catholic Diocese of Antigonish voted $1,500 towards the relief of the strikers; Ron Parsons and his brother Anglican in Arichat, Cal MacMillan, were leading a fresh drive to get welfare payments for the strikers' families. The province and the municipalities had been booting the question back and forth all summer. It was strictly up to the municipalities, said provincial welfare director Don Coulter. The province wouldn't intrude. But the province did uphold a refusal by the Canso officials to grant aid to a striker, and other appeals were left hanging for months on end. The UFAWU, with Parsons and Canon French, wired the federal government to point out that federal assistance was not being given out in accordance with need; and need pure and simple is the only criterion applied to the federal portion of the welfare budget. The union cited a parallel situation in British Columbia in which the province had been ordered to pay welfare

146

to strikers or prepare to see funds under the Canada Assistance Act cut off.

But it looked like a long wait. Canso mayor Jim Hanlon had written to the provincial welfare authorities on July 17, when he saw the problem shaping up; by August 10, when the UFAWU committee reported back, the province still had not answered.

By now, Parsons had been threatened with shooting as well as arson; a petition demanding his removal had been sent to Bishop Davis, and Parsons admitted he didn't dare call a meeting of his parish council.

But he wasn't backing down. The strike, he said, offered a frightening illustration of the pressures that can be marshalled to crush poor people. "The whole Nova Scotia establishment has risen up against these people," he said. After the threats, "the Bishop called me in and said he was concerned," Parsons grinned. "I was too, to tell you the truth, but I said no, I'm not going to back down while the strike lasts." He planned to ask for a later ecclesiastical trial at which he could answer the various charges.

And the negotiations? On September 2, Homer Stevens referred to the "deafening silence from Ottawa. There's been no reply, not even a telegram, from Mackasey. He has not responded in any way to Judge Green's recommendation that he undertake publicly to take necessary legislative steps if the Nova Scotia Supreme Court rules that the issue of collective bargaining rights for fishermen falls within federal jurisdiction." Mackasey was said to be holidaying in Spain.

All the same, the *ad hoc* committee and the companies met in Halifax to explore the prospects for negotiation. The meeting – the first face-to-face encounter between the two parties in the whole five-month strike – was a disaster.

Jim Collins, Raymond Cooper, and Eric and Peter Fitzpatrick came from Mulgrave. Gordon Joshua, Victor Clannon, and Alphonse and Cletus Samson represented Petit de Grat. Canso sent Everett Richardson and Russell Gurney, and nominated Edison Lumsden and Walter Hanlon, but the latter two wouldn't do. They were not acceptable to the companies. Hanlon lived in Canso, but he fished with Booth in Petit de Grat; Edison was an inshore man. Father Lauder was there from Ketch Harbour, but he was barred. So was Ron Parsons, who wasn't particularly happy about the meeting in the first place. The fishermen, he reckoned, had been pressured by the Federation into the *ad hoc* committee arrangement. "For me, the real issue in this strike has been freedom of choice," the fighting Anglican explained, "and now in a sense they've given that up."

The meeting was chaired by Tom McKeough, the Minister of Labour. Leo McKay represented the Federation. Booth sent Charles Gordon and the lawyer, W.H. Jost; Acadia sent Cadegan and Merlin Nunn. The fishermen's lawyer was Leonard Pace.

The fishermen wanted to talk about ways and means of getting the plants ready to function while the talks continued. They wanted to explore the areas which a contract would have to cover – wages, safety, hours, and the like.

The companies balked. Before any of those issues could be discussed, they insisted, the fishermen would remove their picket lines, allow the companies to get on with repairs and servicing, permit the processing and marketing of fish on hand, and send vessels to sea to bring in more fish from Newfoundland or elsewhere.

The fishermen were astounded. Even the Labour Minister seemed startled. After an acrimonious hour, the meeting broke up.

"They didn't want any advisors in the negotiating room," Everett Richardson remembers, turning angry as his mind slides back to those warm September days. "They wanted to eliminate Homer Stevens. Didn't want him in there at all, not even in the building. They didn't want the clergy, they just wanted to take a bunch of fishermen, stupid fishermen as they figured, in there to negotiate a contract for the rest of the fishermen to abide by for the year or two years, or whatever the term of the contract would be. That's all they wanted. Thought it was gonna be an easy pushover, but it wasn't as easy as what they figured it was, because we still didn't give in to the company – "

Yeah. Now –

" – and for to, for to take a bunch of greenhorns in there that had never *drawn* up a contract or hardly even *read* one before is pretty hard thing for a bunch of – of – "

He flounders, choking in his own indignation.

" – I don't know how the hell to put it, a bunch of – I don't know what to call them, but what they done wasn't what they *said* they was doin' at all."

But looking back on it, Everett felt the Federation and the government had been basically dishonest: they were not determined to see the fishermen get their union; instead they were primarily interested in an end to this awkward strike. In agreeing to negotiate as an *ad hoc* committee rather than as a union, the fishermen had already given up their key demand. To be pressed for concessions which amounted to capitulation, and to be encouraged to continue negotiating by labour leaders and the government would enrage anyone.

Nevertheless the fishermen themselves wanted to find some basis for agreement; having gone so far, they were unwilling to give up the prospect of a settlement. The next day they returned to McKeough with a set of further proposals. They would agree to see the companies prepare the plants, boats, and equipment for operation while the negotiations were underway, and to allow final processing, packaging and marketing of frozen fish already in the plants. They would keep their picket lines up, but would guarantee passage through the picket lines for these purposes.

The companies rejected these proposals, too. The fishermen were to remove the picket lines as a precondition to the other negotiations.

With an almost perceptible sigh, the fishermen agreed to take down the picket lines, provided negotiations began in earnest the following week. Work in the plants, they stipulated, was to be done by Seafood Workers' Union members, trawlers were to be moved only with regular crews, the companies were to permit fishermen bearing passes from the *ad hoc* committee into their premises, and no new fish was to be brought in or caught until negotiations were complete. Refits of the boats were to be done in union shipyards in Nova Scotia, and no rigging of fishing gear was to be done until an agreement was reached. Given these common sense safeguards, the men would drop their picket lines – though they reserved the right to reinstate them if the companies violated the ground rules. They suggested further meetings be held in Antigonish or Port Hawkesbury, for the convenience of all concerned.

149

"We consider this to be more than just bending over backwards to get serious negotiations underway," said the fishermen in a press release. Few observers disagreed.

On September 9, the two sides met again in Halifax at Province House, the old Georgian Legislature. The pressure was by now intense: two days earlier Local 110 of the Seafood Workers, the Mulgrave local, had joined its colleagues in Petit de Grat in calling for the fishermen to be represented by a CLC union, and asked that the UFAWU "be removed from union activities" in Nova Scotia. The move took the form of a petition with seventy-nine signatures which, said Alphonse O'Neil, the local's president, represented 90 per cent of the Seafood Workers still in the Mulgrave area. A similar petition was circulating in Canso, although the Canso local had not long before reiterated its support of the UFAWU. And Roy Keefe had announced his resignation as president of the shore union as a result of what now appeared to be a division between his own convictions and the wishes of a large proportion of his members. Time, it appeared, was running out for the fishermen. The strike was in its sixth month; there must be a limit to the endurance of the men themselves, and there was clearly a limit to that of their most important supporters.

But what CLC union did the Seafood Workers propose? The Brotherhood had just voted $1,000 to the fishermen, and in an interview with the *Highlander,* a member of the national executive of the Brotherhood, Dick Greaves, reported that his union had also pledged "full and unequivocal support" to the UFAWU. "One or two of our own Brotherhood representatives see the fishermen as a big membership grab here," Greaves admitted. "It's as mercenary as that, and that's what I'm going to say at the upcoming convention. But the UFAWU has done a tremendous job, and in an organizing situation like this there's no room for labour people to equivocate, from the CLC right on down the line."

The conciliatory position of the fishermen cemented their relationship with the Federation; as John Lynk put it, there was no way the companies could reject their proposals. Going into the September 9 meeting, everyone was optimistic. "The weight of the moral argument has always been 100 per cent on the side of the fishermen," remarked Father Morley, and "the companies now have no more excuse not to bargain seriously."

But the meeting broke up in disorder once again. The companies insisted that in addition to the various concessions the fishermen had already made, the companies also be allowed to catch and process new fish. The fishermen's conditions, said the companies, were "inconsiderate and unrealistic." If they were met, the 800 plant workers could not go back to work, so the companies could no agree to anything less than full operation of the plants "without breaking faith with the plant workers." It's an interesting argument: if the plant workers can't work, the strike must continue, in which case the plant workers can't work.

After the meeting, Canon French summed it up. "The companies," he told reporters, "have told the fishermen, in effect: first you surrender. Then we'll talk."

J.K. Bell, who had represented the Federation this time around, declared that "the full and complete onus" for the breakdown rested with the companies. If the fishermen gave up now and allowed new fish into the plants and permitted the trawlers to sail, it could mean the companies "dragging their feet indefinitely." He pledged the Federation to continuing support of the fishermen, and reminded everyone that a general strike had still "never been ruled out."

Labour Minister McKeough glumly admitted that no date had been set for any further meetings, but he believed that the talks hadn't broken down completely and that there might be further meetings.

"How far can you go?" demanded a furious Reg Carter, returning to Mulgrave after the talks. "How far can a poor fisherman go? We gave up our union – we never should have done that. We gave in on Con and Homer – we never should have done that. We gave in on the inshore fishermen. We gave in on the advisors. We lifted our picket lines – all to please the Federation of Labour, and McKeough, and the companies. Then they tell us that we're going to go back fishing. Well, that's bullshit!"

Next day the reasons for McKeough's concern became obvious. Premier Smith dissolved the legislature and called a provincial general election for October 13. Rumour had it that Smith would retire after leading the Tories home to power again, and that McKeough was a likely candidate to succeed him. The Liberals were given small hope of unseating the government. Commentator Bruce Little reported from Ottawa that

Maritime Liberals here are putting few bets on the chance of a Liberal government in Halifax. The feeling is that Gerald Regan is simply not the man who can lead the Liberals to a victory. No one appears to be making any overt moves to get rid of him, but no one expects him to do any more than trim Premier G.I. Smith's majority in the Legislature.

As for the seatless NDP, the pundits thought Jeremy Akerman might just conceivably win personal election, but the NDP was whistling in the dark to expect anything more than that.

The impact of the fisherman's strike was considered by the backroom strategists to have peaked. The fishermen, one source reportedly said, were by now "isolated enough not to affect the outcome of the election."

Some fishermen had already made their own plans for election day. Because of Ron Parsons, people like Everett Richardson were going to the Anglican church; because of Jeremy Akerman, people like Eric Fitzpatrick regarded the election as important and the NDP as worth supporting.

"Us fishermen, we never paid too much attention to politics before the strike," Eric explained. "When we came on shore we'd never talk about politics, we'd just get drunk and try to forget about everything. If a program that had anything to do with politics came on TV we'd turn to another program – Donald Duck or something. At election time they'd come around and offer us a quart of rum or a case of beer and tell us who to vote for – I'd vote for whoever came around first. But anyone who takes his vote seriously wouldn't sell it like that. Now I wouldn't sell my vote for five hundred dollars. If somebody offered me five hundred dollars I wouldn't lie to him, I'd tell him how I'm going to vote – NDP."

The strike percolated on for another two weeks. The union appealed for clothing, now that autumn was coming on and the children were going back to school: its supporters in Halifax and Sydney sent truckloads of good used garments. Steelworkers' president Winston Ruck was especially active in the clothing drive, and continued to insist that the steel union would support the UFAWU until the men themselves were satisfied. The battle for welfare continued – and Richmond County agreed to pay welfare benefits to the most deprived of the Petit de Grat fishermen and shoreworkers.

The companies charged that the fishermen were tightening the noose by refusing to allow even maintenance workers who had been in and out of the plant all summer to cross the picket lines; the union retorted that the companies were as usual distorting the truth, and explained that the strikers had issued additional passes to replacement maintenance people when the regular maintenance workers went on holiday. Now that the regular workers were back, they were withdrawing the extra passes, and the number of maintenance workers allowed in the plants was the same as it had always been.

"The union has every interest in keeping the plant in operative condition," Edison Lumsden pointed out. "We are still hopeful of a settlement in the not too distant future." Thirteen people had passes, and "this is the original number." If the company wanted to close the plant because more men weren't allowed to enter, "then that's their business, but any responsibility for fish spoiling must rest with them."

Across the bay in Arichat, Anglican rector Cal MacMillan said that despite the virulence of Alfred Martell's comments the majority of the shoreworkers still supported the fishermen. "In fact," said Father MacMillan, "a majority of the people of this area want to see the trawlermen win their struggle." He thought he also detected "a new spirit of hope in the community as a result of the initiatives taken by the fishermen to end the strike," and felt that even the union's critics had realized that the union was making large and important concessions which hadn't been met by the companies.

The fishermen held fish sales in Sydney on September 16 and 17. Meanwhile Ron Parsons had been helping the Canso women in their battle to get welfare benefits, a venture which on September 15 evoked a sit-in at the Town Hall.

"We weren't leavin' until we had the welfare," Linda Gurney remembers, laughing. "We took cow-bells and fog-horns, everything that we could. Oh, we made such a racket! And they wouldn't let us in the court house –"

"Well, the first day we went down there they let us in," Jean Richardson corrects her. "But the next day they wouldn't let us in, and the third day was Wednesday, so Frank Fraser was there." Fraser administers welfare for both the Town of Canso and the County of Guysborough; Wednesday is his regular visit to Canso. "We went in about ten o'clock and we asked what time he would be in his office. He said, 'Ten o'clock,' We said, 'Well, it's five after ten and the door isn't open.' 'Mrs. MacDougall is away,' he said, 'and we don't have any authority to open the door,'" Margaret MacDougall was town clerk of Canso and no friend of the union.

"You can't let us in?" laughs Linda. "Well, we're not letting you guys out."

"But Elsie Ryan's wife came along." Ellsworth Ryan was one of the striking fishermen; his name comes to the forefront again the following spring. "We had fastened the door to the court house with wire, and her, she went to work and unfastened the door so they could get out. Anyway, we kept kicking up a stink, and finally Frank Fraser came out and he said he'd let us go into the court house if we were quiet, you know. Well, that's all we were reaching for, to get in there, 'cause we had it in our mind that when we got in there we weren't coming out. We got in there, talking to Frank Fraser and having a meeting – and Elsie Ryan's wife came in. We told Fraser that she was the whole reason the wire was on the door in the first place, put the blame on her. If there's any names to be taken down for trouble or anything, we said we'd put her down at the top of the list. So she got savage and took off."

"Several of them came and try to get us going," says Linda, "but we wouldn't leave."

"A couple of Mounties came at dinnertime," says Jean.

"Yeah, the Mounties came and told us we were leaving, and we said 'No, we're not leaving.'"

"He said 'I'll give you ten minutes and if you're not out we're gonna have you arrested,'" Jean recalls. "But in that ten minutes – we didn't know it, but he went down and talked to Edison and tried to get Edison to make us leave. Edison said it wasn't his doing; he didn't tell us to go there, and he couldn't make us leave."

"Well, that was a long ten minutes gone," declares Linda. "He must have been gone an hour. Then he came back and he said that we were up not only for trespassing or something – being on the property when we're not supposed to be there, that we were also up for obstructing an officer. We said, 'We didn't touch you!' Then he explained it, that we had disobeyed his orders. But that didn't bother us. We were still hell-bound we were gonna stay there, and they turned the water off, we couldn't get any water in the bathroom –"

"We weren't allowed to use the phone," says Jean.

"We weren't allowed to have the windows open, it was just like the black hole of Calcutta. But that didn't bother us then. We still stayed there. So Father Parsons, he snuck sandwiches into us, which he wasn't supposed to. They got them in by the window. You see, Father Parsons had come up to this Mountie – Kelly his name was, and that's one capital P altogether – and what did Kelly do but slam the door right in his face! Now you talk about a bunch of savage women –"

"If he hadda said much more," Jean grins, "we had it in our head we were gonna lock *him* up in a cell. We wouldn't have cared! Oh, did we ever fly into him! Telling him there was no man into him, we said *everything* to him. After a while he went and got Jim Hanlon, the mayor, and brought him in.

"So Jim said, 'We'll have a meeting tomorrow,' and we said, 'Well, we're not taking your word. Write it out in writing that you'll have a meeting with us tomorrow.' And that was the only condition we would leave."

"Then we went down to see Father Parsons," Linda continues. "He was mad about Kelly, you know, and I don't know who all he called about it. And we weren't there very long when who should come in but Kelly, and he apologized to Father Parsons, for slamming the door in his face."

"I think the Mountie was shocked that we stood up to him," says Jean. "You know, there are very few women standing up to him. We were staying till we got – well, we were going to spend the night in –"

"– in the clink," said Linda.

"Well, in the clink, if you want to call it that."

"That Kelly," chuckles Everett, shaking his head. "You get stuck with a bunch of angry women, now, they *know* how to get under your skin."

Smaller events continued to make the news. Homer Stevens addressed the National Farmers' Union, thanking the NFU for its solid support of the fishermen in the form of tons of food which were still flowing into the three ports. He told the NFU regional meeting that farmers, fishermen and industrial workers had common goals and supported one another's struggles, a view endorsed by NFU president Roy Atkinson. In Glace Bay, the United Mine Workers voted $500 to the fishermen, and a three-man delegation took the cheque to Petit de Grat, where they handed it over to Father Arsenault. Arsenault apparently gave the money to fishermen of his own choosing in the three ports. He was no longer supporting the union, whose officers said they knew nothing about the contribution except through newspaper accounts.

In the *Highlander*, Professor Doris Boyle published a commentary questioning the ability of Homer Stevens to "separate his work as a union leader from his political convictions." An American and long-time Sydney resident who taught economics at Xavier College, Dr. Boyle argued that "the Communist Party is a conspiracy and not a political party at all." Her article initiated the clearest discussion all summer of a theme which was usually merely a matter of dark mutterings.

> The function of unions in the Communist schemes is to mobilize worker support for the Communist party and to serve as an instrument of day-to-day combat with employers. The employer is the enemy. The duty of the union is to harass him in every way possible, to undermine his position in the plant and build up bitterness toward him among the workers, and eventually to dispossess him . . .
>
> If some well-known friends of labour in this province have not spoken out more strongly on behalf of the fishermen, it is . . . because they know from experience that unions led by men with a record of Communist political persuasion, even if they

are certified, can create problems for workers, for employers, and for the public . . .

Look at the record, retorted George Hewison, a west coast UFAWU organizer who had come to Nova Scotia to help out during the strike. "The UFAWU has demonstrated its concern for the public welfare by its consistent fight on issues far beyond the fishing industry." He cited the union's ongoing campaign for conservation of natural resources, and he pointed out that the union's advice was often sought by government in areas where it had made itself particularly expert. Homer Stevens was, at that point, advising the federal government; he was also scheduled to address a Toronto conference on racism and war.

"The companies' social responsibility and conscience extend no further than their pocketbooks," Hewison charged. "They do not open plants to create jobs. They do it to make profits. Neither do they close plants down in the public interest."

Hewison admitted that a Communist might well use his power base in a union presidency to advance political views. But, he suggested, companies do exactly the same thing – and with vastly greater resources of power and money. "If an officer of a union uses his position as president to counteract some of the powerful propaganda of the employers, naturally that should be considered legitimate. Anything less is to sell the workers the short end of the stick."

But Dr. Boyle's most serious charge, Hewison felt, was the implication "that Homer Stevens and the UFAWU do not accept the democratic system." On the contrary, said Hewison, "the UFAWU is noted as one of the most democratic unions on the continent – up to and including the right of the membership to remove Mr. Stevens or any other officer."

At the time of the strike, Homer Stevens was not, in fact, a member of the Communist Party; he had been one, however, and by the 1974 federal election he would be the Party candidate in his BC home riding. But Dr. Boyle's whole view of Communist efforts in the labour movement is, in terms of Canadian history, not very well founded. During the early years of this century, the movement was peppered with Scottish Communists, mostly from Glasgow, and their energy and commitment were responsible for

157

many of labour's advances during the period. J. B. McLachlan, the towering figure of the Cape Breton coal union, was such a Clydesider; so was George Miller, the UFAWU's first president.

During the 'thirties, Communists were largely responsible for organizing the new, militant unions of the Congress of Industrial Organizations (CIO) – and the old Trades and Labour Congress, far from welcoming such new vitality, joined with companies and governments to crush them. Irving Abella, one of our leading labour historians and by no means a Communist himself, has pointed out that Canadian workers owe a great deal to the Communists, who took on tough organizing jobs and carried them through with skill and dedication at a time when nobody else was willing to touch them.

"Communism?" scoffs Eric Fitzpatrick. "This is another way they have of scaring the people. There's lots of religious people around Nova Scotia, and if you're a Communist you're not supposed to believe in God, you're not supposed to believe in truth. I think it was just another way the companies had of dirtying up Homer Stevens' name. They say in this country you got a right to be what you want to be – well, if Homer Stevens is a Communist, that's Homer Stevens' business. As long as he don't tell me what church to go to, that's okay.

"I've heard people say that Homer was leading the fishermen into something that they didn't understand and didn't know about," Eric continues. "Well, this is goddam wrong, because there wasn't a fisherman did anything without Homer briefed him a dozen times on it, to make sure he knew what he was doing." Everett Richardson agrees: he remembers meeting after meeting in which Homer would explain a situation "and then he'd turn to us and say, 'Now what are we gonna do?' And we'd argue about it till everyone was satisfied."

Such procedures contrast sharply with the meetings of the Petit de Grat Seafood Workers under Alfred Martell. Martell had held no meetings at all in the six weeks after denouncing the UFAWU, but he had withdrawn his local from the Seafood Workers and demanded that the CLC send in the Canadian Food and Allied Workers to organize both shoreworkers and trawlermen at Petit de Grat. Martell's move was backed by the local Lions

Club, the Knights of Columbus, and the Isle Madame Board of Trade.

Why no membership meeting? Martell told the *Highlander* "with apparent seriousness," as the paper drily noted, that the members hadn't asked for a meeting in the proper way. They had asked for a meeting "to discuss the Seafood Workers' involvement in the fishermen's strike." But, said Martell, he couldn't call a meeting for that purpose "because we spent ten weeks convincing the UIC that we weren't involved in the strike." On what basis, then, was he denouncing the UFAWU and pulling out of the Seafood Workers? Martell said that of the 280 shoreworkers, 240 had voted in the "Do you want Booth to leave" vote, which had voted "No" with only one exception. But the vote was set up by the Committee of Concern, not the union: and anyway, how does a vote to keep Booth in Petit de Grat become a vote to get rid of the UFAWU? "Because they can't have both Stevens and Booth," said Martell. Who decided that they couldn't? The Seafood Workers' executive, meaning Martell and three other people.

But if Booth and Acadia – or Martell – thought the CLC was going to bring in another union to break the impasse, they were mistaken. CLC executive vice-president Joe Morris was in Nova Scotia, and was said to have handed company representatives a sharp statement telling them to forget about any such plan and get down to serious negotiations with the fishermen. On September 23, talks began at St. Francis Xavier University in Antigonish.

This time the companies dropped their demand to bring in new fish for processing. The fishermen dropped their picket lines for a trial period of ten days.

"There was quite a load on your shoulders," Everett recalls. "All the time, whatever was brought up, you wondered; well, when you take this back to the membership, what're they gonna think about it? Are they gonna accept it, or say, 'If that's as good as you can do we might as well not have a union at all.' All this stuff is going through your head. And Cadegan right there – different times he picked up and walked out and said, 'I'm not coming back any more.' That was all right for him, but if *we* hadda done it, they'd have been right in their glory, see, if we knocked the negotiations off. But after he went outside and talked to the government crooks for a little while longer, he came back. He was cooled off when he come in. We never recessed, and he'd cool off and come back in. He wore his dark glasses all the time. He couldn't face you without them."

"Yeah," sighs Linda. "I noticed that he'd always come down to the picket line with his dark glasses, like the day after Everett and them were sentenced."

"Well, if there's one thing I'll always remember," laughs Everett, "it was when Ed Johnston, Charlie Crowell, Leo McKay and all that was in the board room with the company men, and Eric Fitzpatrick let out at 'em and told them off. Every word Eric said there at that time come out true. There was no blood left in their faces when he was through. Yeah!" He gives a deep rolling chuckle, savouring the memory. But no, he doesn't remember just what Eric did say.

Eric does, at least in outline. "We're here, I said, talking to a bunch of men that's got twenty years of negotiating these things, and you got twenty years of experience of screwing the rich *and* the poor. You got a bunch of fishermen in here now, I said, and you're tryin' to walk all over us. You should be ashamed of yourselves. It's a disgrace to the community and it's a disgrace to the whole country." The company men got up and walked out, and had to be cajoled into returning.

"Yeah," chuckles Everett. "They mighta had a lot of stuff told to them, but they'll never have anything told to them like Eric Fitzpatrick told 'em off that day."

Ten days came and went, and the fishermen kept talking. In Halifax, the Federation of Labour had its annual meeting at the Hotel Nova Scotian. The fishermen's strike was never brought before the conference, but subterranean dissatisfaction with the Federation's failure to take militant action bubbled to the surface at several points. John Lynk was challenged by Chester Sanford, a Dartmouth alderman and head of the Halifax-Dartmouth Trades and Labour Council, but Lynk won re-election, holding Sanford to about 40 per cent of the vote. "Factions within the labor movement feel the executive has been weak-kneed in its stand on the UFAWU," reported *The 4th Estate,* "and is letting its hands be bound by the CLC." The paper also mentioned "heavy

160

behind the scenes politicking by the Canadian Labour Congress" to keep the issue off the agenda.

Lynk argued that public discussion of the strike could only hurt the negotiations going on at Antigonish, and asked the delegates, "Who are you going to strike against with a general strike? Whose jurisdiction does it come under? This Federation has done more for them than any Federation across Canada would have attempted to do." Nevertheless, an appeal for funds netted $1,475 for the strike fund, about $400 of which came out of delegates' own pockets. "Union locals," reported *The 4th Estate's* Pauline Janich, "tried to outdo each other, racing to the microphones to throw their contribution onto the pile."

In Antigonish, events were slowly moving towards a contract, although the fishermen were reported to be dissatisfied with the constant pressure from the labour movement and the government to concede or modify each of their demands as it came up. In Ottawa, the federal NDP blasted Bryce Mackasey for his continued failure to give the undertaking called for in the Green report. "Recommendations on a labor matter made by a commission appointed by the federal labor minister," it commented acidly, "are being ignored by the minister himself." Mackasey's silence had now lasted seven weeks.

The companies wanted an eighteen-month contract: the union was not prepared to go beyond the following April. The companies wanted mates and chief engineers excluded; the fishermen said "No." On October 6, Homer Stevens said that "the committee's view is that no progress yet has been made toward improving fishermen's earnings." Disagreements over length of lay-ups between trips, check-off rights, Canada Pension, and the right to solicit union memberships aboard company vessels, all had to be dealt with. Stevens suggested that the companies were deliberately dragging out the talks until after the election; then they would bring fresh pressure on the government.

The fishermen were still hungry; on October 22 three UFAWU men from Canso were caught shooting a cow and butchering it for the meat. For the UFAWU, re-opening the Mulgrave plant, with its 275 jobs afloat and ashore, was a condition of settlement. Dr. McKeough told the negotiators that provincial money would be available. The companies agreed to drop civil damage suits

161

against fishermen, but not against union officers – though they hinted that if the union were suitably docile, the suits would be dropped; if not, the union itself, Homer Stevens, Con Mills and Jim Allen could expect to go to court.

"On the one hand management agrees to drop damage suits against individual fishermen," said one of the committee members, "and on the other, threatens to bleed the union which we're all a part of. When we finally went on strike, it was by our own decision – no one had to come and tell us to take that action in support of our rights. And the union president didn't arrive in Nova Scotia till we'd been out two weeks – and then only at our request."

Shortly before the October 13 election, however, Labour Minister McKeough was able to announce that an agreement had been reached. Nova Scotians took that to mean that the strike was over; in fact it was not, since no agreement covering the inshore fishery had been achieved. It would be another two weeks before the fishermen would go back to sea.

The trawl agreement itself, said Con Mills, was "nothing to write home about." Cadegan himself said it didn't represent any great change in the conditions the men had always known, and on the whole he was right. Its features included some increases in fish prices, and for the first time, floor prices. The crew members were to receive detailed settlement sheets, showing exactly what they were being paid and why; their own nominees were to be present at the unloading and grading of their catches. Cadegan says those were the accepted practices anyway; the fishermen say they weren't. Grievances were to be processed under a committee and boat delegate organization; the crew was to shop where it wished for its food; no deductions from wages were to be made except those spelled out in the agreement. Crewmen were to be paid 75 per cent of their earnings when the ship docked, the remainder to be calculated and paid after the unloading and grading of the catch. Medicine chests, cool fresh water and adequate beds and bedding were assured. And there would be an eight-day holiday guaranteed at Christmas.

On October 13, Gerald Regan did what no one thought he could do: he defeated the twelve-year-old Conservative régime in Halifax. When the votes were counted, Regan's Liberals held twenty-three seats, one short of a majority. The Tories had been reduced by twenty seats, from forty-one to twenty-one. And the NDP, to the astonishment of the pundits, had elected not only Jeremy Akerman but also Paul MacEwan, a young school teacher who had knocked off Mines Minister Percy Gaum in Sydney.

Nobody was attributing the defeat to the fishermen's strike, though it clearly had been a factor. Both Canso Strait incumbents held their seats for the Tories, Gerald Doucet being returned in Richmond and Angus MacIsaac in Guysborough, but the NDP, which had hardly existed in the strike area in previous elections, picked up a thousand votes in the two ridings. Dr. McKeough won personal re-election, but in Halifax a coalition of Liberals, leftists and students submerged their differences in a joint effort to get rid of Attorney-General Donahoe, who was resoundingly returning to private life. And the new Labour Minister would be Leonard Pace.

The trawl contract had been submitted to the trawlermen; the committee had been authorized to sign it only in conjunction with a similar contract in the inshore fishery. The companies flatly refused – worried, the fishermen said, that such a contract would utterly destroy the co-adventurer concept. After further meetings with the locals, the committee bluntly told the companies that the trawl agreement would not be signed without an inshore agreement.

With a new government in power – a government which soon let it be quietly known that Acadia Fisheries was not one of its favourite organizations, but that it might all the same be obliged to help it re-open the Mulgrave plant – the fishermen quietly dropped their insistence about the matter. The companies conceded that although they would not sign any contract with the inshore fishermen, they would issue a memorandum of agreement, spelling out improvements. Its major feature was recognition of their fish as "premium" quality, which meant a penny a pound more, roughly speaking, for their catch – a difference of perhaps $50.00 on an average day's work for three men. The memorandum also provided for improved berthing and unloading facilities and a lower price for bait.

All the pieces had been put together, except a lingering uncertainty about the return of the three Booth trawlers from Fortune, Newfoundland. The settlement, said the union in a statement, "cannot be described as a victory or a defeat, but rather as a toe-hold for the future . . . An organized return to work under signed contracts is a major achievement in the face of the 'codfish aristocracy' with all the power it wields in government, the courts, and throughout all phases of life in Nova Scotia."

Homer Stevens' own comment was that this had been "the first time in the 300 year history of the Canadian Atlantic fisheries that a strike of fishermen was not totally smashed and its leaders blacklisted."

"We had a contract, see?" says Everett Richardson, his hand wrapped around a mug of strong, dark tea. "That's one thing we did have. It's not as good as what we wanted it to be, but we had working conditions and all this other stuff in it, provisions like that. Which is better 'n what we were sailing under before."

On the last day of October, 1970, after shaking up their native province for seven hot, hungry, exhilarating months, the fisher-men announced that their strike was over.

Their struggle, however, was not. Its next act would be even more murky and bitter than the long strike itself. Their next adversaries would be the people they had thought were their friends.

INTERLUDE
Country Cunning and Unofficial Life

"Then hurrah for your grog,
Your jolly, jolly grog,
Hurrah for the rum and tobacco,
For I've spent all my tin
On a lassie drinking gin,
And across the western ocean I shall wander."

– Nova Scotia folk song

Dear Everett,
By now you've surely figured out that I respect and admire you
and Jean and your family – and the other fishermen and their
families, too, as far as I know them. In fact it was meeting people
like you that made me decide I wanted to live somewhere around
the Strait of Canso. Five years later, I still love it here: the sea
and the woods, the little inlets and harbours, the villages and
farms, the trim unpretentious houses, above all the people.

What kind of people? That's what I'm going to try to talk
about – but I want to make sure you understand that I think of
myself as *part* of this community now. I'm going to say some
things that I think are true but that our more proper neighbours
will find rude. We don't say such things aloud. It's like a family,

in a way. We may all know that Cousin Vicky is a drunk, Uncle Fred is a lecher, and Grandma is a boring old moralist. We chuckle about such facts in private, but we never admit them to strangers.

Well, the writer's job is to tell the truth, as far as he can figure it out, and the truth is that I love my neighbours not because they're polite, dutiful and mealy-mouthed, but because they're warm-hearted, raucous, vital and vulgar. The suburbs are full of walking corpses, but our people are *alive,* and they have a sound set of values. And I think people who don't know the area may need a bit of help to understand the setting in which the strike occurred. Because the life of Canso Strait is a long, long way from the city.

For instance, the work force down here is supposed to be unreliable and irresponsible. You can read in almost any issue of the *Comical Herald* about all the terrible things we do. Is that true?

Of course it is – and thank God for it, too. A steady round of eight-hour shifts in the mills of Port Hawkesbury isn't what life is all about. I'm told that on the first day of the deer season absenteeism at the plants skyrockets: all the boys call in sick and go out hunting. Production suffers. The barons of industry foam at the mouth.

The boys know that the Swedes who own the pulp mill, the Americans who own the oil refinery and the gypsum plant, the proprietors of the various chain stores – they're making the profits. Management gets double and triple the income of the fellows in the plant, and also gets the two-hour liquid lunches, the business trips to interesting places, the stock options and the assistance in moving from one job to another. All the boys want is a day in the woods. It's a small enough pleasure. So they take it.

And if the plant doesn't operate at full capacity for a day, what's that to them? Shag that, b'y, let's wildcat and go swimmin'.

I know a fish plant in New Brunswick – organized by Roy Keefe's union, as a matter of fact – where one of the big productivity problems is that the men and women tend to sneak off into the fields when the weather is fine, and make love.

Meanwhile the fish, unfilleted, come down the conveyor belt and slither onto the floor. Plop, plop, plop . . .

I'm all for it. Most lives include too much boredom and too few outdoor orgasms.

In a way, life in the rural Maritimes – and particularly here, I suspect – is like an anarchist society operating *within* a liberal capitalist framework. People have their own rules and live by them. They obey the law when the law matches the rules.

If you were driving home one night and found a total stranger lying drunk in the middle of the road, you wouldn't leave him there. If you did, and people found out about it, they'd let you know in their own way that you were a miserable son of a bitch. If I fence in land that I own but I'm not using, and try to keep people out, I'll be in for a rough time. (Actually Nova Scotia is the only place in Canada where there's no offence of civil trespass. As long as you're not harming my interests, I have no right to bar you out. If you let the cattle loose, of course, that's different.)

People drive when they're paralyzed drunk. That's within the rules. I remember one time lately a car went off the road with four people in it. They weren't hurt. They had open liquor in the car and they were roaring drunk. The man who owned the house nearby is a very upright citizen, a bit prim in some people's estimation, a pillar of his church, a man of substance and reputation. He came out, urged them all to beat it, took the liquor and hid it, and when the Mounties happened along he told them that No, he didn't know whose car it was or where they'd gone. Except in dire emergencies where someone is going to get hurt or killed, you don't co-operate with the Mounties. Them's the rules.

Bootlegging is okay. Moonshining is okay, except with women whose husbands are alcoholics: those are the ones that turn in the moonshiners. You don't have to lock your doors around here: nobody's going to steal from you. (There are exceptions: eight-track tapes in unlocked cars seem to be fair game, and I've seen some heartbreaking garden raids – but those things aren't approved, though they do happen.) When someone needs help to launch a boat, or control a grass fire, all hands pitch in.

We're remarkably honest with individuals. But it's always

open season on governments and large companies. It's okay to shoplift at Canadian Tire, but not at the village canteen.

"Hey!" cries a man to his brother. "That's my pipe wrench in your toolbox."

"No it's not!"

"It *is*."

"No, Lord Jesus, I stole that from Acme Construction when I was working on the heavy water plant."

"You're crazy! *I* stole it from the pulp mill."

I'd give either one of them the keys to my house. Or loan him money or my car.

Tools turn up missing, materials vanish from construction jobs, the paint on Oscar's barn looks suspiciously like what they were putting on that new building in Sydney. If you can get away with sleeping on the job, fair enough. If a man's drawing pogey – unemployment insurance – and if you'll pay him in cash, he'll do that little job for you quite reasonable. He's 'workin' for the government' anyway.

I remember a fellow in a woodworking shop, working on some little government contract. He was looking over various pieces of wood, trying to find the right one for the next stage. Finally he picked one up.

"Good one, is it?' I said conversationally.

He shrugged his shoulders, sucking on his pipe. Then he offered an opinion.

"No, it ain't a good one," he said. "But it's good enough for d'gov'ment."

People down here consider government an unavoidable affliction, like fog or the flu. The government collects taxes from you and me, then gives them as DREE grants to IBM, builds wharves for Booth Fisheries and Shaheen Natural Resources, takes over the Sydney steel mill after British capitalists have creamed off its profits and let it deteriorate, sets up Anti-Inflation Boards to hold down our wages and shows its own restraint by hiring an army of bureaucrats to staff the bloody thing. Pierre Trudeau lolls in his swimming pool, given by some nameless friends, says he's hired Pierre Juneau at about $50,000 a year and soon he'll figure out what Juneau does for a living. Now if you'll just make a few sacrifices, my friend, we'll beat inflation and the universe will again unfold as it should . . .

Mind you, the bastards have the power. You want a job on the highways, work as a poll captain. Can't get a winter works grant? Remind Allan MacEachen he owes you a favour.

"I see Bert's got a big contract there to haul fuel oil to the power plant."

"Well, you know about *that*, eh? He's on the right side of politics."

The system is corrupt, we all *know* it's corrupt, and we'd really rather live more honestly. I think that was your great strength in the strike: that 235 fishermen could say "No, this is unjust and it's got to be changed"; that was a moral example to the whole province.

In a sense, the strike was a peasant's revolt. Don't be offended. My mother said to me not long ago that we're a peasant family. "I come from a farm," she said, holding her chin up, standing very erect. (She believes good posture is important, and she believes in setting an example.) "My parents worked on the land. They worked hard and they never had very much. They were honest, loving people and they did everything they could for their children. They were peasants and I'm proud to be their daughter."

Amen, Mom.

I think a lot of people made a mistake during the strike. They thought the fishermen were – like most trade unionists – part of an urban industrial proletariat. I don't think so. I think we're just in the process of joining the industrial revolution around here – but people your age and mine aren't workers in that sense. I think our people are peasants who are *becoming* an industrial proletariat.

What's a peasant?

I reckon a peasant is a poor person who lives in the country, operates largely outside the cash economy, and knows how to survive. His people have been in that place for centuries: they've learned how to use the resources around them. They *know* the country as well as they know their own bodies. They've developed traditional ways of doing things. There's an interesting phrase people use around here that tells you a lot.

"Where you from?" someone will ask me.

"I live in D'Escousse."

"But you don't *belong* to D'Escousse."

It's not an insult, it's a statement of fact. You, on the other hand, *belong* to Canso. Canso has formed you, shaped you, determined your style. You know who's related to whom, where you can get foxberries or eels or rabbits or bakeapples; you know where the good stands of timber are, you and Jean know how to preserve food without refrigeration. You know where to find mackerel, lobsters, scallops. You know what can be grown in a foggy garden in Canso, you understand who fits where in the structure of the town.

I've known peasants in Europe, and that's what they're like, too. They *know* the country, they're as much at home in it as a bird or a tree. They belong to it. I don't think it's possible to "belong" in the Nova Scotian sense until a country has been settled for generations, and that's why it sounds a bit odd to think of English-Canadian peasants. (French-Canadian peasants, now, that's a much more widely-accepted concept.) I don't think there *is* a peasantry in the West in this sense. But I do think there's one east of Quebec.

Another thing: peasants have a code of ethics which shifts according to the situation – but it's always based on loyalty to one's own people and suspicion of the squire and all his works. Acadian Fisheries is the squire, the government is among his works. When the squire and his toadies look at the peasants, they see lazy, shiftless liars. Thieves. Con artists. Poachers. Smugglers and bootleggers and drunks. Parents of illegitimate children. Truants from school. You name it: companies and governments want us to lead orderly lives, but peasants' lives aren't orderly.

But when the peasant looks at his friends and neighbours and relatives – the very same people – he sees generous and friendly folks who know how to have a good time, who are realists about sex and death, who don't get all hung up over laws and regulations, who rather enjoy winkling a few extras out of the squire, by fair means or foul. People who don't reckon that a lot of the foolishness that passes for education is really all that important. People who understand that when you have to protect yourself against power it pays not to be *too* candid. People you can trust.

170

In approaching power, I think our people regularly use what I call "country cunning." You fall off your house when you're shingling the roof, and break your leg. It's three o'clock and you have to be at work at four. You go: and you stage another fall on the job. The company nurse rushes you to the doctor. X-rays reveal that your leg is broken – and since you broke it on the job, you get Workmen's Compensation.

That's country cunning.

I know a fellow who was driving around one night drinking with two friends. He put his car in a ditch on a back road, couldn't get it out, and decided that was about as good a place to drink as any other. They sat in the car baling back the booze. After a while the local Mountie – a super-efficient eagerbeaver who had managed to make himself thoroughly unpopular in less than a month with the detachment – arrived on the scene. The two guys in the front jumped out and ran into the woods. The fellow in the back seat simply slumped down onto the floor and went on drinking: the cop never knew he was there.

That's country cunning.

And the other two knew the woods the way a person knows the quirks of his own car. They led the poor Mountie a merry chase. They ran up to a swamp and then split and passed on each side while the poor lawman ran straight ahead into the muck. They yodelled and chortled at him from the thickets. They speculated about his parents' failure to marry. Finally silence descended on the scene. One of the fugitives crept through the woods and bumped into someone else.

"Hey!" he hissed. "That you, Artie?"

"No!" snapped the Mountie. *"Mounted Police!"*

"Ooops!"

The fellow scampered off briskly through the bush, eluding the Mountie's grasp, and laughing as he went.

"Halt!" shrieked the distracted Mountie. He fired a shot into the air. CRACK! *"Halt in the name of the Queeeeeeen!"*

"Fuck the Queen!" cried his quarry, in full flight. The story was all around the county before dinner the next day. The Mountie was ceaselessly ragged about it until he left the area a few months later.

That's country cunning.

Country cunning is a way of defending unofficial life. Unofficial life is the kind of life that goes on below the level of newscasts and government policies, the life that ignores the law. Unofficial life is based on common sense and the concrete facts of our existence. Kissinger is in the Middle East, flitting about on peace missions. That's official life. Peter's pig is down inside his well, and we gotta rig up a block and tackle, maybe a tripod, get three or four fellers, get him up out of there. That's unofficial life. Official life is remote and mysterious; when it comes close it's snotty and unfair.

Unofficial life is the fellows swapping stories in the garage. It's bingo games and forty-fives in the parish hall. It's out-of-season lobsters eaten with a horde of friends. It's the neighbour who quietly takes care of the old man next door. It's kids running off to work as deckhands on freighters and coming home with tattoos all over their arms. It's a bake sale to raise money for the volunteer fire department, a lottery to build a skating rink,

Unofficial life is the *real* news, and the real news isn't in the papers, it's in the mouths of the people around you. Who is this Kissinger, anyway? Hey, did you hear 'bout Pete's pig, Lor' Jesus, thought I'd crap meself!

Unofficial life, peasant life, was varied, tough and interesting. You had a couple of pigs, a cow, some chickens. You raised their feed yourself, as far as possible. You pastured the cow on common land, owned by the whole village. You did a little fishing, a little woodcutting, a little "outside labour." Maybe you had the post office in your kitchen, or drove the school bus, or delivered mail, or worked on the roads. You built your own house with lumber milled from the land you'd inherited from your grandfather. You went to church and respected the priest but you didn't take it all *too* seriously.

Who are you? Little Arthur. *What* are you? Jesus, b'y, don't ask such hard questions.

Even twenty or thirty years ago it was like that. There's a good bit of it left even now. But really, we've been hit by the Industrial Revolution. Heavy industries at Point Tupper. Television. Paved roads. Consolidated schools. Automatic oil furnaces. Electric appliances. Nine-to-five jobs.

It's happened before, that gradual consolidation of local

traditions into massive institutions, the gradual reduction of rounded human beings into workers and consumers. It was happening in England a century and more ago, when Karl Marx was hounded out of Germany and went to the British Museum in London and sat there year after year writing his books. He thought England would have a revolution, as the industrial working class found its condition progressively more unbearable. Children of ten and pregnant women slaving away in the mines and the factories. Farmers forced off the land, driven to seek employment in the dark satanic mills, as the poet Blake called them. Marx knew nobody could stand that kind of degradation forever. Sooner or later they'd revolt.

They did – but not by overthrowing the government. Instead of making a revolution, they formed unions and elected reformers to Parliament. That ought to sound familiar, because that's what was happening in Nova Scotia in the summer of 1970. Fishing had been industrialized. When you started, thirty years ago, one last two-dory schooner was still fishing out of Canso. By 1970 you were fishing in huge mechanized ships that were very like factories. You started as a peasant, you were becoming an industrial proletarian. You did what people have always done in the circumstances: you formed a union.

I said just now that the power of the fishermen derived from their moral courage, but your extraordinary resilience – and that's what made the strike work, your capability for sheer endurance – came from country cunning and unofficial life, from the old Maritime culture. "You can't starve a fisherman." They came close – but in fact they *couldn't* starve you out, not quite. Between what you did for yourselves and what your various sympathizers were able to give, you were able to hold out, against all the odds, for seven months. Ventures like the fish sales are the result of country cunning. And unofficial life presented itself in a dozen unexpected ways. At one point the banks and finance companies were about ready to call in the loans owed by the fishermen in Petit de Grat. They went to see Carl Boudreau, who manages their credit union.

Carl is a native of Petit de Grat, and he remembers the days before the credit unions, when everyone in town was in hock to the merchant and the banks regarded fishermen as a form of waterbug to be kept from sullying the temples of commerce.

When the moneymen came to see him about calling the loans Carl refused to join them. "I can't do that!" he said. "It's *their* money. This is *their* bank." During the strike Carl had been getting cheques in the mail from all over the continent, from former residents of Petit de Grat who wanted to help the fishermen. Not small cheques, either: $400, $500, $700. Put this towards the interest on fishermen's loans, the letters would say. Give this to a family which needs it. Maybe this will help tide the credit union itself over the strike.

So Carl refused – and all the others backed off. And Carl refused because he knew in his bones what the strike was all about, what kind of person was involved, why they needed a union.

That's unofficial life at work. Or look at your own family. Both Bertha and Kenny worked in the plant. Once your picket lines were set up, they weren't going to cross them. I've heard Marxists celebrating the class solidarity of the plant workers, and to some extent that's exactly what it was. But it was also a result of the unofficial but profound personal connections between the shoreworkers and the trawlermen. If you love and admire your old man, and he's down there working sixteen hours a day to keep the picket line *up*, you're not going to cross it.

It's easy to spin fancy theories about what the strike meant. It's all the easier because the strike was a classic strike, the kind of strike which almost seemed *designed* to substantiate a theory. But if we're going to have theories about it, they'd better be complex and sophisticated theories, because the way of life in which the strike had its roots is a great deal more complex and sophisticated than it appears to the casual eye. The strike didn't only spring from politics and economics; it also had its roots in history, geography, language, tradition.

And yet, when all the complexities are considered, there's something very simple, too, at the core of the whole conflict. You fellows had been rooked for generations, you were being rooked worse than ever. You saw a chance to stop it, and you stood up and said, this is wrong and we *will* stop it. You endured what had to be endured and you wouldn't quit. You stood there long enough to become for Nova Scotians what Mahatma Gandhi and Martin Luther King had been in their communities – or, nearer to home, what Joe Howe and J.B. McLachlan had been earlier in Nova Scotia's own history. You became symbolic figures, reminding us that the brotherhood of man is an ideal which has not been achieved and may never be achieved, but for which people still think it worthwhile to struggle and suffer.

That's why so many of us down here are proud to be friends of the fishermen. We owe you a hell of a lot.

Love,
Don

GRADUATE STUDY
The Spring
of the Jackals

(November 1, 1970 – July 21, 1971)

"We suffer for that Yankee brood
Those sharks that bore our wealth away,
And punished tho' our cause was good,
To coward Yankee tricks a prey."

– Miramichi folk song

The raids began almost at once.

After so long, striking had become almost a way of life. "The house is just like a funeral home," said Jim Collins' wife. "One of the neighbours asked me how I was going to stand going back to the old grind again. I told her I lived with it for thirteen years and I guess I can live with it some more. But it's not going to be easy. You get to like having your man home to look after things and you get used to your family being all together. Now I'm in charge again for two and three weeks at a time and I really feel the responsibility after being away from it so long. And nobody knows how much you worry about storms and troubles while your husband is at sea."

The union officers had gone home too – Homer Stevens, Glen McEachern, George Hewison. Homer Stevens used to stay with the Collins' family when he was in Mulgrave, and three-year-old Mary Collins had a morning ritual of waking up her father and her friend Homer. A week after Jim sailed, she was still crying every morning when she realized they weren't there.

"She got so used to travelling around with Jim and Homer," said her mother, "that she fought to go in the car when Homer was leaving for BC. And she got on her boots and cried to go on the boat when Jim sailed. It almost broke her heart and mine too.

"The people here are going to miss Homer something awful. No matter what anyone else says about him, we saw him working night and day and half the time not eating or sleeping. He done that for us and I don't think you'll see many that'll turn him down."

The province was tying up loose ends and assessing what had happened. Bryce Mackasey still had given no undertaking to provide bargaining rights for fishermen, but in late November, Nova Scotia's new Attorney-General, Leonard Pace, announced that the government would withdraw the reference to the courts. Instead, the Liberals would, as he said, "seize jurisdiction" by introducing provincial legislation to bring fishermen under the Trade Union Act. The action brought a mighty cheer, with one prominent exception – Pace's defeated predecessor, R.A. Donahoe.

The UFAWU, said Donahoe in a full-page *Chronicle-Herald* article,

> was a militant union with a reputation for extreme demands and disastrous results upon the success of the Pacific Coast fishing industry. Its leader in Nova Scotia was Homer Stevens, an avowed Communist. It is clear in retrospect that the fishermen of these areas were used as pawns in a struggle by this union to secure a strangle hold upon the fishing industry in this province and that hundreds of Nova Scotians were unfeelingly caused great and unnecessary hardship in the process.

Pace's decision, said Donahoe, was

> not surprising when it is recalled that Attorney-General was solicitor for the UFAWU. He advised the fishermen to refuse any apology to the court for their actions. He accepted the position of his clients that the provincial legislature should act. He has now, in his new capacity, clearly advised the government to act, regardless of whether it has the authority to do so or not.

Donahoe was wrong about Pace, who had only been retained as counsel *after* the contempt sentences. He cited his reasons for believing that the federal government did indeed have jurisdiction – but in the end, he was wrong about that, too: in the spring of 1976, a federal appeal court finally ruled that labour legislation for fishermen is in fact a provincial responsibility.

After this last stern lecture to the wayward children who had thrown him out of office, Donahoe fades from the scene. The contempt sentences against the fishermen were quietly dropped in late November, when the men agreed – now that it didn't matter – to apologize. Things were returning to normal – and yet, as Linden MacIntyre pointed out in a pair of wrap-up articles for the *Chronicle-Herald*, the UFAWU was no closer in real terms to recognition as bargaining agent for the trawlermen than it had been at the beginning of the strike. The contract was "at least as good as, if not better than, anything that has been negotiated to date in the Nova Scotia fishery," but it was not a union contract, although it had been negotiated entirely by union members. Conceivably the conflict was only waiting for the following spring before bursting forth again.

How much difference did their contract actually make to the men, now that they were back fishing?

"I'll tell you," said Everett, "I was on the *Acadia Tern* all one winter, and I'd say we had a thousand pen-boards piled up on one side of her, just held with a little piece of rope. Pen boards for to go in the fish room for to pen the fish in. The first winter I was on her I was all winter trying to get someone to build a rack for to put these pen-boards into, and they couldn't get time to do it. Now there's lots of times that when they were loose all those pen-boards would go hell-ways and crooked all over the deck, and if you were in line with them, you could be killed or smashed up.

"But when we had our contract through the *ad hoc* committee, before we sailed I made sure that this was done, and it *was* done. The marine superintendent said he was pressed for time to get the dragger out. 'Well,' I said, 'I don't care how much is the pressure of time, it's gonna be done before we sail. It was brought up in negotiations and Cadegan promised.' So he went right to work and ordered the man down to do it. It was only a couple of hours when he had this made.

"Well now, why fight a whole winter for to get this done when it took one man a couple of hours? So there's one reason we should have a union. They wasn't worried about a man's life, or about him getting smashed up. You had no say, because if you disputed too much you were put ashore. But once we had our contract, then they *had* to do it."

In the meantime, the future of fishing unions was still very much in the air. At its fall convention, not only had the Brotherhood praised the UFAWU's work in Canso Strait and supported it financially, but had also endorsed continuing talks of a merger between the two unions.

Such a merger would make obvious sense. The Brotherhood already bargained for crews on coastal boats and tugs, and in Nova Scotia had signed up trawlermen in Lunenburg and Lockeport – which it heartily denied it would "hand over" to the Canadian Food and Allied Workers, as CLC vice-president Joe Morris had suggested earlier that fall. (With labour officials making such remarks, it's easy to understand how outsiders may become confused about labour's own commitment to the union of the workers' choice, democracy within the unions and so forth.) The UFAWU would immeasurably strengthen the Brotherhood's marine branch, and the muscle of 33,600 Brotherhood members would provide important backing for the fishermen who – with fewer than 10,000 members in a world increasingly dominated by conglomerate corporations and massive unions – obviously cannot stand alone forever.

The marriage which the CLC was promoting, however, was between the fishermen and the Canadian Food and Allied Workers, the union the CLC intends to develop as Canada's sole food union. Merger talks had been held in Vancouver while the Nova Scotia strike was in its second month, and they looked promising. The CFAWU declared that it needed the expertise of the UFAWU "which has done such a good job in BC" to complete organizing the fishing industry across the country. The fishermen could "practically write their own ticket," Joe Morris is reported to have said.

"The CFAWU is mostly Packinghouse," says a veteran official in the labour movement. After the American Federation of Labor and the Congress of Industrial Organizations merged in 1955, it was logical that their food-industry unions, the Amalgamated Meat Cutters and Butcher Workmen, and the United Packinghouse Workers respectively, should also merge. But the two had been at war during most of their histories, with the Meat Cutters on several occasions undercutting Packinghouse organizing efforts by signing voluntary recognition agreements and contracts less attractive than Packinghouse was seeking. In 1952, for instance, the Meat Cutters signed up 10,000 clerks at the A&P Food Stores through an arrangement with the company which guaranteed a forty-five-hour week for the next five years. The CIO union at Safeway had just signed a contract calling for a forty-hour week. The Meat Cutters' contract is said to have saved A&P several million dollars.

Nevertheless, the two unions did merge in 1968, and the Canadian branch became the CFAWU. In Canada, Packinghouse had been much the stronger union, with what one observer describes as a record of "reasonable militance, integrity, and social concern." Homer Stevens agreed that a single union in the fishing industry would be a benefit to the fishermen, and he was prepared to consider the CFAWU merger very seriously – although not as the price of admission to the CLC, as the CLC brass were insisting.

"If there's to be discussion of merger, on the basis of building bigger, stronger, more effective unions," Stevens explained, "then we should have the right to discuss that as equals, and not be in an unequal position where the Congress is saying to us 'you can only come into the Congress that way.' If the Congress is serious, there shouldn't be any inequality about it at all.

"They have a tremendous field to work in. There are over a hundred affiliates, where they are talking about narrowing it down to perhaps eighteen or twenty. We don't see that as a process of shotgun marriages. We see it as a process of equals sitting down to discuss, within the framework of the needs of the workers involved, the kind of structures they want, structures that are suitable to local conditions. It can't be forced."

In the spring, Linden MacIntyre pointed out, the race to represent the fishermen would be on again – and there would be three contenders: the UFAWU, the Brotherhood, and the Food Workers. "It is, however, impossible to assess at this stage," MacIntyre noted, "just how the contenders will rate in the eyes of the people who will make the final choice – the trawlermen who work for Booth and Acadia." A further complication, he pointed out, was "the over-riding hostility of the two companies to the UFAWU and their implicit assurance that they are still determined to shut down rather than deal with that union." But they would

Left to right: Father Tom Morley, Father Robert Lauder, Father Ron Parsons.
Credit: Jim Haggarty photo, courtesy *The 4th Estate.*

Credit: Jim Haggarty photo, courtesy *The 4th Estate*.

Credit: Jim Haggarty photo, courtesy *The 4th Estate.*

have to deal with *some* union; the strike had clearly destroyed the myth of the co-adventurer.

MacIntyre obviously expected an honest horse race – but what developed was quite different.

The Food Workers first raided the UFAWU local at Petit de Grat, always the weakest of the three locals. Even during the strike the Food Workers had some overtures; as soon as the agreement was signed they stepped up their activities. In Petit de Grat they could count on the support of such shoreworkers as Albert Martell; Booth Fisheries had repeatedly indicated its willingness to deal with a CLC union, and the Food Workers could expect easy recognition. Disgruntled UFAWU members like Lloyd Power, a trawler mate who had decamped for the Great Lakes during the strike and who would not be welcomed back into the UFAWU local, were obvious targets. Above all, Father Arsenault, who had already worked actively to undermine the UFAWU and who had attended meetings with the provincial government directed against it, was willing to put his best efforts into assisting the Food Workers' organizing drive.

Food Workers' organizers Jim Coles and Jim Bury called a meeting in Petit de Grat in November. Virtually nobody came; Coles and Bury were told that the fishermen had a union and didn't need another. Power and Arsenault kept pointing out to the men how easy it would be simply to join the Food Workers and have their union accepted by Booth; if they stayed with the UFAWU, Booth would again refuse to recognize them and might even close the plant. On December 23, Arsenault called a meeting, and Coles attended. A shouting match developed, and the meeting broke up inconclusively.

Arsenault kept at it, in close co-operation with Booth manager Earl Lewis; on one occasion he is reported to have visited Lewis five times in a single day. On December 28, one trawler was held behind while UFAWU members attended the provincial council of their union in Antigonish. When they returned, they were told that all but two of the vessel's crew had joined the Food Workers before the vessel sailed. That was apparently enough: shortly thereafter, Booth announced that the Food Workers had signed up a majority of the trawlermen, and that the company had granted the new union voluntary recognition. Earl Lewis said he was "very pleased" about the arrangement. "The future of Booth Fisheries," he remarked "is much brighter." He even ordered the three wayward trawlers home from Newfoundland.

Lloyd Power emerged as the president of CFAWU Local P-268. The union said it would enter negotiations at once and would be looking for higher fish prices, better union security, and effective safety measures.

One of the fishermen told UFAWU officers that he had signed up with the Food Workers, "because if I don't, I'll get fired after the second trip." Nevertheless it appears that the men did agree – albeit under heavy pressure – to accept the new union. They were broke and weary; the last thing they wanted was another extended and inconclusive battle.

Reactions to the raid were quick and furious. The Steelworkers denounced the Food Workers as "jackals"; Cape Breton Labour Council vice-president Jack Eddy called them "a pack of vultures." The raid was widely considered to have had at least the tacit backing of the CLC and the Nova Scotia Federation of Labour; and John Lynk pointed out that the Federation had undertaken to protect the UFAWU only against the companies, not against other unions. Eddy disagreed. He had been a participant in the talks which ended the strike, and John Lynk was "off base."

"Homer Stevens and his union were to have full say in that area – period," Eddy declared. "Nothing about just till the strike was over or anything like that. As far as I'm concerned the United Fishermen have the jurisdiction at Canso, Mulgrave, and Petit de Grat."

Homer Stevens reacted as much in sorrow as anger. "On the basis of reports, we must assume that with few exceptions Petit de Grat members have signed up with the Meat Cutters' Union," he said. "But the raid by the Meat Cutters completely reverses assurances given by the CLC and the Nova Scotia Federation of Labour during the strike that no affiliated union would interfere. Booth Fisheries has for a long time been issuing public invitations to other unions to move in and drive out the UFAWU. The glee expressed by Earl Lewis at developments shows how company interests are being protected. It may well be a brighter future for the us-owned corporation, but it will be the opposite for fishermen and their families. Improvement of fishermen's living standards can't be achieved through cosy arrangements with a company."

Glen McEachern, who was in Nova Scotia at the time, took a similar position. "If some of our people decide to go through with something like this there's not much you can do," he reflected. "When unions start fighting each other there are no winners, and all the workers will be the losers."

"This is a pathetic and ignoble whimper on which to end a fight for justice which had captured the imaginations of people right across the country," editorialized the *Highlander*. "It is a measure of the cynicism of the CFAWU, of its hosts in the community and of the Canadian Labour Congress. They have used to exploit the weakness of the workers the same technique they claim to find so reprehensible when used by management. . . . There is no question that a conspiracy exists among certain elements of the community, Booth management and the CFAWU."

The Food Workers, of course, see the events in a different light. Conspiracy? No, says one of their staffers, but "there is a community of interest between the government, the companies, and our union."

"I know what happened there," says a labour man in Ontario. "I'm sure the word just went out, Get down there and smash the Communists. It's part of the old labour wars. When an anti-Communist labour leader is out to get a Red, practically anything goes. Of course, in fairness, that's generally true the other way around, too."

No doubt – although one of the left's main criticisms of the Communist Party of Canada is its unseemly willingness to forge unity and common fronts at almost any sacrifice to its own principles. Perhaps the CLC and the Food Workers were indeed on an ideological binge; if so, they were remarkably stupid. In the end, they looked like sleazy manipulators, while Homer Stevens and the UFAWU stood alone as the moral examples of principled trade unionism.

If there had been any doubt about the complicity of the CLC and the Federation, it vanished on January 5, 1971, when representatives of both organizations – and of the St. Francis Xavier

Extension Department – met with the Food Workers in Arichat "to hear reports of progress made by the trawler fishermen of Petit de Grat regarding the state of their union." Contract proposals had been drawn up, and negotiations were to begin two days later. The statement released by the local after the meeting ended, "If the Canso bunch want to join they are welcome."

It was, of course, to Mulgrave and Canso that attention now turned. On January 11, the Food Workers announced they would begin organizing in those ports as well. "Let 'em come," replied Edison Lumsden: Canso fishermen were "100 per cent behind the UFAWU, and if those fellows come here they'll be shown the way out just as fast as they came in." Edison suspected that Acadia would be just as happy as Booth to give voluntary recognition to the Food Workers, but he saw the whole venture as a ploy to show the provincial government that bargaining rights for fishermen needn't be legislated, since unionisation was going ahead anyway.

Meanwhile, the Food Workers were still working in Petit de Grat, raiding the Canadian Sea Food Workers. Even unionists who had been undisturbed about the raid on the UFAWU – a maverick union anyway – were dismayed at the raid on the Seafood union, which was a CLC affiliate itself. Arsenault once again was involved, and the Food Workers claimed the shore people wanted out of Seafood because of poor service and because they wanted to be able to vote on any further actions by the trawlermen.

Seafood president Roy Keefe appealed to an impartial umpire under the CLC constitution, H. Carl Goldenberg of Montreal. On February 22, Goldenberg found that the raid was, "in the absence of justification," a violation of the CLC constitution. If two-thirds of the CLC Executive Council approved of the raid, however, it could be held to be justified – and on March 9, Donald MacDonald wrote to the Food Workers to say that "the application for justification is granted, two-thirds of the membership of the Council having voted in favour.

"The effect of this decision. . . is that the Canadian Food and Allied Workers' Union cannot be proceeded against under the Constitution of the Congress as a result of any organizing activity" against the Seafood Workers in Petit de Grat. The CLC, in short, had legalized the raid.

The Food Workers called meetings in Canso and Mulgrave, but cancelled them when the fishermen demonstrated no interest. Then they went to the men individually – "rather quietly," said Jim Bury. "You don't go after the strong ones first. A majority of the Canso trawlermen don't live in Canso – they're in Linwood, Guysborough, Glace Bay, Isle Madame. I went around with Jim Coles and Sinclair Allen and we signed up people."

In February, however, Jim Collins was telling a rather different story. "The UFAWU is as strong as ever in Mulgrave and Canso," he wrote to *The Fisherman.* "The Canadian Food and Allied Workers were in trying to get the fishermen to join their union, but so far, no success. They had the help of the CLC, but they haven't made any headway. They tried all the fishermen individually, but so far I don't think they got a man to join them. I wouldn't know what to call it except raiding."

Acadia Fisheries, meanwhile, was sizing up the Food Workers. An internal document outlined the union's history and reputation ("The reputation of the CFAWU is one of tough leadership in negotiations combined with responsibility. This has not been confirmed with management of any Maritime plants but has been confirmed in Toronto and Ottawa.") and went on to assess its probable impact on Acadia.

> The CFAWU has fought for parity in wage settlements across the country in each specific industry it represents and is reported to have achieved some success. Probably, if the CFAWU were to become representative of fishermen there would be some attempt at national parity, but as the industry is located on both coasts (some 3,000 miles apart) this should not present a major problem.
>
> The CLC as well as most labour leaders in central Canada quietly support the CFAWU as the union to represent workers in the fishing industry.

The conclusions are obvious: Acadia must face the prospect of a unionized fleet; and the CFAWU is a union it can live with.

While union matters hung fire, the company was also involved in negotiations with the province about the future of the Mulgrave plant. In early December, Guysborough MLA Angus Mac-

Isaac had called for government funds to re-open the plant: with less than a month till Christmas, the employees were running out of unemployment insurance benefits, and nothing seemed to be happening regarding the plant. The Regan government was said to be studying Acadia's request for further aid for both Canso and Mulgrave, although the company still had not even paid its full interest on the $9 million already loaned by the province. Just before Christmas, Trade and Industry Minister Ralph Fiske said the government had been talking with Acadia's British parent company, but he had nothing to report.

In fact, the Liberals were in a bit of a bind. During the election, Regan had made a considerable fuss about the province's aid to lame-duck industries, chiefly operated by outsiders. In Acadia's case, fish prices were high and the fishing was good at the time; why should the government be putting money into what ought to be a profitable operation?

Yet 230 people were out of work in Mulgrave, and Acadia's Canso operation was said to be in shaky condition. *The 4th Estate* reviewed the problem, and then – with almost palpable distaste – concluded that "this blackmail must be paid." Ron Parsons, however, called for the government to take the company into public ownership instead. Parsons found it "difficult to accept" that the company wasn't making "tremendous profits." "An extremely high protein is being produced at an extremely low cost to the company," Parsons argued, "and it is marketed in North America at excellent going prices. The plant is ideally located in a winter port, with short transportation hauls to some of the world's best markets. Only absolute mismanagement or an unreasonable demand for an extremely wide profit margin could run this plant into difficulties." And A. L. Cadegan, despite his "decidedly nineteenth century labour attitudes," Parsons felt had "no peers on the East Coast in the production and marketing of fish."

Some suspicions seem to have affected the government, too. In early January, two officials from England flew to Halifax for talks, and though Fiske said no new snags had developed, the talks arrived at no obvious conclusions.

The Petit de Grat trawlermen concluded an agreement with Booth on February 11. The new contract provided for a minimum of $5 a day per man, plus a $50 Christmas bonus and some improvement in fish prices. It also contained a closed shop clause and the check-off of union dues. Lloyd Power said the contract was "a step in the right direction" and opined that "now it is only a matter of time until we have the assistance and support of all trawler fishermen in Nova Scotia." As he signed the agreement, Earl Lewis remarked that he was particularly grateful to Father Arsenault for bringing the two sides together.

Ron Parsons, meanwhile, had received his own bishop in Canso, and the riled feelings among his parishioners seemed to be calming as the strike faded into memory. The fishermen's wives raised enough money to send him to Vancouver on March 25, the first clergyman ever to attend a UFAWU convention. Back home, the CFAWU was still working on the Acadia trawlermen. From a post office box in Mulgrave, Jim Coles mailed all the trawlermen an application for membership and a form letter.

"You have after seven long months of strike been out fishing for several trips," Coles wrote, "You now know that the trawler fishermen of Petit de Grat have signed up in our union, the Canadian Food and Allied Workers. They did this to make sure of a signed agreement with the Company and to get into a union that is growing in this industry." The Food Workers were anxious: the Provincial Assembly was already debating the legislation that would give bargaining rights to fishermen.

On March 8, while Ron Parsons, Everett Richardson, Edison Lumsden, and Con Mills were in Vancouver, Acadia Fisheries granted voluntary recognition to the Food Workers. A . L. Cadegan, announcing the voluntary recognition, said he was "pleased" and "ready to negotiate a new contract." On March 12, the company signed a collective agreement with the Food Workers. On March 17, the new legislation received third and final reading; the next day it was given royal assent and became law.

What the hell was going on?

Nothing unusual, said the Food Workers; they had signed up a majority of the trawlermen, demanded and received recognition, and negotiated a contract. The contract, they said, was a good one, providing a union shop, increases in fish prices, a first aid kit and a first aider "where possible" on each boat, leave of absence to attend school, 5¢ more an hour for work in port, $15,000 free life insurance for each crewman, and a $200 bonus for any crewman making twenty trips in a calendar year. The contract was signed by Ellsworth Ryan, for the crewmen – the same man whose wife had made herself so unpopular with the women at the welfare demonstration.

Jim Bury said that the contract talks had been "friendly, but difficult," and that he didn't anticipate any difficulty signing up the rest of the Acadia fishermen. "It's a good contract," he said. "We made real, solid progress."

With its wounds from the original strike still unhealed, Canso was ripped open once again. Dozens of trawlermen denounced the Food Workers and walked off the boats. When the *Acadia Gannet* pulled into port in Newfoundland, thirteen men left her. The *Acadia Crest* landed at the Canso Causeway to put a sick crewman ashore: her crew jumped ship en bloc. As other trawlers docked in Canso and Mulgrave, their crews were told to join the CFAWU or be fired. The whole crew of the *Acadia Thunderbird* was fired. In Harbour Breton, Newfoundland, the crew of the *Acadia Cormorant* departed.

Everett Richardson knew his union brothers: when the first reports of the fresh raid arrived in Vancouver he didn't take them seriously. He returned home to find himself involved in a dispute over which seven men had been fired, and in a meeting with Cadegan the *ad hoc* committee managed to have six reinstated.

"At that time, when we left," Everett recalls, "Cadegan told me, 'The first boat that comes in, you'll be going out onto it.' And then when we were goin' out the door, he said, 'This'll be the last time I'll be meetin' with you fellers. It'll be CF,' he said. 'Before the boat sails from now on, they'll all be joined up CF.' That's when I knew it was right down in earnest.

"Then they come for me to sail on the *Acadia Thunderbird,* but they didn't approach us at that time for to join the CF, because they wanted to get her out, get her clear of the wharf and fishing. We were gone ten days, and when we come to the wharf Adrian Armsworthy [trawler supervisor] come down, chest stuck out. We were all standing on deck.

"He give us our advance pay, and he said, 'Boys,' he said, 'if

191

you don't join that CF card, you won't be sailing.' Well, we said, 'We won't be sailing, 'cause we're not joining.' We went in and packed our gear and went ashore. I think there was twelve or thirteen on our boat quit at that time. The skipper and the engineer, and I think the cook, they stayed aboard."

The UFAWU analysis of the situation runs like this. In an industry which is not under the Trade Union Act, a voluntary recognition agreement doesn't have to be reviewed by any third party. The Labour Relations Board can't force the union to show it has a majority of the workers; the LRB has no power at all. If the union officers and the company are happy, the agreement stands, regardless of what anyone else – including the workers – may feel.

Normally a company which did not *have* to recognize a union wouldn't do so unless it were obliged to by a show of force – a strike, say, of its workers. The workers would hardly support a strike by a union they didn't approve. The interplay of power usually assures that the union *does* represent the workers. The UFAWU's entire Pacific Coast structure was built in this fashion.

In Canso and Mulgrave, however, the situation was quite different. Any agreement with a union signed after March 18, when the Trade Union Act amendments were proclaimed as law, *would* have been subject to the scrutiny of the Labour Relations Board. Because the UFAWU was the fishermen's choice, it could be certified simply by showing the LRB it represented a majority of the trawlermen; Acadia would be powerless to prevent certification, and would have to bargain with the UFAWU or defy the law itself. By setting up a *voluntary* collective bargaining agreement a few days earlier, the company had stolen a march on the UFAWU; even though the Food Workers did not represent a majority of the workers, the company was free to recognize it – and by doing so, it was able to keep the UFAWU out permanently. The "union shop" provision in the contract – which meant that every trawlerman *must* belong to the union – permitted the company to fire any stubborn employee who refused to join the company's chosen union.

As evidence that this was indeed the neat package worked out jointly by the Food Workers and Acadia (with the backing of the

CLC and the Federation), the UFAWU pointed to the unseemly haste with which both recognition and the new contract had been rushed through only a few days before the new legislation, and to the troops of trawlermen leaving the boats rather than join the new union. If the Food Workers *did* represent a majority of the trawlermen, they had nothing to lose by going through the usual process before the Labour Relations Board; their haste proved that their arrangement would not stand up to impartial scrutiny.

To this whole interpretation the Food Workers raised one fatal objection: they contended that they held fifty-seven signed membership cards, enough to give them exactly 50 per cent of the company's 114 fishermen. The whole thing was perfectly legal, they pointed out, and, given that number of members, perfectly in accord with trade union principles.

But the turmoil in the fishing ports was obvious. UFAWU organizers were kept from the docks, while Food Workers and company men together met the returning trawlers and told the crews they would have to join or quit. Con Mills and Edison Lumsden took a lobster boat out to sea, met the trawlers outside the harbour, boarded them and told the men what was going on. "They had heard on the radio at sea that they had joined the CFAW and signed a new contract," Mills said. "They didn't know what to expect when they got home. But believe me, they didn't hesitate about telling those meatgrinders where to go."

An angry Homer Stevens decried the Food Workers for "the worst form of company unionism," denied that the Food Workers had a majority, and denounced them for standing by while the men who had left the ships were replaced by crews from Newfoundland – some of whom belonged already to a Food Workers' affiliate in the island province. Thirty-seven of forty men landing in Canso had signed a statement saying that they had not joined the Food Workers; Con Mills put the figure at fifty-two, with four trawlers still at sea. Mills also reported that an Acadia trawler crewed by Newfoundlanders had been held up when the second engineer refused to sail; picking up a replacement, the ship had not gone to the wharf in Port Hawkesbury but had stood off while a launch brought the new man out. The reason? Fear that the whole crew would walk off if they had a chance.

"As soon as they get that legislation in action," said Mills, "we'll apply for certification, and I can't see any way anyone can stop us."

"Our members," Homer Stevens echoed, "intend to challenge the validity of the so-called agreement and its 'closed shop' conditions. The 'unfair labour practices' of the Acadia Fisheries and the Meatcutters will also be challenged."

As the UFAWU prepared its legal moves, the familiar round of charges, counter-charges, leaflets and demonstrations, began again. The Food Workers condemned Stevens' union as strike-happy, weak and irresponsible. J.K. Bell called on the province to nullify the Food Workers' contract, and require certification by the Labour Relations Board before either union was recognized. Premier Regan told Opposition Leader John Buchanan that the situation was "serious" and that he was studying it closely. NDP leader Jeremy Akerman called for immediate action on any certification bid.

The Vancouver local of the Brotherhood "unanimously voted to condemn the CFAW for its raid on the UFAW at Canso Strait," chastised the CLC for supporting the raids, and called for a free vote. Local 624 of the Canadian Union of Public Employees expressed itself as "sickened." The Sydney Steel Local 1064 condemned "in the strongest terms the cowardly and disruptive raiding tactics of the CFAWU in the Strait of Canso area," and declared that "every acceptable principle of democratic unionism is being violated by elements in the Canadian Labour Congress." In the Vancouver Labour Council, delegate Jack Lawrence got up to call for a free vote for the fishermen. His union? The Canadian Food and Allied Workers.

CLC president Donald MacDonald told CBC Halifax that it was "not convenient" to talk to them, but opined that the Food Workers *were* the choice of the fishermen. Then why had the crewmen been leaving their ships? MacDonald said he had heard nothing about that: the CLC had given the Food Workers jurisdiction in the fishery, and as far as he was concerned, that was that.

Federation president John Lynk was more talkative. He confirmed Homer Stevens' claim that the labour movement had agreed to stay out of Canso Strait for six months, or until after the fishermen had bargaining rights. And were the Food Workers raiding, he was asked?

"I think it depends on which side of the fence you're sitting on, whether there's raiding or not," Lynk explained. "If I was a member of the UFAW I guess I'd say there was raiding, but then if I was strictly an arbitrator looking at the agreement that the *ad hoc* committee of the fishermen signed with Booth and Acadia I would have to say there was no raiding."

Technically, he's correct. Where no union is recognized, no union can be raided. But a letter from Canso to the *Comical-Herald* cut through the legal niceties.

Mr. Cadegan and Acadia Fisheries did all the bargaining with the union behind the backs of the fishermen. They were not asked if they wanted to join another union or not. The company has recognized this union and the men are told to sign up or get ashore.

The contract was signed by one fisherman. There have been no meetings with the fishermen. The fishermen have not even seen a contract and do not know what they are signing for.

The CFAWU wouldn't attempt to organize the fishermen until another union came in and laid the foundation for bargaining rights for the fishermen. After all the hard work is done, it wants to step in and take over with the help of Mr. Cadegan.

We would rather be married to unemployed Communist fishermen than spineless, transplanted meat cutters.

And it was signed by Jean Richardson and Linda Gurney.

Jim Collins reported that Acadia's men were being replaced by "inferior, inexperienced fishermen from Newfoundland" who had been told their union was "accepted up here and there was no trouble. When they get here and find the truth they want no part of scabbin' on us." Some of the men, Collins said, had signed up with the UFAWU, and "a lot more are packing up and going back to Newfoundland." The UFAWU went out of its way to underline that it had no objection to Newfoundland crewmen: indeed, many of its Canso Strait members were emigrant Newfoundlanders. The objection was to "the degrading of Newfoundlanders by using them as scabs."

On March 25, the UFAWU applied to the Labour Relations

Board for certification as bargaining agent for the trawlermen in Canso and Mulgrave. At the same time, forty-two fishermen filed complaints of unfair labour practices against the company, charging that they were fired for refusing to join the Food Workers. On April 1 and 2, and again on April 8, the Board held hearings on the Canso Strait fishery. The transcripts of those hearings are a drama in themselves. Charles W. MacIntosh, QC, appeared for the UFAWU:

"(Cecil Wilneff called and sworn)

Mr. MacIntosh:	What's your full name, sir?
Mr. Wilneff:	Cecil Wilneff.
Mr. MacIntosh:	Where do you live?
Mr. Wilneff:	Mulgrave.
Mr. MacIntosh:	How long have you been a fisherman?
Mr. Wilneff:	All my life.
Mr. MacIntosh:	How long did you work for Acadia Fisheries?
Mr. Wilneff:	Nine years.
Mr. MacIntosh:	When did you last work for them?
Mr. Wilneff:	The nineteenth.
Mr. MacIntosh:	The nineteenth of March?
Mr. Wilneff:	Yes.
Mr. MacIntosh:	Where were you when you were laid off?
Mr. Wilneff:	Grand Bank, Newfoundland.
Mr. MacIntosh:	Who told you you were laid off?
Mr. Wilneff:	The Captain.
Mr. MacIntosh:	Did he tell you why you were laid off?
Mr. Wilneff:	He came down and told us – he said, 'I guess you heard the news.' Well, we didn't hear anything down there. He said, 'You either have to join – sign the blue card,' was the way he put it – 'or we'll make reservations for you to go back home.'

Mr. MacIntosh:	What did you understand him to mean by 'blue card?'
Mr. Wilneff:	Well, it was the other union – I knew that.
Mr. MacIntosh:	What union was that?
Mr. Wilneff:	Allied and Food Workers.
Mr. MacIntosh:	Was there a meeting of the crew called for this?
Mr. Wilneff:	No, we were all in the galley at the time.
Mr. MacIntosh:	I see. The captain came into the galley?
Mr. Wilneff:	And explained to us.
Mr. MacIntosh:	And what did the members of the crew there assembled say to this?
Mr. Wilneff:	They all said the same as I did – we're going home.
Mr. MacIntosh:	Did the captain indicate why he was telling you this? Had he been instructed?
Mr. Wilneff:	He said he's been instructed by Mr. Cadegan.
Mr. MacIntosh:	Now, how did you get back home to Nova Scotia?
Mr. Wilneff:	That was a hard trip – by taxi, bus, and boat.
Mr. MacIntosh:	How was your way paid back?
Mr. Wilneff:	By the company.
Mr. MacIntosh:	Why did they do that?
Mr. Wilneff:	Well, according to our old contract, if we were fired away from home the company had to pay us back; if we quit on our own, we paid our own way back.
Mr. MacIntosh:	What were you on the boat?
Mr. Wilneff:	Chief engineer at the time.
Mr. MacIntosh:	And have you worked since?
Mr. Wilneff:	No, I haven't.
Mr. MacIntosh:	Was there a meeting of the crew of your boat by the officers of the C.F.A.W.U.?

Mr. Wilneff:	Not to my knowledge.
Mr. MacIntosh:	You weren't notified of any such meeting?
Mr. Wilneff:	No, I wasn't.
Mr. MacIntosh:	You were on the boat all the time, were you?
Mr. Wilneff:	Yes, I was.
Mr. MacIntosh:	Were you asked to vote on a Collective Agreement with Acadia Fisheries?
Mr. Wilneff:	No, I wasn't.
Mr. MacIntosh:	Were you shown a copy of a Collective Agreement between Acadia Fisheries and the C.F.A.W.U.?
Mr. Wilneff:	I wasn't at the time, no.
Mr. MacIntosh:	Or at any time before this?
Mr. Wilneff:	No.
Mr. MacIntosh:	Your witness.
Mr. Nunn	[counsel for Acadia Fisheries] No questions.
Mr. Matheson	[counsel for Canadian Food and Allied Workers] No questions.

(Eric Fitzpatrick is called and sworn . . .)"

The UFAWU brought a parade of witnesses, telling similar stories about different boats. Jim Collins, Eric Fitzpatrick, and John Drudge from the *Acadia Condor*, Fred Gurney and Arthur Ryan from the *Acadia Thunderbird*, Clayton Haines from the *Acadia Gannet*, Maurice Kavanaugh from the *Acadia Cormorant*, Ivan Ryan from the *Acadia Gull*, and two familiar faces from the *Acadia Albatross* – Everett Richardson and Russell Gurney.

The evidence was overwhelming: crew after crew had picked up their gear and left the ship rather than sign up with the new union. The shrewdness, candour and good sense of the fishermen repeatedly illuminated the hearings, and evidently impressed the Board. MacIntosh asked Eric Fitzpatrick whether he knew Food Workers' organizers Bury and Coles. Oh, yeah, said Fitzpatrick.

He'd seen them with Adrian Armsworthy, trawler supervisor for the company.

"Mr. MacIntosh: And on the occasion when you saw them with Mr. Armsworthy, what happened?

Mr. Fitzpatrick: Well, Mr. Armsworthy said that – said to me, 'There's two gentlemen here wants to speak to you.' Well, I couldn't repeat what I said then, because I think I'd be put right out of here and be put right down in jail."

Merlin Nunn, acting for Acadia Fisheries, cross-examined Fred Gurney. The lawyer led the fishermen into an exchange which circled around and bit the lawyer from behind:

"Mr. Nunn: Do you know that some of the people we are talking about may have had two cards – a C.F.A.W.U. card and a U.F.A.W.U. card?

Mr. Gurney: It could happen.

Mr. Nunn: It could happen. If they had a C.F.A.W.U. card which permitted them to go to work, why do you think they didn't go to work?

Mr. Gurney: Because they were paid up with the U.F.A.W.U.

Mr. Nunn: But they could go back if they had a C.F.A.W.U. card, couldn't they?

Mr. Gurney: Yeah, they could.

Mr. Nunn: Well, why do you think they didn't?

Mr. Gurney: Because they *wasn't* joined up with the other union."

The point of Nunn's questions here – unintentional comedy aside – is the Food Workers' claim that they *did* have a majority, but that Canso people who were ready to abandon the wicked Red union of Homer Stevens were afraid to admit they had joined the new union and wanted Stevens to leave. "We want to give evidence that there's intimidation down there," Nunn told the Board. "We want to give evidence that even a secret ballot would not reflect the true wishes of the people down there at this time. This is a community afraid, and we want to give this evidence to the Board."

The Food Workers' strategy was to claim, first, that since it already had what amounted to certification, the Board couldn't hear a second application for certification. Second, even if it *did* hear the UFAWU application, it could only concern itself with events after March 18, when the new legislation had taken effect. Third, the Food Workers shouldn't *have* to show that they represented a majority of the trawlermen, because, as Merlin Nunn pointed out, many a union is recognized and signs an agreement when it has no members at all – construction unions, for instance, negotiating with companies coming into the province for a particular project.

Fourth, the Food Workers claimed they *did* have a majority of the trawlermen among their membership, and fifth, those members were not prepared to stand up and be counted because they were afraid of the UFAWU.

"You should see some of the testimony that was given *in camera*," Jim Bury told me, four months later, smiling indulgently at me in his office in suburban Toronto. "Many of our people who had signed cards with us walked off the boats with them, because they were scared shitless. You should see the testimony." Bury is very insistent that the UFAWU is a violent union, alluding to the nervousness he felt standing on wharves waiting for boats to come in, "with a couple of Homer Stevens' great big fellows standing right there." He indicated darkly that the *in camera* testimony was thoroughly chilling.

The *in camera* evidence occupies fourteen pages of transcripts. The only witnesses are Ellsworth Ryan, president of the Food Workers' Canso local, and his wife Evelyn. Ryan says that he's been in the new union since March 6 – just two days before the voluntary recognition – and that the men "all want to get a union, but nobody would go back on strike, they said they definitely would not walk a picket line no more for nobody. Apparently the same fellers today's out with Homer, out there" in the hall. Of people in the community "most of them wants Homer to leave."

And the threats of violence? "This fellow said he would burn the house down to get even with me . . . . I couldn't say right for sure who he told it to, but the people he told it to come and told the wife and the mother . . . then the priest come in about it, and they had the Mounties down."

"Now this talk about burning your house," said MacIntosh, on cross-examination, "that's something somebody else told you somebody else had said, is that right?"

"Yes," said Ellsworth Ryan. Earlier he had said he had seen the UFAWU crew "put some dandies on some poor fellows . . . beating up some poor fellows for no reason at all." Pressed for names, he mentioned Eddie Grant, production supervisor at the plant. Pressed further, he reported that Grant and Cadegan had broken an arrangement to allow maintenance and clerical staff into the plant, and so the fishermen had decided to keep the two men out of the plant. Grant tried to go through the picket line, and "the men grabbed him."

As for the Food Workers' agreement, Ryan said it had been ratified by "meetings on the boats according as they came in. We went right aboard the boats." "Who went aboard?" asked John Lynk? "James Bury and James Coles," replied Ryan. But, as the questioning went on, it emerged that only the crew of the *Acadia Tern* had voted on the contract, and even their votes had never been tabulated.

Evelyn Ryan took the stand, and testified that Father Robert Wicks had heard threats about burning the house and had called the RCMP. And she had had a call from Jean Richardson a couple of weeks earlier.

"Mr. Matheson: What did she say to you?

Mrs. Ryan: She called me up, and she said that Ellsworth was one of the first suckers to join this new union, and she said, 'I hope they go to sea and never come back,' and she said, 'If there's anything that I, or we' her and the other women that goes with her, you know, she said, 'If there's anything that we can do to stop this new union from going in,' she said, 'we'll do it.' "

Joe Kavanaugh would join the new union, Mrs. Ryan said, but he's scared to, and several other wives are "afraid of the members of the U.F.A.W.U."

That's the *in camera* evidence. All of it.

By mid-hearing, Board Chairman Horace Read was beginning to make some alarming sounds, from the Food Workers' viewpoint. What's a voluntary recognition? he mused. It means a union "purports," as the Act says, to represent a group of employees, and the employer concedes that it does, and agrees to bargain collectively.

"What is that employer's recognition founded upon?" asked Dr. Read. "It's founded upon a statement of fact by the union that it represents the employees in the Bargaining Unit. If that is false, the whole thing falls flat, because it's fraud."

And after a brief recess, the Board dropped a bombshell.

"The Board has decided," Read told the hearing, "that it has heard enough evidence from the Applicant to raise a doubt in the mind of the Board as to a majority. The Board, however, would like to have evidence from the Canadian Food and Allied Workers' Union as to whether or not, at the date that the union purported to represent the employees – that's on March eleventh – they in fact did represent a majority of the employees in the bargaining unit."

The 4th Estate summarized the hearing for its readers by saying "the fishermen who were called on to give information were so strongly behind the UFAWU that the Board caught the CFAW completely by surprise and asked them to prove their claim that they represented the men. At this point, the UFAW appears to be in a strong position to gain certification."

Meanwhile the legislature was quickly passing a bill to provide that in future, unions gaining voluntary recognition might be required to prove that they did actually have a majority. But the bill was not made retroactive, and had no effect on the fishermen's dispute. On April 13, the Labour Relations Board handed down its decision.

Where a valid collective agreement is in force, no competing union can apply for certification until within two months of the expiry of the agreement, except under special circumstances and with the consent of the Board. The whole point of the UFAWU's had been to show that the Food Workers' agreement was *not* valid, that the circumstances *were* special, and that the Board should allow an early application. But, despite the actual hearing, the Board found that a valid agreement did exist, and pronounced itself "not satisfied that there was some reasonable basis" for an early application. The UFAWU had lost the first round.

It was a bitter blow. James Bury, however, said that "the important thing now is the men will be able to go back fishing . . . and the industry will have some stability. The Board has recognized the correctness and the legality of the position taken by our union."

The UFAWU had hoped their application would result in a vote in which the fishermen themselves would demonstrate which union they wanted. "But which fishermen?" asked a labour lawyer. "Maybe the men on the boats on March 8, when CFAWU was recognized, were mostly United Fishermen supporters. But by the time the UF got its application to the Board on the 26th, all their men had walked off, and everyone on the boats was CFAWU – *had* to be, you see? The contract required it."

The Acadia trawlers, in fact, did precious little fishing in April. Crewed by young Newfoundlanders who generally went home as soon as they saw the situation, the trawlers had sailed rarely, and not very productively. Late in the month crews were being brought in from the Gaspé. As Edison Lumsden pointed out, the fishermen could talk to the Newfoundlanders. But the Gaspésiens were whisked into town by car and straight onto the boat; the few times the Canso men got a chance to talk with them, they found the outsiders spoke very little English.

The week after the Board's decision, eleven Anglican priests from across the province issued a statement calling for a free vote by April 27. Prominent among the eleven were Ron Parsons, Gordon Neish of Port Dufferin, Cal MacMillan of Arichat and Canon Mel French of Halifax. Their call for a free vote was supported by the Seafood Workers' executive in Canso, by the Marine Workers' J.K. Bell, and by the *Highlander, The 4th Estate,* and the *Scotia Sun* of Port Hawkesbury.

That Saturday, the fishermen and their supporters marched in Canso: UFAWU IS OUR CHOICE. *OUR* PEOPLE HAVE

BEEN HERE 200 YEARS: *WE* SUPPORT A FREE VOTE. That night, forty-two trawlermen showed up at a rally in the town, though many of the 114 Acadia trawlermen had already gone elsewhere temporarily for work. They were receiving no unemployment insurance, no welfare, and no strike pay. A Halifax citizen's committee had raised $1500 to help them endure, but families which had not yet recovered from the strike had already gone six weeks without pay.

On April 29, the *Chronicle-Herald's* red headline screamed
ACADIA FUTURE 'UNCERTAIN'.
Over the by-line of managing editor Alvin Savage, the lead story revealed that Premier Regan and Trade and Industry Minister Ralph Fiske had been holding top-level talks with Acadia's British owners. Company officials were said to have "expressed concern that the present 'labour unrest is also aggravating the whole situation.' "

And Everett Richardson: "They think that after what we've been through, we'll go back to work with that kind of sweetheart contract. It's crazy." But what would happen? "I wish I knew," said Everett. "I just wish I knew."

"They keep saying how bad Communism is," mayor Jim Hanlon told reporter Stephen Kimber, "but what could be worst than what's happening right here? What are the people in this town supposed to do? It seems such a simple request to me: give the fishermen the right to vote for the union of their choice. Then we'd settle this thing once and for all. This whole thing has caused a lot of serious problems in the town – breaking up families and such – and for what?"

As April ended, a Citizens' Committee for a Free Vote for Fishermen, supported by the Cape Breton Trades and Labour Council, announced that a free vote would be held under its auspices. Father Bob Lauder, spokesman for the group, announced the vote would take place May 3, and all Acadia trawlermen employed at the time of the Food Workers' voluntary recognition would be eligible. Father Lauder said the vote should really be undertaken by the province, "but we are forced to become involved because of the failures of the provincial government to meet that responsibility."

The vote would be supervised by a committee whose integrity

was beyond reproach: three college presidents, Clarence Nicholson of Pine Hill Divinity College, Graham Morgan of King's College, and Edmund Morris, now mayor of Halifax, and at that time acting president of St. Mary's University; plus Dr. John Savage, president of the Catholic Social Services Commission; and June Callwood, freelance writer and a member of the National Executive of the Canadian Civil Liberties Association.*

If the Labour Relations Board had been conducting the vote, it would have required a turnout of at least 60 per cent of the eligible workers, and required a majority of at least 50 per cent of the voters to certify a union. The Committee sought to meet these criteria, and despite the obstacles – many of the fishermen were away, some who had signed cards were at sea, because Acadia kept its trawlers out of port – sixty-nine of the 114 fishermen voted, some having returned from as far away as Ontario. Each one had to produce identification and sign an affidavit to the effect that he was who he said he was. One fisherman showed up to vote, and even though he was able to prove he had worked for Acadia before March 9 he was turned away, because he was not on the prepared list. "According to our terms of reference," said Edmund Morris, "we were to follow certain procedures, and we didn't deviate from those in the slightest. This election was conducted more scrupulously than even a provincial or federal election."

"Usually around here votes were sold for a pint of rum," said a young radical from Halifax who had been working with the fishermen for over a year. "But you couldn't have bought one of those votes for a million dollars." Even so, the Food Workers' Jim Bury charged that the UFAWU had intimidated voters and had bought votes. Not so, said Con Mills: "I'd have to have Bury's kind of money to do that."

The sixty-nine fishermen represented 60.5 per cent of the eligible voters. And they voted for the UFAWU by the overwhelming margin of sixty-six to three. The sixty-six votes, in fact, represented an absolute majority of the men employed by Acadia on March 8.

---

*As it turned out, a death in June Callwood's family kept her in Toronto.

The Food Workers called the results meaningless, and said they were surprised that even three of their members had braved the intimidation to cast their ballots. But Stephen Kimber, covering the vote, saw no evidence of intimidation or harassment. "I don't think there's been any attempt to intimidate fishermen by either union," Edison Lumsden said. "I certainly don't know of any. The only people who can intimidate the fishermen are the company, and they've tried every trick in the book to do that."

Father Lauder said that "the fishermen have now spoken to the world. They have said clearly and unequivocally that they want to be represented by the UFAWU. It's now up to the Labour Relations Board to take some action to ensure the men their human rights." No doubt that was true enough. But if the Board felt its hands to be tied, and the company chose to ignore the vote, and the government continued to ignore the problem, what difference would the vote make?

Stephen Kimber quoted a top labour organizer to the effect that the only real solution would be a general strike – and that, now the squabble was within the labour movement itself, was not very likely.

"Let's face it," said Don MacPherson, an executive with the Cape Breton steel local, "they fought the companies and the government and they won. Now they have to fight people within our own labour movement. There are some good people within the Canadian Labour Congress, but there are also some rats. Unfortunately, right now the top is infested with rats who don't know what trade unionism is all about."

Nevertheless, Acting Labour Minister Peter Nicholson, after an hour-long meeting with the Citizens' Committee, said that it was "significant" that the Labour Relations Board had not officially turned down the UFAWU application, and suggested that they might review its status when they heard the unfair labour practices charges against Acadia Fisheries.

On May 6, the Board took up the matter of unfair labour practices. Merlin Nunn, acting for Acadia, made a spirited defence. The UFAWU claimed its men had been fired for belonging to the union: that wasn't true, he said.

"Have we intimidated anybody, to compel them to refrain from becoming or cease to be a member of the union?" he demanded. "Which union? We haven't done anything to compel them from being members of the U.F.A.W.U., or to cease from becoming members of the U.F.A.W.U. All that we said, by a contract that we honoured and that we were bound with, was that the contract says you must become a member of the C.F.A.W.U. They could have paid dues and still been members of the other union."

Nunn told the Board that "Mr. Stevens and his crowd" were "trying to use every bit of the law . . . to corner you until you make a decision that he can use to support him – and this is what's going on, and the Board has to know this. . . . "

Matheson agreed with Nunn, and carried matters even further: at one point he suggested that labour peace was so important, and the UFAWU such a danger to it, that even if the UFAWU *could* prove that it had a majority the Board should refuse to certify it.

He referred to a recent petition by 350 people in Canso who "have pleaded for stability in the community." By now, Canso was bitterly divided, with most of the fishermen still demanding justice while many of their neighbours wanted only peace and quiet and an end to conflict. "The whole thing has been so confusing and divisive it's even got God confused," Matheson told the Board. "God is squarely down on both sides of this issue. The Roman Catholic clergy are down on both sides of it. It's got everybody divided and confused."

Ron Parsons chuckled when he heard that.

"No," Parsons commented, "God is concerned and distressed by what's happening to the fishermen. But He is *not* confused."

Ultimately, the Board dismissed the complaints on the grounds that the men had been fired not for belonging to a union, but for *refusing* to belong to a union. The former would have been an unfair labour practice, but the latter was merely observance of a union shop provision.

On May 15, Ron Parsons was fired. Bishop William Davis announced that the fighting Newfoundlander would be removed from his parish effective August 31, because of "a breakdown in the pastoral relationship."

"I didn't know you could be fired from a church," Parsons reflected, "but I *have* been, so I guess you can."

The Bishop said Parsons was being removed as a result of

pressure from within his own congregation – and Parsons admitted that was partially true. Even Canso has its Establishment, which is largely Anglican. "The Bishop has been under the most tremendous pressure for fourteen months about me," Parsons mused. "I don't know how many conferences we've had. I've forgotten. But he's stood it for fourteen months." The pressure was not all, or even mostly, from within his own parish. The codfish aristocracy is well represented in the Anglican Church: the Morrows, who operate National Sea Foods, and the Lewises, one of whom was Booth Fisheries' manager, were prominent Anglicans, and such people, Parsons pointed out, could withdraw financial support the Church could ill afford to lose.

"I stand solidly with the doctrines of the Church," Parsons explained. "I have no quarrel with them at all." But he did argue that the Church had become burdened with fine buildings and ornaments to the detriment of its mission to mankind. He mentioned massive mortgage payments, the $40,000 repairs to the organ in Halifax, gold chalices and stained-glass windows.

"When you see him with the fishermen," said Bishop Davis, "he's – well, he's very like Our Lord. But he's a sort of Jekyll and Hyde." He mentioned specifically the ferocity of Parsons' attack on privilege in synod meetings. Parsons himself laughed about that, but he admitted that at one point when he was arguing that the synod was dominated by retired admirals and judges, he had asked for all the fishermen present to rise. Nobody stood up.

"The Church," he concluded, "is not representative of the people of Nova Scotia."

Parsons was distressed by the implications of his dismissal: it would be a sobering example for other clergymen tempted to speak out for the dispossessed, and Parsons sees the church's ministry to such people as vital to its very survival. The fishermen circulated a petition calling on the Bishop to reverse his decision, claiming that the petitions from Canso parish were at least in part signed by frightened people who stood to lose their jobs. Nothing worked: Parsons was to go at the end of August.

Articulate, intelligent, full of laughter and faith, Parsons had meant a great deal to the fishermen. The elite had left his church, but many of the fishermen were attending. He went to meetings with them, advised them in negotiations, fought their cases with welfare and unemployment officers. The Richardsons had attended the Anglican Church – "but now," declared Jean, after Parsons' departure, "if the dog died I wouldn't have it buried Anglican."

May rolled past, with the trawlermen once again trying for unemployment insurance and welfare, and appealing to their supporters for food and money. At the end of April, Health Minister Scott MacNutt had said that "emergency welfare services" would be available to men who could demonstrate a need and who were registered for work with the Unemployment Insurance Commission. But the two towns and the county of Guysborough had policies of giving no aid to strikers, and the Acadia Fisheries dispute was being, for the time being at least, treated as a strike. Local welfare director Frank Fraser said welfare budgets were "tight," and Margaret MacDougall, Canso's town clerk, was more forthright yet. "The majority of taxpayers are not behind welfare payments for the UFAWU," she said. "They are behind Acadian Fisheries. Let the province pay 100 per cent of welfare payments if they think they should get it. The present situation is heartbreaking – Canso is getting a black name, but it is certainly not the people of Canso behind the present agitation."

The welfare office in Canso simply did not open the first and second weeks of May. During the third week, thirteen families applied for welfare; none received it. Health Minister MacNutt threatened to pay welfare directly to the fishermen and deduct it from the town's allotment. An appeal board came down from Halifax, its members receiving $45 per day each, plus expenses, to hear Jean Richardson's appeal. The board arrived at no decision, and went back to Halifax. Two weeks later, all the Richardsons had received was a handwritten message on a form. Neither Everett nor Jean could decipher the handwriting. Perhaps that wasn't surprising: when Everett took it back to the official who had sent it, the official couldn't make it out himself.

Unemployment insurance was equally frustrating.

"We were fired off the draggers on the 24th of March," explained Everett Richardson late that June. "On the 28th of March, I applied for unemployment insurance, and after a month or so, and making two trips to New Glasgow, to the unemployment insurance office, I was still refused. Not enough contributions. I was gettin' forms to fill out, I was sendin' them in every two weeks.

"When we were in Halifax, we staged a demonstration against the unemployment insurance office in Halifax. We were up and talked to the head man there, to see what he could do to get it straightened away, because we figured the company was stalling the whole thing for to starve us back on the draggers. I told them in Halifax that computer cards was pretty hard to digest after being off for two months. Well, they promised they'd do all they could for to help us out.

"So it was about a week or so after that, I did receive four cheques in the mail and a notice also with it: as of May the 15th, our unemployment would be cut off. And first I said that computer cards was hard to digest, but they ain't so hard now because I'm not even getting them for to digest.

"We had an appeal board set up in New Glasgow which took one man up and if the appeal board would pass him for regular benefits then all of us would receive regular benefits. But he was turned down, so that turned us all down. The way I understood it when they come back was that the laws of the unemployment is so erratic that the appeal board couldn't even understand them. So I'm still not gettin' any unemployment. I'm not even gettin' any computer cards any more."

Meanwhile Jim Bury was appearing on paid-time television with Ellsworth Ryan, putting the Food Workers' position. CLC president Donald MacDonald offered his own analysis of the issue. "If the people of Nova Scotia want to usher in a decade of violence and confusion which could spell ruin for the fishermen," said MacDonald, "the way to do it is to permit the UFAWU to grab control of the industry." He described the UFAWU as a divisive force in the campaign to organize Strait fishermen – a curious comment about the *first* union to organize in the area. Atlantic organizer Ed Johnston filled in the blanks: in BC, he told the press, the UFAWU had used physical threats, intimidation and coercion "without parallel in the history of the trade union movement of this country." Terrorism in BC ports had reached such a pitch that some clergymen were afraid to answer their doors without firearms. As the *Highlander* noted,

Observers find the increasing fury of the Congress attack on the UFAWU more than passing strange since it is little more than a year since the union was being wooed by the CFAW because of its admitted and proven expertise in the fishing industry. No mention of 'terrorism' or any similar evil entered discussions surrounding the UFAWU's application to join the CLC, and indeed the Northern Fishermen and Allied Workers' Union in Newfoundland [an affiliate of the Food Workers] cited the UFAW's outstanding work in B.C. as a rebuttal to Premier Joey Smallwood's contention that a union was not workable in the fishing industry.

The virulence of the attack was modified a few days later by CLC vice-president Joe Morris, who admitted the UFAWU had "a fairly good reputation" on the West Coast, where "nobody's complained about the kind of operation they run."

Ron Parsons, who had always liked to refer to the "fish barons" of Nova Scotia, now adjusted his metaphor.

"If the barons of Labour want to show their authority," Parsons said, "let them move out amongst the people who need help so badly in the ghettos and slums. Less than 30 per cent of the workers in Nova Scotia are organized. They don't have to show their power in Canso, where our trawlermen were damn well organized and put up the best fight this province has seen since the end of the Second World War."

But the CLC and the Food Workers continued to draw support. Their position, and the decisions of the Labour Relations Board, were praised by the Labour Councils of Truro, New Glasgow, and Amherst, by locals of the Quarry Workers and the General Workers, by 650 petitioners from the town of Canso, and by a group of clergy including Anglican Edward Burton of Mulgrave, Rev. Henry Whiteway of the Christian Mission, Canso, and Catholics Robert Wicks of Canso and Georges Arsenault of Petit de Grat. On May 25, Frank Fillmore of *The Scotian Journalist,* who had been one of the first newsmen on the strike scene and had always been strongly in support of the fishermen, ran a full-page analysis of the current situation.

Fillmore argued that, in general, the UFAWU had fought an admirable fight. But he pointed out that some of the most vocal critics of the Food Workers' alleged "sweetheart" contract – he mentioned Ron Parsons and Edison Lumsden – hadn't actually read it. The contract wasn't all that bad, said Fillmore. Nor was the Food Workers' union all that bad: it had done well in the meat industry, and it could be expected to be tough and effective in the fishery.

Fillmore concluded that the UFAWU, if it continued to struggle for justice, would only wrench the fishermen, their families, and their communities apart without achieving any result. "The UFAWU has made important contributions to Nova Scotia, and no honest Nova Scotian should forget that," said Fillmore. "But the best it can do for us now – and I say this with the utmost regret – is to withdraw."

Coming from Fillmore, this was startling indeed. But not everyone agreed. On May 12, the Halifax Labour Council heard a speech from Jim Bury, who told his familiar story. The Food Workers had come to Canso Strait at the request of the fishermen, and had organized fairly and freely, in accordance with good trade union principles. Charges of collusion with the companies were mere UFAWU propaganda.

The council executive had recommended that the council refrain from issuing any statement about the dispute, but after Bury's speech, representatives of the Canadian Union of Public Employees and the United Auto Workers moved that the council urge the Labour Relations Board to reconsider its decision against hearing the UFAWU certification application.

In the course of the debate, J. K. Bell lit into Bury and his union, denying the accuracy of Bury's story. "There is no question that international reps came into the province at the end of a seven-month strike because a reactionary character like Cadegan would not recognize the union of the workers' choice. If a man like Cadegan now determines which union is to represent workers, I want no more part of the labour movement."

Bell said the facts were clear. "On March 7, Cadegan met in a hotel with the CFAWU. Two days later the CFAWU said it had a majority of the workers signed up – but it has yet to substantiate its claim." The Food Workers, Bell charged, had "become an agent of the boss," and he disclosed that his own Marine Workers' Federation had been offered "the same deal" by Acadia Fisheries.

"It was offered to us," Bell said. "Cadegan made no bones about it, and when we pointed out we didn't have the membership he said he would fix that up. To our credit, we told him to go F* himself."

The motions and hearings before the Labour Relations Board went on: bids to revoke the Food Workers' certification by both the UFAWU itself and the old *ad hoc* committee; applications for reconsideration of various Board decisions. The UFAWU hopes rose when, at a hearing on May 28, the Board directed the Food Workers and the company to produce the cards and crew lists it had first requested early in April, and again on May 5. Matheson and Nunn argued vigorously that the Board had no right to make such an order, and Homer Stevens pointed out that the Board had set no deadline. Stevens also doubted that the Board had the legal power to compel the two parties to provide the information, but remarked that "a refusal to do so in itself would seem to be pretty clear evidence of the recognition pact's real nature – and under those circumstances it's hard to see how the Board could refuse to approve the UFAWU application for certification."

It was also clear that the UFAWU would *not* see the cards, even if the Food Workers produced them. And that, in turn, would leave them unable to challenge the fraud they suspected.

Meanwhile, Donald MacDonald was addressing the annual convention of the Canadian Food and Allied Workers in Montreal. "You already represent the vast majority of the Atlantic fishermen," he declared, "and you have a strong organization here in Canada to support them. But it does not end there. The Amalgamated Meat Cutters is a large international organization which has contracts with some 120 units in the North American fishing industry. This includes nineteen plants in the New England States which are part of the Consolidated Food chain to which Booth Fisheries is directly connected. This is an illustration of the importance of strong international union ties."

Ironically, on June 4 the Food Workers struck for a first contract with Burgeo Fish Industries, in Burgeo, Newfoundland. That battle had many of the qualities of the Canso Strait strike.

*Bell didn't say "fuck"; he said "F."

213

However, if its conduct in Burgeo did somewhat redeem its image after the raids in Nova Scotia, the union nevertheless saw its own argument about its irresistible power fall apart in Burgeo, for the strike was disastrously lost in November when the fish plant owner simply closed the plant and threw the whole community out of work.

By now the UFAWU men had been out of work for three months. On Saturday, June 5, at 4.00 a.m., eleven fishermen boarded the trawler *Acadia Gull,* warped her out twenty feet from the company dock, and occupied her, vowing to hold her until the government or the Labour Relations Board took firm action on their demand for certification. They decked the boat in UFAWU flags and signs. The night watchman called production supervisor Eddie Grant, and Grant told the fishermen they'd have to leave, then called A. L. Cadegan. Cadegan came down and ordered the men off. The only reply was a few laughs and some loud snores.

About 7.30, company men slashed the lines holding the ship away from the dock, and pulled it in. Four Mounties went aboard, demanding that the men leave. They refused. An hour later, Cadegan ordered shoreworkers to turn high-pressure hoses on them. One of the men was Terrence Hanlon, vice-president of the shoreworkers' union, and son of the mayor; he refused, and was suspended for six weeks. Finally a couple of men obeyed, drenching the men, but they stayed put. Union supporters came up to the boat by water, on the side away from the dock, and brought dry clothes, food, and oilskins.

A crowd gathered, watching and cheering. Three more fishermen bolted past the surprised Mounties to join their colleagues in the occupation. Maintenance workers came aboard to work on the ship. About 11.30, five more carloads of Mounties arrived, and after a scuffle, removed the men and took them to Guysborough jail, after running through a blockade of fishermen's wives at the plant gate. That afternoon, an information picket line of the wives tried to persuade the crew members not to sail. It succeeded: several men returned to Halifax, and the skipper booked off "for personal reasons."

The men were charged with mischief, and released on their own recognizance. Con Mills was additionally charged with

214

resisting arrest, and Stanley Cooper, who had aided Mills, with obstructing justice. Ultimately the mischief charges were dismissed on a technicality, and Cooper and Mills were convicted and fined $25.00 or twenty days each.

Edison Lumsden told the press similar protests were "possible" in the future, while A. L. Cadegan rumbled that "these people committed piracy . . . It was a big publicity gimmick to them, but it was really a very serious matter." The union and its auxiliary met that night, and declared themselves pleased with the occupation and its results. The Committee for a Free Vote released a statement the next day blaming the incident squarely on government inaction: no welfare, no unemployment, and unconscionably long pauses in the Labour Relations Board's processes. It quoted a fisherman as saying that "the boats are our only source of livelihood, but the company won't let us fish. The company has milked this province of $9 million so that it can starve us out. By rights, these boats belong to the people of Nova Scotia." The Committee agreed and reiterated its conviction that the matter was not complicated: the men had chosen a union, and wanted to work under it. And the company was denying them that right, with the help of government.

On June 7, the Labour Relations Board issued four decisions. In two, it dismissed the applications to revoke the Food Workers' certification. In another, it dismissed the complaints of unfair labour practices. In a fourth, however, it reiterated what it had said at the May 28 hearing: "The failure by the Canadian Food and Allied Workers' Union, Local P-268, to supply the Board with the cards and of the Respondent [i.e. Acadia Fisheries] to supply the membership list has raised doubt in the minds of all Members of the Board." The Board was prepared to reconsider its decision on the UFAWU's initial application for certification.

Two days later a brawl broke out on the wharf in Canso, the result of a clash between UFAWU fishermen and some plant workers. A. L. Cadegan denied a union statement that the company was "attempting to muster goon squads to fight with the fishermen," but Rev. Whiteway of the Christian Mission said "the plant workers realize their jobs are in danger – and they don't want to be out of work seven months again." Another clergyman who was "unwilling to reveal his identity" said he feared further

215

violence and had called for increased RCMP protection for the town.

On June 20, Jean Richardson still had received no welfare, and food was hard to come by. The Richardsons are generous people, happy to feed a guest or put him up overnight or longer. But in June of 1971, they didn't invite visitors to eat with them. They were embarrassed about their situation, judging from their looks, but they plainly couldn't afford to share their food.

"On the 5th of May I went down for welfare," Jean explained at the time. "Everett wasn't home, so therefore I had to go – because Wednesday's the only day that he's in, Mr. Fraser, the Welfare Officer. I went down, and I didn't fill out any forms or anything. He just told me that we didn't qualify. So then they set up an appeal even though we hadn't filled out an application.

"The next Wednesday, a couple of men come down from Halifax, and there was an appeal. They told us that the report would be in on Thursday and we should know by Saturday the results of it. But we didn't know; it was about ten days after which when we found out that in their opinion it should be granted.

"Then, the next two weeks, we went down but Mr. Fraser wasn't in, and we were told that he would call to the houses. But he didn't. We didn't see him. In the meantime they decided that they should have another appeal, that this was only a recommendation and it should have been an order.

"Well, since then we've had another appeal and we got word back that it should be given us, that we should be getting welfare. But we were down last Wednesday and it's still turned down."

In mid-June the owners of Acadia Fisheries met in Halifax with the provincial government. Trade and Industry Minister Ralph Fiske said "no new developments" came from the meetings, and denied rumours that Acadia had laid down an ultimatum that if further aid were not forthcoming the company would pull out of the province. "There was definitely no ultimatum," said the minister. "We just had discussions about their business in Canso."

Premier Regan said he believed the parent company had the financial muscle to put more money into its subsidiary; Boston Deep Sea Fisheries was pleading difficulties in exporting the capital from Britain, but the Premier said other companies had managed. He also remarked that if Acadia did pull out, he'd prefer another private operator over public ownership of the plant.

On June 25, the Labour Relations Board made its four final decisions about the fisheries dispute. The Board dismissed three applications to reconsider earlier decisions, and announced that it had

> received the certified lists of the names of the persons who comprised the trawler crews employed by Acadia Fisheries Limited on the relevant dates and the signed membership cards of those who were members in good standing of the Canadian Food and Allied Workers' Union, Local P-268, on the same dates. The Board having processed and examined the lists and the cards . . . is satisfied that a majority of the employees . . . were members in good standing of the Canadian Food and Allied Workers' Union, Local P-268 on the relevant dates.

The Board's decision contained an explanatory note: the relevant dates were March 19 and March 26, when the Food Workers' and the UFAWU applications were filed. That choice of dates ensured that the Food Workers would emerge victorious, even though hardly anyone has ever believed that they represented a majority of Acadia's normal work force. By March 19, most of the work force had left Acadia; with a closed shop arrangement, the Food Workers unquestionably had a majority by then.

And so the great strike died away. The struggle that had rocked the province was given a single column at the bottom of page fifty-three of a fifty-four page *Chronicle-Herald* on June 29. That same day, in a last burst of defiance, a group of fishermen and students demonstrated outside the legislature in Halifax, chanting "Laws for workers, not for companies" and "Government hacks, off our backs." Then they entered the public gallery, while the Speaker, George Mitchell, interrupted the debate to tell them they were welcome, but they must keep their signs out of sight.

Instead, the demonstrators shouted slogans while Edison Lumsden attempted to read a statement. Mitchell ordered the galleries cleared, and the government members began leaving their benches. Word spread that the police were coming, and the demonstrators left, pausing to bandy angry words with Finance Minister Peter Nicholson, Labour Minister Pace, and Premier Regan.

"We were called up to go down and demonstrate at the Problem House," Everett remembered a year later. "I don't call it Province House because that's not a very good name for it. Problem House, as far as I'm concerned. That's where you take all your problems at."

"And come back with bigger problems," murmured Jean.

"But we were led to believe that we were just going to have our demonstration outside of the Problem House, and then go in and set down – "

"Quiet," said Linda Gurney.

"Quiet," Everett nodded. "Not make any noise or anything. But the moment we went in the Problem House, we kinda split. Edison got up for to read his piece, and the students started singing songs and a-hootin' and a-hollerin' – and the plaques, they wouldn't put them down and last goin' off, the House cleared out.

"I don't know if I was surprised or stunned, or whatever the hell it was, you know, for to get in a snarl like that. Then afterwards the students said that we knew what was gonna take place, but we *didn't* know. If I hadda know'd that they were goin' in there to do that, I'da never went in. And I know Edison didn't know anything about it, and none of the fishermen knew.

"I didn't feel too good about that. I think it was goin' a little bit too far. They said it was the first time that was ever done in the history of Nova Scotia."

"It was bad publicity," said Linda.

"All the good the students done for us, they kind of hurt us right there," said Everett. "We got out just before the police got there – we were going across the street to the lawyer's office and the police cars were comin' up the street and they wasn't stoppin' for stop signs or nothin'. They were jumpin' out and runnin' down to pick us up, but we got clear of it anyway, by the skin of our teeth."

And now the blacklisting began. One fisherman said he was told by Cadegan that "no United Fishermen supporter will ever work here again," but Cadegan's comment to me was milder:

"Acadia has the right to hire *who* it wants, *when* it wants, *where* it wants," he said. "And the boats are fully crewed. I admit that there are men I wouldn't want back. But Eric Fitzpatrick is strong UF, and I'd hire him anytime."

However, Eric stood in the kitchen of the bungalow he was renting in a woodyard in Mulgrave and told me he wasn't going back. Some of the men had signed cards – one told Edison Lumsden that "It's gonna hurt me more to sign that card than it did to sign my father's death certificate. But what the hell else can I do?" Eric's alternative was no easier. He was broke: he and Gail were more than $700 behind on their rent alone. The UFAWU had promised to loan air fare and help find jobs for any of the trawlermen who were willing to come to the union base in British Columbia, and Eric was going. He stood in the kitchen on July 8 as his six children coursed in and out, pestering Gail, and said he was leaving next morning. How did he feel?

"I used to think there was half-way respect at least in this country for democratic rights," he said. "I thought you had a democratic right to the union of your own choice. Now when the politicians talk about democratic rights, why, it just makes me sick to my stomach. There aren't any democratic rights in this country. Not for fellows like us.

"It has something to do with Homer, too. To think that for twenty years, the only man that had guts enough to come to Nova Scotia to try to organize the fishermen – well, you just *couldn't* turn coat on him. I'd rather starve than join the CF. I didn't like the principles of it, I didn't like the way they came in here. Another thing about the UFAWU, it's an all-Canadian union. I don't see why we have to have the Meatpackers come up from Chicago to organize fishermen on the East Coast. I just can't join the CF, that's all there is to it. I don't think I could sleep at night – and I like me sleep."

The next morning Edison Lumsden and Con Mills drove nine fishermen to the airport in Sydney. After fifteen months, Eric Fitzpatrick's fight was over. He had gone to the other coast, and Nova Scotia was the poorer for his going.

Down in Canso, I asked Ron Parsons if it was game over. "It's game over *here,*" he replied. But then he thought that he'd maybe been so preoccupied with his own problems that he was unduly pessimistic. His wife was going to hospital the next Monday for a serious operation and she was suffering from nervous hives. Anything new on Ron's own future? Yes, he said, though it wouldn't be announced for a while yet, he expected to be going to Coalition for Development, a Halifax ecumenical venture involved in social action.

Edison Lumsden wasn't home, but his pretty wife Louise reported an unhappy man: he hadn't eaten for several days, he can't eat properly when he's drinking. Last night, she said, he got in at a quarter past one, made himself spaghetti and couldn't eat it. She thought that sometimes all he'd really like to do would be to get back fishing himself again. "That's the thing he really loves."

Edison came in, and while we talked Jim Collins called from Mulgrave to say he'd just landed a job on the Shell Oil boats supplying the drilling rigs on Sable Island – $600 a month now, $700 after a few weeks. He had intended to go to BC and perhaps to stay and move his family, but now he wouldn't. But Homer had phoned to say he'd lined up another four or five jobs and who wanted to go? A couple of guys from Mulgrave were going, one or two from Petit de Grat. Edison called Art Ryan and another chap, and told them the news, since they'd indicated they'd like to go.

The town, said Edison, was full of rumours and stories. Six or seven UFAWU fishermen had applied to Acadia for work, sailing under the Food Workers. Cadegan had told them they weren't blacklisted and they weren't fired, but there was no work for them at Acadia. That at least made the welfare situation easier, and Everett and Jean had at long last had a cheque for $75.00. There were stories that the Food Workers had sewed up Prince Edward Island, and Joe Rideout, the skipper who had left the *Acadia Gull* after the sit-in, had taken a crew with him to the Island, looking for work: they had been told no fishermen from Canso would be hired. And meanwhile the Food Workers were launching a raid on the Canadian Seafood Workers' local in the Acadia plant: I might ask Ted Nickerson about that.

It was painful to be with Edison that day. The previous night he had decided to sell the boat, mortgage the house, and give the money to those in worse need. "I don't know how some of them are living," said Louise. Edison is a proud, impulsive, fiery man: one sensed the boil of thoughts and emotions that chased through his mind. He's competent, and shrewd, and tenacious as a bulldog, and these were perhaps the hardest days of his life.

I went to see Ted Nickerson, remembering, as I drove, the day Edison had confronted A.L. Cadegan on the Acadia Fisheries wharf and shouted to a watching crowd of plant workers that the Food Workers' raids on the fishermen should be a warning to them: if it were the fishermen today, it would be the plant workers tomorrow. Nickerson was a tall, lean, brown man who had been born in Canso, quit school at Grade 3 and gone to work in a little fish plant at the age of nine, wheelbarrowing salt for 15¢ an hour. He considered himself a strong union man, and had served as president of the shoreworkers' local; he was particularly grateful to the union for the various educational experiences it had offered him – trips, conventions, and the like.

"I'm not against the fishermen at all," he said. He'd fished himself, briefly, and he felt the fishermen had been badly treated from time immemorial. It was time they got more. But he also felt they should have signed up in the Food Workers for a year, and voted for the UFAWU at the end of the contract if the Food Workers had proven unsatisfactory.

That idea, in retrospect, was probably an excellent one. Suppose the men had not left the boats, I said to Cadegan at one point, suppose they had joined the Food Workers and petitioned the Labour Relations Board for a vote – which the UFAWU would surely have won? "They'd have had us cold," snapped Cadegan. "They'd have had their union. And we'd have fought the fucking strike for nothing."

The shoreworkers, said Nickerson, had lost $1,000 to $3,000 each during the strike, and though it was right to do that once, they shouldn't be asked to do it again. "The Seafood Workers," said Nickerson, "should be looking out for the shore plant workers, not for the fishermen. The fishermen got a lot of money, food, clothes – hell, the shoreworkers didn't get none of that, and we weren't gettin' strike pay either.

"My one resource is to keep this plant goin' and keep people employed. A lot of people here just can't keep going without it. I don't care who takes it over, if Acadia leaves – Acadia, National Sea, or Ed Sullivan, I don't care. All I want is for the plant to keep goin' and for people to keep workin'." He reckoned the shoreworkers were about evenly split in their allegiance, half preferring the Seafood Workers, half preferring the CFAWU.

The meetings of the UFAWU, which he attended, were militant and democratic, he said. He referred to Homer Stevens with respect: Homer was tough and able, and interested in educating people; he had given Nickerson a lot of literature.

"Me, I'd go into the CF tomorrow," he said. "But I tell you, if we had a union that'd stick together like the fishermen did, I wouldn't care about anything else."

Everett Richardson was gloomily defiant.

"Things are lookin' pretty bad," he admitted. "About six or seven of the boys will be able to work at inshore fishin', but that's about it. The rest, I guess they'll have to go away." He was one of the lucky ones, being well-established as a summertime inshore fisherman.

"I still don't believe the CF had enough support to get a majority here," Everett declared. "I'm not sure, because we couldn't see the cards, but there's probably taxi drivers and guys who've fished once in the last sixteen years down as CF members. That's the only way they could get enough. If it was a true count, they'd probably have twenty men at the outside."

Would he do it again?

"Sure I'd do it again. The UF is a good union; and the CF ain't no union at all."

The Canadian Food and Allied Workers, it seemed, had won throughout the Acadia operation. But it was a hollow victory, after all. On July 20, less than a month after the Labour Relations Board's final ruling, plant workers were handed a mimeographed sheet as they punched off shift. The first sentence stunned them.

"It is with regret that we announce that the company must discontinue business."

The notice to the employees was taken up with outlining the few days' work remaining, processing fish already in stock or expected from the trawlers then at sea. But in a press statement

222

the same day, the company went into more detail. It said it had been forced out of business by

> the disastrous financial effect that the seven months' strike and continued labour problems since the strike, both organized by the United Fishermen and Allied Workers' Union, has had on the Company's finances, which has cost them $2,000,000. This has now also cost the 850 loyal employees at both Canso and Mulgrave their livelihood.
>
> Acadia had hoped to transfer the activities of their operations to a major Canadian Company, so as to ensure a continual livelihood for their employees, and did reach agreement with a company concerned. The government of Nova Scotia did not, however, accept the terms offered.

The company had also offered a plan for the reconstruction of Acadia itself, but the government had preferred to see the company bankrupt.

The government retorted that the "major Canadian Company" had insisted, as a condition of taking over the plant, that the province write off its $9 million claim against the plant, or, alternatively, that repayment of the loan be tied to fish caught. And the "reconstruction of Acadia" could be translated to mean "more provincial funds." That, said Premier Regan, did not interest the province while the company remained under the same management.

Totting it up, Boston Deep Sea Fisheries claimed to have dropped $4 million in Canso. But anyone who has read the basic texts on the behaviour of foreign companies in semi-colonial countries like Canada – Kari Levitt's *Silent Surrender,* for example – realizes that the multi-nationals have dozens of ways to siphon funds out of a subsidiary without seeming to be doing so. Management fees, royalties on technology, artificially low prices paid for the subsidiary's product, often coupled with artificially high prices for anything sold to it – those are only a few of the techniques. Was Acadia really bankrupt, or was it bled white by its parent? Cadegan says it *was* bankrupt, but he also says (p.47) that Suddaby thought he could live with the union long enough to get out of Acadia what he had to, which suggests Boston Deep

Sea was extracting a very high rate of return from Acadia and could do so even with the union in place.

How can one figure out the truth? Presumably only by getting a cracking good accountant to go through the books, an exercise neither the Boston group nor the Nova Scotia government is likely to encourage. Another point: if Boston didn't *want* to fold and didn't think it could survive the strike, why did it persist? Cadegan never gave me an adequate explanation of the point.

But whether or not Boston Deep Sea had taken a beating, the taxpayers on all three levels certainly had. Various Canadian governments had put in nearly $13 million, and other creditors claimed another $2 million – against a plant worth perhaps $4 million to $5 million. The town of Canso also had a tax bill against the company which by now amounted to $111,000.

The day after the announcement, I had a long interview with Donnie Cadegan. The atmosphere was curious: the plant was winding down perceptibly, and everyone I spoke to seemed soft-spoken and uneasy, as though in the presence of a corpse. Cadegan's office had plywood panels over the broken windows, legacies of the strike. Cadegan himself was furious, pacing back and forth, barking out comments. He had been portrayed as a monster, and certainly he is a tough, outspoken man who is accustomed to being obeyed. But the overwhelming impression I had was of a man at bay, and in pain.

"No matter what we do, we're suspect," he declared. "We're the Simon Legrees. But who leads the field? There was nothing in the *ad hoc* agreement that we weren't doing already. The *ad hoc* agreement was *better* than the CBRT contract with National Sea."

He denounced Homer Stevens: "He didn't win the day but he did destroy the industry. Now that's a signal victory for any Communist." He was contemptuous of Roy Keefe, and his failure to organize the trawlermen years earlier: "Roy Keefe is directly responsible for the fact that Acadia Fisheries today doesn't exist." The mention of J.K. Bell threw him into an ecstasy of name-calling. Above all, Bell was only a tool of Homer Stevens, who had "fired all the balls that Homer Stevens made."

He riffled through some letters on his desk, and groaned.

"When I look back at these letters I get sick to my stomach. We were comin' right along. Look, here's a letter from February 13, we were dickering with the Fisheries Loan Board of PEI for three new $850,000 stern trawlers. You know, this plant was bankrupt when I came, and I've kept it together for three years. All I did was break my back to feed 850 people. I never had a vacation in three years. And until the strike we were in pretty good shape. We went from a $1,600,000 deficit to an $800,000 cash flow in one year. Sure I'm a strong leader. The only day I ever got catcalls and whistles in the plant was this morning, because they figured I was no longer in charge."

He went into his private washroom, talking over his shoulder.

"Boston Deep Sea should have closed the Mulgrave plant ten years ago," he said. "But Sir Basil Parkes told me, 'I have a moral responsibility to the community.' They invested $4 million here and lost it all. They even paid their own fares back and forth. They lost money on Mulgrave every year."

He stalked back into the office.

"Acadia ran the old BC Packers plant in Canso for one year; then it burnt. They bused workers to Mulgrave for two shifts, for three years or so while the new plant was being built, and it cost them a barrel of money. They lost their shirts."

The province, he said, permitted the company to defer some of its loan payments in consideration of the strike. But the plant was always undercapitalized. "I never had a day when I had enough money to run the place. It was what my father called 'frenzied financing to keep the door open.' "

What was the future of the plant?

"Why don't you ask the Premier?" snapped Cadegan.

The 4th Estate had reported that Cadegan was bitter about the fact that he was out of a job: the Boston Group had no place for him in its organization. Toward the end of the interview he alluded to it. "They're over in England," he muttered. They couldn't care less. And who's left in Canada?

"Me. Universally despised."

EPILOGUE
January, 1977

"In our hands is placed a power greater than their hoarded gold,
Greater than the might of atoms magnified a thousand fold,
We can bring to birth a new world from the ashes of the old,
For the union makes us strong!"

– "Solidarity Forever"

Almost seven years after the strike, I drove into Mulgrave on a brilliant winter day. All that remained of Acadia Fisheries was a set of seven metal tanks on the hillside, standing like the tombstones of a forgotten enterprise, for the bankrupt plant burned in the fall of 1971 and was never rebuilt. Mulgrave has an unemployment rate of nearly 50 per cent, and its angry citizens regularly harangue the government and all the talk shows with invective, but these are hard times everywhere and nothing seems to work for Mulgrave. Eric Fitzpatrick's bungalow in the woodyard is boarded up. I haven't seen Eric or Gail for years.

Down the shore in the sunlight, a stunning panorama of snowy woods and frozen harbours with the cold blue waters of Chedabucto Bay open on the left clear to Ireland. Pirate Harbour, Sand Point, St. Francis Harbour, Port Shoreham, and so into Boylston, where I lived when I wrote my first reports on the strike, and Guysborough, where the fishermen went to court.

Something eternal haunts one along this rocky shore: things change, but the sea and the woods endure. Is there a prettier village in Canada than Guysborough, cupped by its hills and rooted by its harbour like an old, miniature Vancouver? Can anything be more crisp than a clear winter day along the Guysborough shore?

From the bluffs of Cook's Cove, I could almost see the water tower of the Petit de Grat fish plant, far across the Strait. Booth Fisheries won the strike, but pulled out anyway. In 1974, it consolidated its operations in Fortune, Newfoundland, and again the province found itself pushed into public ownership, unable to find a buyer for a rundown industry. Usen Fisheries of Boston

226

operated the plant for two years and finally bought it. And Booth, I reflected cheerfully, got to Newfoundland just in time for the bitter 1975 strike by the Food Workers' affiliate there, which revolutionized the whole Newfoundland fishery by winning approval of the principle that, as the conciliation report put it, "the trawlermen should negotiate with the companies not the price of fish but rather the income level that will be attained for full-time work."

Earl Lewis had retired. The Food Workers still held their sway in Petit de Grat, and the strike had faded into a bittersweet memory. Father Arsenault was gone; he now worked for the Citizenship Branch of the Department of the Secretary of State. One of his colleagues was Ron Parsons, who also left church work after a couple of years of hell-raising with Coalition for Development.

Memories and reveries, as the villages appeared and vanished into the rear-view mirror, clustered around dents in the shoreline like visions of tranquillity: Dort's Cove, Corbett's Cove, Halfway Cove. The UFAWU is no more than a memory now, though Homer Stevens occasionally visits Nova Scotia. Edison Lumsden and Con Mills continued as full-time organizers, and in 1972 made a bid for certification for scallop draggermen at Comeau's Sea Foods of Meteghan, on the south-west shore. The application was denied, amid a flurry of accusations and counter-accusations. That September, a small group of inshore fishermen in Canso was the subject of the union's only successful certification in Nova Scotia. Con Mills later moved to British Columbia, where he is now Northern Representative of the union, and Edison went back to fishing in Canso.

Homer Stevens, too, was going back to fishing. He announced in the fall of 1976 that he would not stand for re-election at the union's annual convention in February, and as I drove I wondered idly at the odd episode in which Stevens announced his candidacy for president of the Canadian Labour Congress, and then withdrew under pressure from his own executive. For the CLC at last bowed to the pressure from the BC Labour movement and re-admitted the UFAWU in December 1972, just a year after condemning it so furiously. Stevens hailed the re-admission as "a real victory for a principled approach to fraternal solidarity within the labour movement," and I was amused to read that a

CLC officer had extended "a warm welcome to officers and members of the United Fishermen and Allied Workers Union," feeling "confident your affiliation with us will be beneficial both to you and to the labour movement of Canada." A decade of violence and confusion. . . .

And the other actors in the drama? A. L. Cadegan was owner and manager of Highland Fisheries in his native Glace Bay. The students of the NDY had dissolved and re-formed in various combinations, into various leftist groups in Halifax, most notably the East Coast Socialist Movement, which during its two years or so of existence put out a punchy little paper, *The East Coast Worker*. Now they were doing such work as would fit their consciences, and several were heavily involved in such ventures as a co-op daycare centre, for the students of yesteryear are the parents of today.

Father Poirer of Arichat had retired. Father Morley was parish priest of River Bourgeois, not far from Petit de Grat. Father Bob Lauder studied at Saul Alinsky's Industrial Areas Foundation in Chicago, and subsequently left the church to teach at Memorial University's new college in Corner Brook, Newfoundland.

Both Richmond and Guysborough Counties had gone Liberal. Guysborough was captured in a by-election by A. M. "Sandy" Cameron – no relation of mine – a Dartmouth businessman who served first as Minister of Fisheries and later as Minister of Development. He and the Regan government were both re-elected in 1974.

Peas Brook, Queensport, with its lighthouse on a bulbous rock in the harbour mouth. Not that Queensport has much of a harbour; in fact there's not a decent shelter anywhere along the shore from Guysborough till you get right out to Canso.

Canada's new 200-mile limit was less than a week old: I wondered what difference it might make. K. C. Lucas, federal Deputy-Minister of Fisheries, had said that "on the East Coast our fish stocks have been depleted like hell. We are inheriting a disaster."

True enough. The fish, it seems, are gone. Whole villages once reliant on fishing have one or two fishermen left. The 1976 lobster season was the worst in a series of terrible seasons. Haddock, cod and herring are little more than a memory along vast stretches of the shore. Swordfishing has been closed because of mercury pollution, salmon closed because there are hardly enough fish left to ensure survival of the species. In 1976, the federal government had to impose a limit even on "redfish" – ocean perch – once considered an inexhaustible junk fish, but now a valuable and diminishing part of the catch.

So the inshore men now wanted a limit within the new limit, a fifty-mile zone reserved for the small shore-based boats. One of the stronger units of this inshore fishermen's movement was in Canso, and one of its strongest members was the only fisherman in town who made good catches when the 1976 season opened: a particularly able gentleman by the name of Edison Lumsden.

Philip Harbour, Half Island Cove, Fox Island Main. Then Hazel Hill, with its old telegraph company buildings, and Canso. And the little house by the road just past the new Fishermen's Memorial, a house externally unchanged in half a dozen years, the home of Jean and Everett Richardson.

Everett has changed more than Jean. He wears glasses steadily these days, he's a bit thicker at the waist, his manner is somehow more reserved. We catch up on the news: Russell and Linda spent a season on the West Coast, then came home and took over Everett's parent's place. They have a boy and a girl. Bertha married Eddie Dort, one-time president of the shoreworkers' union, and they have a little daughter. Everett Jr. is now a lanky fourteen-year-old, and John is a rotund, mischievous twelve: both of them were small boys when I was here last, and now they are only a few seasons from manhood. Kenny is still working at the plant.

"I haven't seen Eric Fitzpatrick for a year or more," says Everett. "Gail's living in Auld's Cove, I hear, and Eric generally comes home for the winter. He's probably around now, if you went to look for him."

The house has changed inside. The kitchen renovations are finished, and though the combination oil and wood range still purrs in the corner, vents here and there reveal a new oil furnace in the cellar. Off the dining room there's a curtain, and behind it is a complete new bathroom. Yes, they *have* done a great deal of work, Jean concedes; they stripped all the plaster off the living room walls, insulated thoroughly behind it, and panelled it over.

Everett is going down to overhaul some gear in the bait shed: would I like to come? Of course. We slip into his geriatric Dodge and drive slowly through the town. There's Linda's house, newly painted. Bertha and Eddie live in one of the new houses up the hill. That's a new tavern they're just building.

"You know," I say to Everett, "Canso looks really good." "Things ain't too bad," he admits. A member of the codfish aristocracy recently told me that during the last five years Canso has destroyed its bad reputation as a town full of drunks and layabouts, where no venture could ever hope to succeed. One of the owners of Canso Seafoods apparently claims that of all the employees in the various plants his family owns around the Maritimes, among the best are in Canso – competent and conscientious people.

Canso Seafoods is a subsidiary of H. B. Nickerson and Sons Ltd. of North Sydney; it took over the former Acadia plant in December, 1971. When the trawlers went back to sea, ironically, the crewmen were members of neither of the two warring unions, their bargaining agent was the Brotherhood, with which Nickerson already had contracts elsewhere. Even the former Acadia building looks more trim and proud; and the wharves are jammed with boats – seiners from the Sou'West shore, refurbished Acadia draggers under new names, draggers from the Gaspé. Over the sunshot water wheel thousands of startlingly white gulls, plummeting to the freezing water for scraps from the ships and the plant. The ground, the shoreline, even the tops of the wharves are coated with iron-hard ice, but the gulls are not discouraged.

Everett turns down a little alley between the old Acadia plant and the former Cardinal Protein plant.

"Nickerson got the Cardinal plant for $100," Everett grinned. "It cost the government nine million. That's about the most expensive storehouse ever I seen."

The bait shed is a new plywood building with a freezer room in one end and a heated work area in the other. Inside are half a dozen fishermen; Lloyd Richardson, Everett's cousin, and his son Purvis, who share a big boat; red-headed Freddy Munroe; stumpy, quiet Howie Jackson, whose boat exploded at the wharf last fall; Leo Quann, who I last saw in the courthouse in Guysborough six years ago, charged with mischief over the *Acadia Gull* affair. Others come and go – Clayton Haines, who I last saw as a co-defendant with Leo; Fuss Richardson, Lloyd's brother, who has given up his gas station, bought a boat and gone fishing; Jamie Mackenzie; Edison Lumsden and his brother Clyde.

"Get outa me way, yah stupid Newfoundlander," grins Everett, muscling Leo aside.

"Jesus Christ, you fat bastard," yells Leo, brandishing a knife. "I'll cut out yer friggin' t'roat, how'd ye like that?"

The two of them get into a tussle, hauling one another back and forth across the floor, offering to make up to each other's wives for their husband's deficiencies, calling one another down on grounds of moral character, professional competence and personal hygiene. They break apart, still muttering abuse and grinning, Everett to re-nail a trawl tub, Leo to mend a net with the long wooden needle, everyone else smiling and shaking their heads.

For me, it's a bit of a reunion. I went fishing, once, with Lloyd, Everett and Purvis, before Everett bought his own boat, and if there are better companions anywhere I don't know how to find them. Lloyd looks like a gumbooted leprechaun, his greying hair curling up outside his peaked cap, his mouth naturally falling into a grin. Purvis, in the full flush of his manhood, has inherited his father's easy nature and dry humour, and watches me watching Leo and Everett. Purvis winks at me, and shakes his head.

Everett did buy a forty-foot boat, and fished her three years. "But she's too big," he explains. "Can't get nobody to go fishing with you."

"Who'd go wit' *you,* you lump o' lard?" demands Leo.

"So I got a twenty-eight footer, I can fish that alone."

"She's open?" I ask.

"Yeah, only got a little shelter at the wheel onto her, what we call a shithouse, that's all."

"You ever get calls to go back on the draggers?"

"Oh yeah, maybe a couple of times last year. But I ain't goin'. I said it right out to them. You had a chance to fire me once, I said, you ain't gonna fire me again. Next feller that fires Everett is gonna be Everett."

The men settle into a steady rhythm of work, and the stories

231

begin to flow. If a fellow spent the winter in that bait shed, by spring, he'd be able to write the funniest, most poignant novel in Canadian history. Freddy is a pool shark, and talks about the almost frightening ability of some of the town kids. Howie Jackson is a skinflint, and suffers a terrible ragging for pulling the plug on the electric kettle before it even boils.

"You ain't payin' the power bill," Purvis protests.

"Well, I – " Howie explains.

"What a man to be cheap," grunts Everett. "He goes fishing, all he takes is a quart bottle o' oil fer 'is stove. An' some days he's too cheap to use *that* much, he just fires the bottle overboard."

"Well I – " Howie interjects.

"We ain't all tough like you," says Freddy. "We can't go all day wit'out a cup o' tea."

"Tough?" declares Everett. "Howie's tough. He's tough as a boiled owl."

"I can't stick around all day listening to this bullshit," cries Leo. "I got work to do."

"What work?"

"Gotta cut some wood."

"Cut your leg off, more likely," Everett mutters. "You'd be some woodsman, you would."

"Aaarghh," growls Leo, taking a run at him.

"Heh, heh, heh," chuckles Everett, ducking. Leo goes to fetch the borrowed chainsaw.

"What a feller," Everett sighs. "He'll be like old Cece now. Met Cece one time comin' out o' the woods, chainsaw lyin' on the back seat of the car. 'LorJesus, Everett,' he says, 'that chainsaw works some good.' Give a little pull on the cord and by God she started. Cut the whole back seat out o' the car. Heh, heh, heh."

Leo returns. He can't get the chainsaw to run above an idle. He and Freddy take it out on the bitter icy deck of the wharf, and after a moment we hear its bark, see blue smoke drifting by. Freddy comes in.

"No wonder she wouldn't go," he announces. "You shoulda seen the fuel filter in it. Dirty? It's a wonder she'd even idle."

Leo sticks his head back in the door.

"I'm through wit' yez," he states. "No more fishin'. From here

232

on I'm a mechanic and a lumberjack." He claps the door too.

"Lumberjack," snorts Everett. "Mechanic."

An hour or so later he looks up from his work.

"Hear the ambulance yet?" he asks the company. "No? Guess Leo ain't cut his foot off yet, then."

Then we go home for supper – steak, plenty of it, a hearty meal – and Everett remarks in passing that he hardly drinks at all any more. That's a shame, I say, because there's a quart of Bacardi in the car, and Everett concedes that a sociable drop might not come amiss, and after I've got a good one inside me I come down to business. I mailed them a copy of the draft manuscript of this book last May: what did they think of it?

"Well," says Jean, "it was pretty good. One thing, though –"

"Go ahead."

"Well, I thought at first you made us sound like a bunch of Newfoundlanders. But then later I thought, well, how *would* you write it down, the way we talk?"

"That's right," I explain. "You *don't* sound like Newfoundlanders, but I don't know how to show the difference on the page."

"I know," says Jean, "but that's the thing that struck me right away."

"Everett?"

Everett sighs. "You want to know the honest-to-God truth of it?" he demands. "When I come right down to the facts of it, I never heard the whole thing."

"Everett doesn't read very fast," Jean explains. "So I was reading it out in the evenings, to the whole family."

"Don," says Everett, "it woulda taken me a month to read that whole thing, now that's the actual fact."

"But then it got to be summer," Jeans says, "and visitors and what-not, and we put it aside and just never got back to it."

"You know what I think?" says Everett. "What about if you read it over to us down to the bait shed? Then you'd have not only my ideas onto it, but everyone else. Jamie Mackenzie read it over, but the rest would like to hear it too."

Why not?

And so for two days I sat on a workbench, reading aloud to a chorus of comments. *No, that ain't right, that happened earlier. Did you get it in about the companies runnin' down our fish at the*

*fish sales, sayin' it was old and dirty and not fit to eat? Poor old
Ron, how's he doin' now? Yeah, the biggest part of the fellers is into
the Brotherhood now, an' back on the draggers. . . .*

I stopped sometimes, drank coffee, and talked about the book,
about how it was not the God-like overview I might have
wanted, but was instead the book I *could* write. I talked about the
paucity of books on Canadian labour and about the reasons for
it. That's not surprising, said Jamie MacKenzie, who reads a
good deal and thinks about such things: capitalist institutions
naturally serve capitalist values.

Jamie is a quiet, thoughtful man in his fifties, with a thoroughly independent cast of mind. I hadn't met him before, but I
quickly developed a considerable respect for him. On this point
he's certainly right. The skills of the writer and the historian are
middle-class skills, the context in which such people grow and
learn is the middle-class context, and the view of the world they
develop will almost certainly be bourgeois. Our intellectual life is
filled with people who respect the system – which has indeed
served them well – and it comes naturally to them to concentrate
on the lives and works of high officials rather than on the struggles of masses of nameless workers.

"I wonder do you concentrate too much on Everett?" asked
Jamie, turning to where Everett sat. "I'm not saying you weren't
important, Everett, everyone knows you put everything you had
into the strike, but there was another couple of hundred fellows
as well."

He turned back to me. "Some people around here call it 'the
Richardson strike,' did you know that? Well, they do, and that's
not right. We were *all* into it."

I know, I said, that was a problem for me too. I nodded at Edison Lumsden, sitting on a lobster box tying new hooks on a
length of trawl: some people had said Edison would have been a
better central figure, or Jim Collins. They were thrust into posi-
tions of leadership, given unexpected responsibilities, and grew
into the role fate and their fellow fishermen had given them. But
I wanted to follow a man who had fallen into the strike almost by
accident, to watch how it took over his life and reshaped his
thinking. Edison is a gifted natural leader who might well have
become a full-time union officer. I didn't want an organizer; I

wanted one of the boys. I just have to hope the reader will understand there were dozens like him.

And I couldn't tell everyone's stories. By its very nature, a strike involves hundreds of people, and a strike which mobilizes an entire province involves hundreds of thousands. That's another reason for the shortage of labour books, I said: the stories are just bloody unwieldy. To cover every aspect of the strike would take years of research and fill dozens of volumes.

"Good enough," said Jamie. "But for instance, when you wrote about the women taking over the town hall, there – now there was a lot more there that *weren't* mentioned than what were. There was Vera Quann, and Louise Lumsden, Gertie Richardson – "

"Thelma Munroe was there, and Pauline Rose – "

"Right, and Blanche Richardson, June Nickerson, Laura Haines – "

"Marg Gurney – "

"Yes, and a good bunch more besides."

"I know," I said, "I know. You're right. The whole book is just a sketch of the strike."

"Another thing," said Jamie, "I'd like to see a little bit less about drinking."

"How come?"

"I'm not saying we don't drink here. We do, same's anywheres else. But Cadegan used to say we were all drunks and winos, you see? Well, we weren't then, and we aren't now, so why give him an excuse to say that?"

"I see," I nodded. And something suddenly came home to me, a basic thread in the whole story. *The strike was about respect.* Sitting around me were eleven men of great intelligence, courage, and humanity, some of the finest men I had ever known, men who worked appallingly hard under terrible conditions, and who were treated by the codfish aristocracy as though they were scum whose lives and work counted for nothing. That burning tenacity which marked the fishermen's whole battle came, in part, at least, from a profound need to secure the respect they had earned.

"In its fourteen months, it had taken its place among the classic labour struggles of recent times," wrote Robert Chodos. "Like

235

the Newfoundland loggers' strike of 1959 and the Asbestos strike of 1949, it had torn a society apart so thoroughly that that society could never be quite the same again."

Chodos is right – but, sitting in the bait shed, I saw too that the strike was also a classic story in a Canadian literary tradition. George Woodcock has remarked that Canada's epic literature is composed of "epics of endurance, epics of imagination, not in any true sense epics of heroism," and he goes on to say that he "would accept the further argument, which Margaret Atwood later developed in *Survival*, that such heroism as does appear in our epics is also mainly *collective* heroism."

In the end the fishermen were collective heroes and martyrs, who lost the battle for themselves but won it for their brothers. They smashed the archaic prohibition on fishermen's unions and left unionism firmly established on the draggers. They changed the law, changed conditions on the boats, and left the sea saw of power balanced a little more evenly.

They forged an alliance with young urban radicals, adapted to a new relationship with their women, brought two new fish buyers to Canso and dramatically improved the price of inshore fish. And they demonstrated the real relationships between Nova Scotia's most powerful institutions with startling clarity, while revealing that a handful of people, strengthened by their insistence on justice, could bring an entire province to a halt. They showed us what the labour movement was really all about, and in their defeat the complacent labour bosses were forced to parade their own bankruptcy.

They struggled, in the end, to expand people's minds; they succeeded brilliantly. Thousands of Nova Scotians who had dismissed the labour movement as an outmoded idea, a preserve of thugs and opportunists, suddenly saw anew its fundamental glory, its insistence on respect for human labour and its resistance to the moral squalor of exploitation. If the strike was a failure, let us pray for more failures like it.

This is a book about what Everett Richardson and his brothers and sisters learned from the strike, but it is also a book about what Silver Donald Cameron learned from the fishermen and their families.

I sat in the bait shed in Canso and read to my brothers the

236

final pages of the book I had written for them.

Eric Fitzpatrick stood on a deck in Vancouver in the fall of 1971.

"If you're going to fish, this is the only place to fish," he said. "You got so many opportunities for to make a dollar, you know?" He liked BC, and Canso Strait families were arriving all the time. He wondered what Gail was thinking, and he said he had thought of phoning a couple of times, but he didn't want to run up the phone bill.

"I miss the kids an awful lot," he said wistfully. "I see kids sometimes, and I start to feel lonely then. I think about Jeanie an awful lot, you know – I suppose because she's the youngest in the family. I think of her smile, and then I'd give anything, you know . . ." His voice trailed off.

But he didn't regret the strike. "When I tell some people I'd do it again they say, Oh no, Eric, you wouldn't – but I *would,* because of what I *learned* through the strike. And standing up for something you believe in, and standing by it – this is one thing I'm happy about. During the strike, Gail used to say, I know we're having it hard, but you're standing up for something you believe in. I got to give her a lot of credit. I have much respect for her.

"I don't think anybody can figure we lost, because we got bargaining rights, and the only place in North America where the law gives bargaining rights to fishermen is in Nova Scotia today. I guess a lot of things went on in that strike that'll go down in history, and be talked about for years to come. It put me in a kind of bad position, but I don't regret it, and I'd do it again.

"There's another thing I took into consideration," said Eric, pausing for a moment.

"I think that when the kids grow up, they'd like to figure that their father stood up for something he believed in. I figured sometime the kids would say, Well, Christ, my old man stood up for something he believed in, one time. So maybe I'll do the same."

And in Canso that fall, Edison Lumsden and Everett Richardson sat around the kitchen table, while Jean made tea and Bertha and Linda and Eddie Dort listened.

"I got the surprise of my life to see what this came down to, this whole thing," said Edison Lumsden.

"In what way, Edison?" I asked.

"Well, who'd ever thought that a small group of men could stir up the trouble we have in the labour movement today – right across Canada, as far as that goes – and last for seven months. A handful of people! You know, it just goes to show what a bunch of working people can do if they want to stick together and they have good leadership. And support. I admit that without the support of other trade unionists we wouldn't have gotten anywhere, but with the support of farmers, construction workers, steel workers . . . The people around Canso, you know and elsewhere, they just came together and made themselves change."

Everett laughed and nodded.

"If anybody hadda told me a week after we went on strike we were goin' out for seven months, I would have told them they were definitely wrong. No way!"

"I think the strike was Women's Liberation around here," said Jean, "because you sat up and took notice and voiced your opinion – got your mouth open, I suppose, when you should."

"Before that, women didn't get involved with men's affairs?" I asked.

"Well, that's true. It was their business, not ours. I think it *was* that way, but I'm sure in saying it isn't *now*, no!"

"The big changes were inside you," I suggested.

"Yes. That's right."

"How about you?" I asked, turning to Edison. "Do you feel like a very different person than you were?"

"Yeah," said Edison. He thought for a moment before he spoke. It seemed to me he found it difficult to say something that sounded almost pious. "Yeah, I feel more dedicated to my fellow man than what I always have, before this ever happened."

The kitchen was very quiet.

"Everett?" I asked. "You feel a change?"

"Yeah," said Everett, staring down into his teacup. "A whole lot."

"What kind of a change?"

"Well," said Everett slowly, "one time, regardless of what come up you never took no part in it. You just said, 'Oh, hell, somebody's gonna do it.' You'd just walk away and forget about it, let the other feller work for you.

"But once you go through a strike like this here, that changes it. Not only meself, it changed an awful lot around here. They got the same thinkin' on it I have.

"What you see is, everybody's gotta pull together and do what they can. You try to get into it and do what *you* can, too, for to help the other feller out."

We can bring to birth a new world from the ashes of the old. For the union makes us strong.